I0824694

PRAISE FOR *ENGAGED COMPASSION*

"Lobsang Tenzin Negi's *Engaged Compassion* gives us the hopeful message we all need: that while we can't control our circumstances, we can control our reactions by managing our emotions and practicing compassion. This beautiful book might change your life."

—Arthur C. Brooks, #1 *New York Times* bestselling author of *From Strength to Strength*

"For many years, as both a friend and a student of His Holiness the Dalai Lama, I've hoped to see his core message about the fundamental importance of cultivating and actively engaging compassion presented in a practical and accessible way. In *Engaged Compassion*, my friend Lobsang Tenzin Negi does exactly that. Drawing on decades of work bringing the Dalai Lama's teachings to a broader, secular audience, Negi integrates deep wisdom and modern science into clear, actionable practices for everyday life. You'll find this book to be hopeful, inspiring, and deeply needed for our times."

—Richard Gere, actor and humanitarian

"Dr. Lobsang Tenzin Negi opens the chest to reveal millennia of treasures from the Buddhist tradition. Inviting all seekers, he makes the steps forward clear, understandable, and actionable. We are given a wise and experienced guide, hand-picked for this mission by His Holiness the Dalai Lama to help each of us embrace pathways to sacred wholeness. The wisdom within this book may enrich the rest of your life."

—Lisa Miller, PhD, *New York Times* bestselling author of *The Awakened Brain* and founder of the Spirituality Mind Body Institute at Columbia University

"Lobsang Tenzin Negi embodies a marvelous combination of deep expertise in traditional sciences of flourishing with a brilliant integration of the newest findings in developmental science. He brings his magic to *Engaged Compassion*, a practical guide for leading a fulfilled life. The world will benefit from this gift of kindness."

—Daniel Goleman, *New York Times* bestselling author of *Emotional Intelligence*

"Dr. Negi offers a simple and radical truth: compassion begins inside each of us—not as a belief system but as a human capacity to practice everyday choices that become acts of healing. With tenderness and clarity, Dr. Negi reminds readers that even the smallest moments of kindness quietly reshape the world."

—Sharon Salzberg, *New York Times* bestselling author of *Lovingkindness* and *Real Life*

"In a time of deep division and collective suffering, *Engaged Compassion* offers something essential: a practical way to train the heart for courageous, compassionate action. Lobsang Tenzin Negi bridges contemplative wisdom and contemporary science to show that compassion isn't passive—it's a force for healing, justice, and connection. This book invites us to move beyond sentiment into engaged, ethical living. It's a powerful reminder that our shared humanity is not an abstraction but a responsibility we must learn to embody."

—Karen Armstrong, author of *A History of God* and *Twelve Steps to a Compassionate Life*

"This book is a beautiful and timely exploration of the power of compassion. Geshe Lobsang has considerable expertise from decades of research into the science of compassion and he skillfully combines this with his embodiment of the Buddhist tradition. His command of the subject matter and his artful storytelling result in a compelling, life-shifting read. Both intellectually enriching and deeply moving, this book offers a compelling case for us all to live with more compassion—a learnable skill that offers wisdom and guidance in order that we might lead with humanity and build communities characterized by trust and resilience."

—Kirstie Papworth, author of *Compassionate Leadership: For Individual and Organisational Change*

"*Sewa bhav*, the spirit of selfless service, has guided my family and our foundation for decades. In seeking what truly sustains this commitment over a lifetime, we discovered Cognitively Based Compassion Training (CBCT®) and experienced its transformative impact firsthand. In *Engaged Compassion*, Lobsang Tenzin Negi distills this research-based program into a practical guide for cultivating compassion that endures and creates real-world impact. This is an essential book for anyone committed to service and to being a force for good."

—Ajay Piramal, industrialist and philanthropist

"*Engaged Compassion* offers a clear and compelling framework showing that compassion is a trainable skill that strengthens resilience and elevates how we lead, work, and live. Dr. Lobsang Tenzin Negi illuminates the inner foundations required for individuals, institutions, and, ultimately, societies to truly thrive. This book is essential reading for leaders and for anyone committed to building a more humane and flourishing world."

—Jagdish N. Sheth, PhD, coauthor of *Firms of Endearment*

"I have read *Engaged Compassion* with deep appreciation and recognition. Lobsang Tenzin Negi offers a rare synthesis of ancient wisdom, rigorous science, and lived practice that shows why compassion is not a soft virtue but a foundational capacity for resilient, wise leadership. In a time when leaders are under unprecedented pressure, this book makes it unmistakably clear that compassion is not optional—it is essential."

—Rasmus Hougaard, founder and CEO of Potential Project and author of *Compassionate Leadership: How to Do Hard Things in a Human Way*

"As a lifelong practitioner, teacher, and writer in the Tibetan Buddhist tradition, I have witnessed how compassion takes root through sustained reflection and practice. In *Engaged Compassion*, Lobsang Tenzin Negi translates ancient wisdom into a path that is accessible to people of any background. Through these contemplative techniques, gratitude and empathy arise naturally, softening resentment and cynicism while widening the heart. This is a profound and timely offering to His Holiness the Dalai Lama's vision of a global compassion revolution."

—Venerable Thubten Chodron, author of *Working with Anger* and *Open Heart, Clear Mind*

ENGAGED COMPASSION

Seven Practices to Cultivate Resilience, Connection, and a Joyous Life

LOBSANG TENZIN NEGI, PhD

SIMON ELEMENT
New York Amsterdam/Antwerp London
Toronto Sydney/Melbourne New Delhi

An Imprint of Simon & Schuster, LLC
1230 Avenue of the Americas
New York, NY 10020

First Simon Element hardcover edition May 2026

SIMON ELEMENT is a registered trademark of Simon & Schuster, LLC

Interior design by Farzana Razak

Manufactured in the United States of America

10 9 8 7 6 5 4 3 2 1

Library of Congress Control Number: 2025945928

ISBN 978-1-6680-0645-0
ISBN 978-1-6680-0647-4 (ebook)

For those who wake each day
with the quiet courage to serve humanity.

CONTENTS

FOREWORD

BY HIS HOLINESS THE FOURTEENTH DALAI LAMA

In our interdependent world, the need for genuine human connection has never been more urgent. Despite extraordinary material progress, many people continue to experience loneliness, anxiety, and emotional distress. I have long believed—and scientific research increasingly confirms this—that compassion is essential to both personal well-being and collective human flourishing.

Since the late 1960s, I have traveled widely outside India and have come to recognize that emotional suffering is a global challenge. Through my exchanges with educators, scientists, and others, I have seen a clear need for a more holistic educational approach that nurtures both heart and mind, alongside intellectual development.

Soon after our forced escape to India in 1959, with the generous support of the government and people of India, we were able to establish schools and major centers of learning that have enabled us to preserve our distinctive culture of peace and compassion. This remarkable success has been possible due in large part to the resilience and dignity of the Tibetan people inside Tibet.

As one of Emory University's Presidential Distinguished Professors, I have worked closely with the university for many years to support efforts that integrate science and spirituality and develop secular methods for cultivating compassion.

Since the Emory-Tibet Partnership was established in 1998, Contemplative Science and Compassion-Based Ethics have been brought to global academic attention. This has accorded deeply with my vision for education. Among those leading the initiative is Dr. Lobsang Tenzin Negi, executive director of the Center for Contemplative Science and Compassion-Based Ethics. The programs the center has developed for Cognitively Based Compassion Training (CBCT) and Social, Emotional, and Ethical Learning (SEE Learning) have reached many people around the world.

Dr. Negi was just a fourteen-year-old boy when he arrived in Dharamsala from his home in Kinnaur, a remote Indian Himalayan region, to study Buddhist philosophy at our Institute of Buddhist Dialectics. I commend his commitment to contemplative practice and rigorous academic study, as well as his contributions to the development of compassion education.

I am pleased that he has now written this book, *Engaged Compassion: Seven Practices to Cultivate Resilience, Connection, and a Joyous Life*, drawing on his many years of experience. It describes a clear and accessible path for cultivating compassion. May this book inspire readers to help lead meaningful lives with peace and joy.

August 8, 2025

INTRODUCTION

If you want others to be happy, practice compassion.
If you want to be happy, practice compassion.
—His Holiness the Fourteenth Dalai Lama[1]

Imagine becoming the person who instinctively brings kindness into every interaction. One who is remembered for their warmth and generosity. One who lifts up those around them, who remains steady and unshaken, fierce when necessary—for example, in the face of injustice—yet never reactive or consumed by anger. A person who creates a sense of belonging, who connects with others at a deeper level, wherever they go.

This is the essence of leadership—and if we ourselves cannot become the kind of leaders we wish to see in the world, there is little hope for change. It is up to each of us to shift, to grow, to make compassion not just an aspiration but a way of being. This is not an unrealistic ideal, nor does it require suppressing anything within you. Instead, it is a process of bringing forth the best parts of yourself—harnessing the compassion that evolution has wired into us and anchoring it in wisdom and action. As His Holiness has said, "It's not enough to be compassionate. One must act." That is what I hope this book will do: help you along your journey to cultivate your heart and harness the power of engaged compassion.

What you're about to read is the result of more than twenty years of research and practice at the Center for Contemplative Science and Compassion-Based Ethics at Emory University. CBCT® (Cognitively Based Compassion Training) was initially designed in 2004 to help students cope with mental health challenges. CBCT has since become one of the most extensively scientifically studied compassion training programs. This revolutionary meditative practice combines concentration and analytical reasoning. This approach has been tested not just over millennia but also by contemporary medicine and neuroscience. And what sets it apart is that it isn't simply mindfulness. It's not just about being present. While mindfulness and being present are beneficial, they are neither a cure-all nor a sustainable solution on their own.

What makes this protocol different is its ability to reframe thoughts and emotions, literally rewiring the brain so that our best qualities emerge naturally. The results are measurable—not only increased joy, resilience, and fulfillment but also reduced stress, stronger immune function, and improved overall health. And all it takes is fifteen minutes a day. Just you, building a skill that can change your life and the world around you.

Meditation apps can be useful for learning the basics, but if you always rely on them, it's akin to hiring a personal trainer and expecting them to lift the weights for you. At some point, you must build your own strength—which you are absolutely capable of. This book will help you do just that.

And so you can understand how this practice was shaped, I'd like to share where it began for me—high in the Indian Himalayas, where I first learned that compassion wasn't just a value to admire but a skill to be trained, practiced, and embodied.

A BUDDHIST DESTINY

I was born in a remote village in a region called Kinnaur. Our valley was cradled beneath the towering presence of Kinnar Kailash, a majestic, snow-covered peak related to the better-known Mount Kailash in western Tibet that is revered as the abode of the god Shiva in the Hindu tradition and of the deity Chakrasamvara in Tibetan Buddhism. The mountain was a constant companion in my childhood, a silent witness to the rhythms of our daily life.

Our village operated on a barter economy, and we survived mostly on what we grew. The valley was rich with fruit—plums, apples, pears—all thriving in the high altitude and crisp mountain air. We farmed wheat, barley, and corn, and raised goats for wool, spinning it into warm clothing. There was no electricity, no running water—we carried our water from a spring beside our house. My toys were pebbles and sticks; my playground the open landscape. And yet, no one in our village felt poor. We had food, family, and the security of a close-knit community. Life was simple, but it was enough.

Even as a child, I was drawn to the teachings of Buddhism, though I didn't yet understand the depth of their meaning. That understanding would come later, sparked by a school play when I was about nine years old. The play told the story of a young prince named Siddhartha, who would later become the Buddha. He was roaming the royal gardens with his cousin, Devadatta—Siddhartha was known for his kindness, Devadatta for his aggression and jealousy. When Devadatta saw a swan take flight, he swiftly pulled an arrow from his quiver and shot it down. Both boys ran to the fallen bird—Devadatta to claim his prize, Siddhartha to help. Siddhartha knelt beside the injured swan, carefully removing the arrow and gathering herbs to dress its wound. Devadatta was furious. "The swan is mine," he argued. "I shot it."

But Siddhartha refused to hand it over. "It belongs to me because I saved it." The dispute was taken to a judge, who decided that the swan should choose for itself. When the bird was released, it immediately moved toward Siddhartha.

That moment was a revelation to me. Everyone—even animals—prefers kindness over cruelty. Compassion was not just a virtue; it was a force that drew others in, creating trust, safety, and connection. That realization stayed with me, shaping how I saw the world.

Still, I was a restless child. School came easily to me, so I spent most of my time roaming the village, gathering other children to play. I had no fixed schedule, no responsibilities beyond enjoying my days. I would stay out until it got dark, returning home to the safety of my parents' warmth and care. My mother was deeply kind, always invested in her children's development, but she gave me the freedom to follow my own interests and aspirations.

My older brother had become an engineer, working on hydroelectric plants in a town called Nogli, on the other side of the mountains. He had received an education and I wanted one, too. Determined to join him, I hitched a ride on a military truck that could take me only as far as Tapri, near the border checkpoint, about halfway to Nogli. After spending a night there, I was able to get on a bus to Nogli the next day.

When I finally arrived, my brother was shocked to see me standing alone at his doorstep. He was terrified for my safety—and not at all eager to let me stay, as I was only eleven then. He was single at the time, traveling frequently for work, sometimes gone for weeks at a time. If I was to live with him, I had to prove I could take care of myself. If I could do so, he would let me stay.

Within days, I had enrolled in school. Learning Hindi was a struggle at first, but eventually, I excelled. Still, my true desire—the one that had been growing in me for as long as I could remember—was to enter the monastery.

I was fourteen when I hopped into the back of a small pickup truck with two other boys and all my belongings in December of 1974, the coldest time of the year in the Himalayas. The three of us were the fortunate ones whom Geshe Topgyal, a senior Tibetan Buddhist teacher, had handpicked for the journey. To help with the preservation of Tibetan Buddhist culture in this Himalayan region where two of his own teachers were from, His Holiness the Dalai Lama had asked Geshe Topgyal to bring three young boys to study in Dharamsala. The two-day drive was terrifying: At a curve on the Narkanda Pass, at fourteen thousand feet, there was so much snow that we slid backward and barely stopped before rolling off the mountain. It was still snowing when we arrived at the sleepy town of McLeod Ganj at dusk. The cluster of houses snuggled together on the steep hillsides had walls of stone, roofs of metal siding, and dirt floors. These were the early days of the Tibetan refugee community that dominated the area.

Two days later, Geshe Topgyal took us to the residence of His Holiness for an audience. I barely noticed the ornate surroundings, so eager was I to meet His Holiness. I can't explain how moving it is for Tibetan Buddhists to meet what we consider to be the living embodiment of the Buddha of

Compassion. This was such a rare honor—and to this day, I am profoundly grateful to His Holiness and Geshe Topgyal.

His Holiness then instructed Geshe Topgyal to enroll me and my two peers in the Institute of Buddhist Dialectics in Dharamsala. This is where I would spend the next ten years, just a few hundred meters away from His Holiness's residence. The kitchen and dining hall were on the first floor, and we were shown to our beds along the walls of the dining area. On the second floor were the prayer hall and small rooms for our teacher, as well as half a dozen rooms for senior students. There were about thirty of us altogether.

We didn't have clocks, but I remember that the amount of light in spring indicated we woke around 5:30 a.m. for an hour of morning prayers. Breakfast was delicious: thick Tibetan salted butter tea, freshly baked bread, and a generous slice of Western cheese donated by a Tibetan refugee relief fund. After breakfast, we worked on memorizing texts, then engaged in study and reading and a vigorous morning debate in the courtyard. Then lunch, a short afternoon nap, more classes and reading, sweet tea at 3:00, dinner at 5:00, followed by a bit of free time. Evening prayers were at 6:30 or so. Evening debate sessions lasted until 9:30, after which we wound down with black tea and visits with friends. Or we might read quietly and go to sleep by 10:30 or 11:00 p.m.

My teacher, Gen Lobsang Gyatso, would become more than a father to me. He was practical, skillful, and sometimes tough. He was like our parent, best friend, and spiritual guide all in one. He ate every meal with us, played games with us, participated in every ritual, helped us build an extension when the school started to grow, and cried when the health of any of us was in danger. He was a role model for how compassion, understanding, and wisdom were lived.

I didn't know it then, but everything—the lessons of my childhood, my mother's strength, my love for Buddhist teachings, and even my impulsive journey to Nogli—was shaping me for the path ahead. As I reflect on my life's journey, I recognize how fortunate I was to be influenced not only by my early experiences but by the immense influence of His Holiness. His first and most fundamental commitment has always been to promote the well-being of all humanity—not as a Tibetan, not as a Buddhist, not as a monk but as a human being. He has taught that the divisions we create—us versus them, this religion versus that, this country versus another—have caused untold suffering and conflict throughout history. His vision has always been of the oneness of humanity, a deep belief in the interconnection of all people.

His second commitment is to religious harmony and understanding. So much of the world's population belongs to one spiritual tradition or another, and without respect and cooperation, we will continue to see conflict. His Holiness has always urged dialogue, encouraging people of all faiths—and those with none—to recognize our shared humanity.

Finally, as a Tibetan leader, he has carried the responsibility of preserving Tibet's environment and culture while also facilitating the promotion of ancient Indian wisdom. He sees himself not only as a Tibetan but as a "son of India," committed to reviving and sharing the vast spiritual and philosophical heritage that has shaped the region for millennia.

I was raised in this worldview—that our deepest identity is not based on borders or religions but on our shared existence as human beings. That call to unity has shaped every step of my path. I didn't know it when I was a restless child running through the hills of Kinnaur, but I was being prepared for a life devoted to these teachings. It was a journey that would take me far beyond my village, into monastic life, and eventually to the work I do now: bringing the wisdom of compassion and belonging to people around the world.

A NEW AND OLD APPROACH

As I began teaching in the West, I realized that these teachings—this vast, ancient tradition—should not be limited to monks or scholars or those raised in Buddhist cultures. Compassion is a human capacity, not just a Buddhist one. And yet, in much of the world, people are suffering in isolation.

So many people believe that strong emotions—anger, despair, grief—

are unstoppable forces. That once our mind starts spiraling, there is little we can do to stop it from spinning out of control. That life is simply overwhelming, and suffering is something we must bear alone. This is not true.

We are not helpless in the face of our emotions. We are not meant to suffer in isolation. We can stabilize the mind. We can expand our sense of connection. We can create the conditions for flourishing—not just for ourselves but for those around us. This is not wishful thinking; it is a skill that can be cultivated. Inclusivity—bringing more and more people into our circle of care—is not only possible; it is the foundation for well-being, for resilience, for healing.

Right now, our way of living is fraying the fabric of our communities. Anxiety, depression, and loneliness are at an all-time high. People feel isolated, disconnected, unseen. The weight of bias, injustice, economic struggle, and trauma is making it harder and harder to feel safe and at ease. Our nervous systems are on high alert, flooded with stress and fear. When that happens, we lose the ability to solve problems. We lose clarity and start seeing danger everywhere—even in one another.

Fear leads to disconnection. Disconnection leads to blame. And blame fuels a cycle of division, deepening social fracturing and making it harder for any of us to thrive.

If our society is not cohesive, if our institutions are built on fear rather than care, then individuals will struggle to connect, learn, and grow. If individuals cannot flourish, then neither can the systems they create. The more fractured our world becomes, the more we need a shift—not just in policy or structure but in the way we see one another.

Finding a sense of safety is fundamental to well-being. Feeling kinship with those who are different from us, recognizing our shared humanity, is not just a moral ideal—it is a practical necessity. It changes how we relate to others. It changes how we move through the world. When we feel safe, when we feel connected, we become less reactive. Our nervous system settles. Our anxiety lessens. We are more open, more curious, more able to meet challenges with resilience rather than fear.

The power of connection is what makes compassion so transformative. It is not just about being kind. It is about training the mind and heart to see beyond our habitual fears and divisions. It is about recognizing that we are not as separate as we think we are. That was what set me on the path to developing a common language—a bridge between ancient wisdom and modern science. I wanted to take these teachings, these practices that had transformed my own heart and mind, and make them more accessible.

The result of this work was the development of CBCT (Cognitively Based Compassion Training)—an initiative to advance a global culture of compassion through programs that span the disciplines of education, business, health care, and human services. In the beginning, CBCT training for Emory students was offered in collaboration with Emory's counseling center. Then, it expanded into Emory's medical school, where doctors, nurses, chaplains, and hospital administrators began training in compassion—not just as a concept but as a concrete skill that could change the way they approached patient care.

From there, CBCT continued to grow. It is now taught in police departments, hospitals, businesses, and schools. More significantly, it has informed the development of SEE Learning® (Social, Emotional, and Ethical Learning), a K–12 program to cultivate inner values, which has now reached more than twenty million teachers and students around the world. This is what gives me hope.

Compassion is not just an idea. It is not a luxury for those who have time to meditate. It is a trainable skill. And when we cultivate it, it ripples outward. It strengthens our relationships. It helps us meet life's difficulties with steadiness rather than reactivity. It creates safer, more cohesive communities.

We do not have to be trapped in patterns of fear, division, and isolation. We can choose something different. That is the heart of this work.

ACTIVE BELONGING

When we feel safe, we're able to show up for others with openness instead of fear. When we trust in our own worth, we're less defensive, less overwhelmed by life's challenges. Hardship doesn't have to shut us down—it can actually strengthen us, helping us connect more deeply with others who have struggled, too. The tender awareness of our shared struggles is the seed of compassion.

If we understood how powerful compassion is, we would live differently. We'd see that it's not just a "good" idea—it's the key to stronger relationships, healthier communities, and a better world. But even when we practice it, we experience limitations. When someone we love is suffering, our response is immediate. But our empathy tends to be selective, shaped by familiarity and proximity. The brain filters out those who seem different. Yet, in certain moments—like when the world saw the image of Aylan Kurdi, a Syrian refugee child, washed up on a beach—our shared humanity becomes undeniable. More recently, during the early days of the COVID-19 pandemic, we witnessed spontaneous acts of compassion around the world: people singing from balconies to uplift their neighbors, health care workers risking everything to protect strangers, and communities coming together to care for the vulnerable. These moments of recognition move us to act, but they are often fleeting. With training, however, that openness can be sustained.

We can begin by asking ourselves:

- Do I hold a deep yearning for peace and well-being?
- Do I wish to be free of pain and struggle?
- Am I alone in these desires, or do I share them with all others?

By sitting with these questions, we move from feeling separate and isolated to recognizing our profound connection to all human beings. And in doing so, we start to experience something that can feel so scarce in our world today: a deep sense of belonging.

Belonging isn't just about fitting in or being accepted by others—it's about knowing, at the core of our being, that we are part of something larger than ourselves. It's the recognition that our joys and struggles are not ours alone, that our existence is intertwined with the lives of countless others. When we cultivate compassion, we awaken to this truth. We begin to see that we are not meant to go through life alone; that support and connection are available to us, not just in our closest relationships but in our shared humanity. The more we practice compassion, the more this sense of belonging becomes a felt experience rather than an abstract idea. And with it comes a new strength: the confidence that no matter how hard life gets, we are not alone.

This book is a guide to making compassion a way of life—an inner skill that brings stability, connection, and purpose in a changing world. Through its practices, you'll learn how to create a sense of belonging within yourself and become a source of that same belonging for others. Part One explores the forgotten power of compassion, an ancient and often overlooked capacity that holds the key to personal healing and collective transformation. In these chapters, we explore the roots of compassion and the development of CBCT, weaving together ancient wisdom, personal story, and the early scientific discoveries that inspired this work. Part Two guides you through the seven steps of the CBCT process, offering practical instructions, deeper scientific insights, and tools to cultivate compassion as a way of life.

Each of the seven steps in the CBCT process, which we'll explore in depth throughout this book, liberates us from old patterns:

- **Moments of nurturance** free us from insecurity.
- **Stable and clear attention** gives us space between stimulus and response.
- **Self-awareness** frees us from impulsivity.
- **Self-compassion** releases us from self-blame.
- **Expanded concern** breaks down isolation and bias.

- **Gratitude and tenderness** nourish our heart with warmth.
- **Compassion** moves us from helplessness to wise action.

CBCT is one of the longest-running secular compassion training programs in the world; it is also one of the most scientifically validated. For millennia, spiritual traditions have emphasized the value of compassion in fostering a sense of belonging and awareness of our intrinsic interconnectedness. Now, modern science confirms what these traditions have long understood: The human mind is capable of change, and compassion can be trained. Studies show that its benefits complement many other interventions, including mindfulness practices, by directly addressing the root of human suffering: disconnection. Former surgeon general Vivek Murthy has called loneliness the defining epidemic of our time, linking it to anxiety, depression, and even premature death. But loneliness is not inevitable. CBCT is a direct and proven antidote.

CBCT's impact has been studied in foster children, trauma survivors, veterans with post-traumatic stress disorder (PTSD), cancer and suicide survivors, and individuals struggling with depression, anxiety, and chronic pain. The results are undeniable. And in a time of unprecedented uncertainty, the need for this work has never been greater.

Thankfully, times of crisis can also awaken solidarity. They remind us that we are not alone. And when we train ourselves to expand our circle of care, we turn belonging into a choice, not a circumstance. We use it to bridge divides, to move beyond tribalism, to heal wounds of bias and inequality.

Engaged Compassion: Seven Practices to Cultivate Resilience, Connection, and a Joyous Life is the first book to lay out the CBCT process in full. In my tradition, we are taught from a young age that every person we meet is a part of our extended family and that our own well-being is deeply tied to the well-being of others. That understanding stayed with me through years of study and meditation, and later through my work developing this protocol. The impact has been profound—helping people not only reduce stress and emotional suffering but also build resilience, deepen connections, and live with greater ease and purpose. I've seen firsthand how small shifts in perspective can bring people back to themselves, and back to each other.

My deepest hope is that this book will make a meaningful difference in your life. Every act of compassion, no matter how small, contributes to a better world. And when we change ourselves—even in the simplest, most incremental ways—we change everything.

PART ONE

THE FORGOTTEN POWER OF COMPASSION

CHAPTER ONE

COMPASSION—THE GREATEST NOURISHMENT OF ALL

Basic human nature is compassion.

—His Holiness the Fourteenth Dalai Lama[1]

When I first began teaching at Emory University in the early 2000s, depression, anxiety, and suicide were on the rise, paralyzing some of the student population. Despite the fact that so many were struggling, most were trying to cope alone, believing they had to bear their suffering in isolation.

In 2003, Molly Harrington was a student in my course "Tibetan Buddhism: The Psychology of Enlightenment," and she saw this clearly. She was a mental health advocate, deeply committed to raising awareness and ensuring that students could get the help they needed. She understood that shame around emotional suffering keeps us from reaching out—even though connection and belonging are what we need most in order to heal. One day after class, she came to me and said, "Professor Negi, there has to be a way to adapt what we are learning here to help other students. I know we can do it."

Her determination inspired me. It also reminded me of a story from the Buddhist tradition. I come back to it again and again, not because it's ancient but because it feels like it could be happening today. In a way, I think it is.

One day, the Buddha was walking with five of his closest students along a quiet path in the hills. The sun was just beginning to rise, casting soft light over the trees, the rocks, the river below. As they walked, a young man came running toward them. He was dressed in expensive clothes, fine fabrics clinging to his body like they didn't belong. His eyes were wild. He didn't look at anyone. He was running straight for the cliff.

He wasn't just running away from something—he was running toward an end. Just before he reached the edge, the Buddha stepped forward and gently caught his arm. The young man jerked away.

"Why are you stopping me?" he demanded. "Who are you to interfere? You don't know me. You don't know my pain. There's nothing left for me. I'm done."

The Buddha didn't argue. He didn't lecture or shame. He simply held on with quiet strength and said, "This life isn't just yours. It doesn't belong to you alone. Your parents, your grandparents, and generations before them lived, struggled, and loved so that you could be here. If you leave, your pain won't disappear. It will ripple outward. It will break others who love you."

The young man froze. His eyes were still locked on the cliff—but now, for the first time, he noticed what was below. A waterfall, powerful and beautiful, tumbled over the rocks into a deep blue pool. He hadn't seen it before, even though it had been there all along. He looked up. The world was still there—sunlight, birds, trees swaying in the wind.

"Was this always here?" he whispered.

"Yes," the Buddha replied. "It was always here."

In that moment, the young man softened. It wasn't that his pain disappeared—but a seed of peace, or wonder, or simply presence, began to take root. He looked at the Buddha—this calm, grounded man who had shown him kindness when he expected judgment—and asked, "What are you?"

And as the Buddha shared his path—the practices of compassion, wisdom, clarity, and connection—the young man felt something he hadn't felt in a long time: the desire to live. Not just to survive but to live differently. He asked if he could follow the Buddha, to learn from him. And he did. He became a monk. When his parents heard what had happened, they were furious. How could their son abandon the privileged life they had worked so hard to give him, just to join what they saw as a wandering spiritual group?

But one of the Buddha's senior students quietly asked them, "Would you rather your son be dead?"

The question hung in the air. Their anger dissolved into understanding, and then into gratitude. Their son hadn't vanished—he had returned to them. Not the same, but more himself than ever before.

Stories like this remind us that even in our darkest moments, compassion can open a path back to ourselves and to one another. But not every culture, or every philosophical tradition, has emphasized this possibility. While many ancient traditions have centered connection, care, and belonging as the foundation of human nature, others have taken a more skeptical view. Some voices, particularly in the modern Western world, have argued that, when left to their own devices, people will choose cruelty over kindness, competition over cooperation. These assumptions have shaped not just literature and philosophy but also our institutions and policies—and, perhaps most painfully, the way we see ourselves and each other.

But history tells a different story. Humans have not survived because of selfishness—we have survived because of kindness and cooperation. The belief that people are inherently selfish has shaped modern economies, policies, and power structures, reinforcing the idea that life is a ruthless competition. This mindset comes from thinkers like Machiavelli, who promoted ruling by fear, or Hobbes, who described life in a state of nature as "nasty, brutish, and short." Even Darwin's ideas were twisted into "survival of the fittest," when in reality, his work emphasized adaptability and collaboration.

Tibetan culture operates from the assumption that our positive qualities—kindness, sense of connection, and cooperation—run deeper than our negative ones. Though humans can act selfishly, our most natural instinct is compassion. This is one of the central truths that the first part of this book seeks to remember: that compassion is an ancient wisdom that is rising once more to meet our time. Although we can sometimes forget this, when we calm the mind and see reality clearly, we recognize that acts of kindness far outnumber acts of cruelty. This understanding is what allows His Holiness to transform the loss of Tibet into something greater. Rather than dwelling in exile with bitterness, he has dedicated his life to ensuring that compassion is not only a personal value but a subject of scientific inquiry and a focus of education—one that has given rise to the field of contemplative neuroscience.

CBCT is part of this growing movement. It helps us examine the hidden assumptions shaping our lives—assumptions that can either keep us trapped in fear or open us to a more compassionate way of being. Through practice, we learn to reframe our perspectives, shifting away from cynicism and toward connection.

We have a choice: We can see the world through a lens of competition and scarcity, or we can see it through the lens of belonging and care. This is the shift that CBCT makes possible—not just for individuals but for entire cultures.

WHAT IS COMPASSION?

In CBCT, we define compassion as a complex psychological state with three aspects:

> **A Heartfelt Connection (Affective):** This is the emotional part of compassion. It's the warmth or tenderness you feel when you experience connection. It's what happens when you see a friend crying and your chest tightens, or when you hear good news about a loved one and you instinctively place a hand on your heart. This affective connection creates the emotional bridge between you and someone else. Without it, your response may stay detached or purely intellectual. *Example:* You're walking down the street and see someone

sitting on the curb, visibly distressed. Before you even know the details, you feel a pang of concern in your chest. That's the affective, or emotional, component.

An Understanding of Another's Suffering (Cognitive): This is where the mind joins the heart. It's the recognition of what the other person is actually going through. It's about putting the pieces together: What are they up against? What pain, fear, or limitation are they experiencing? This aspect of compassion helps you see context, not just the moment of suffering. It opens the door to perspective-taking. *Example:* You learn that a coworker who's been short with you lately is caring for an ill parent while working two jobs. Suddenly, their behavior makes more sense—not as a personal offense but as a result of deep stress. That mental shift is the cognitive element of compassion.

The Wish to Help (Motivational): This is the drive that turns compassion from a feeling into a response. It's not merely feeling for someone or understanding pain—it's about wanting to do something to help ease it. This could mean stepping in with support, speaking up on someone's behalf, donating time or resources, or even just offering your full presence. It doesn't have to be grand. What matters is the motivation: the sincere desire to reduce suffering. *Example:* After learning about your coworker's situation, you offer to cover for them during a stressful week or bring them a meal. That small, intentional action is compassion in motion.

Bringing all three of these aspects together, **compassion is a warm-hearted concern that unfolds when we witness the suffering of others and feel motivated to relieve it.**

Our need for compassion is as basic as our need for nourishing food or clean water. It is not just an ideal or a virtue—it is a survival instinct. From the moment we are born, we depend on the care of others. Without it, we would not survive infancy, let alone thrive in a complex world.

His Holiness reminds us, "Love and compassion are necessities, not luxuries. Without them, humanity cannot survive." This is not simply a philosophical statement; it is a reflection of how we are wired. Care for one another is as old as life itself. From the earliest forms of existence—single-celled organisms clustering together for protection—to the deeply social nature of human beings, connection has always maximized survival. As pioneering American biologist Lynn Margulis so aptly noted, "Life did not take over the globe by combat but by networking."[2]

Evolution is, in many ways, a story of increasing cooperation. Early humans hunted together, extending their sense of kinship to others who helped ensure their survival. Agriculture required even greater collaboration, expanding that sense of "one of us." Spiritual beliefs, culture, and social bonds emerged, reinforcing who we saw as part of our group. Over time, villages became towns, and towns became cities—living proof that compassion and cooperation are at the core of human success.

Yet today, so many of us feel isolated. We live in a world that, through technology, is more interconnected than ever, but loneliness and polarization are at an all-time high. What we are missing is not connection in the digital sense but a genuine sense of connection—the kind of belonging that comes from knowing that we are not separate from one another. And that is where compassion comes in.

Compassion arises from a deep, bodily understanding that we are intrinsically connected. Even when we don't feel it, something in us recognizes that our lives are bound together. From that recognition comes a natural impulse to care for one another. This isn't merely a choice or virtue, or even an emotion; rather, it is an impulse, an instinct to ease the pain of others. And it is not reserved for those we already know and love—it extends to everyone, even those we may struggle to understand.

We're all taught to be nice or kind. However, this isn't the same as being compassionate. What we tend to define as "kindness" and "niceness" usually amounts to keeping the peace, avoiding conflict, or making sure people like us. While well-intentioned, it is often rooted in appearances rather than real care. Compassion is different. It's active. It's about seeing suffering, staying present with it, and doing what actually helps—even when that means having tough conversations, setting boundaries, or standing up for what's just and right. Compassion isn't about making people comfortable all the time; it's about truly being there for them in a way that matters.

We are all born with the capacity for compassion, but like any skill, it must be cultivated. Despite this, many people struggle with the idea of compassion. Some believe it is something you either have or don't. Others see it as passive, as if being compassionate means accepting injustice or allowing harm to continue. And many feel helpless, overwhelmed by the sheer magnitude of suffering in the world. If we can't fix everything, they wonder, what's the point in trying at all?

But compassion is not weakness. It is not passive. It does not mean accepting injustice or ignoring harm. It takes courage to stay open when the world feels harsh. It takes resilience to keep caring when life gets overwhelming. And history has shown us that compassion, when acted upon, has changed the world.

Mahatma Gandhi did not win India's independence alone. He was inspired by the teachings of nonviolence and worked alongside tens of thousands of others who were committed to the same vision. Martin Luther King Jr. did not lead the Civil Rights Movement by himself—he trained in nonviolent resistance with those who had studied Gandhi, and together, they created change.

Making the Compassion Shift does not mean we will solve every problem overnight. We will not end world hunger simply by wishing for it. But that does not mean we do nothing. Every act of compassion matters. Every choice to be open rather than closed, to reach out rather than turn away, helps create the world we want to live in. The key is not to be overwhelmed by the scale of suffering but to do what we can, when we can, with whomever we can. Compassion is not about fixing everything—it is about being present, being willing, and choosing connection over separation.

THE POWER OF STORIES

Stories have a way of reaching the heart in ways that facts and theories cannot. They make complex truths feel real, immediate, personal. Throughout this book, I will share many stories—some from the Buddhist tradition, others from the lives of people who have been deeply affected by this practice. All of them are meant to remind us that doubt, struggle, and the longing to help—even when we feel overwhelmed—are part of being human.

I don't expect you to take the tale I'm about to share literally, but I do believe stories carry the power to speak across centuries, across cultures, and straight into the heart. This one has always resonated with me, especially in times when I've questioned my own ability to help.

Avalokitesvara is a name many may not know, but his story is one we can all recognize in some form. He is a central figure in the Buddhist tradition—a *bodhisattva*, which means someone who devotes their life to easing the suffering of others, not for personal gain or spiritual achievement but out of a deep sense of responsibility and care. He represents compassion at its most expansive: limitless, unconditional, and enduring.

But even Avalokitesvara struggled. According to the tradition, he had already made an extraordinary vow: to bear witness to the suffering of every living being and to do everything in his power to help. He wasn't some far-removed ideal—he was someone who wanted, more than anything, to relieve pain wherever he saw it. He meditated with this intention, focused and sincere, trying to strengthen his heart with every breath.

But one day, something shifted. Maybe he had seen too much suffering, or maybe he simply felt the weight of how much pain there was in the world. War. Poverty. Injustice. Everyday cruelty. The kind of slow, grinding sorrow that doesn't make headlines but breaks lives all the same. The more he took it in, the more overwhelmed he felt. His vow began to feel impossible. The desire to help was still there—but so was a creeping sense of inadequacy, even despair. And in that moment of doubt, his head shattered—splintering into a thousand pieces.

The story says that this was a physical transformation, but haven't we all had moments like that? When something inside us gets to the breaking point—not from anger but from trying too hard to hold everything together? When our will to do good, to be present for others, suddenly feels too fragile to carry on?

Amazingly, Avalokitesvara didn't remain broken. Even in that moment of despair, he never lost his connection to his spiritual teacher. It was this enduring connection to Buddha Amitabha that became the source of strength that allowed Avalokitesvara's shattered form to reassemble—now with ten faces and a thousand arms, each hand bearing an open eye. The arms represent his deepened resolve to reach all who suffer; the eyes his ability to truly see their pain. Amitabha appears as the eleventh face at the top, a stabilizing presence and source of guidance.

Through this transformation, Avalokitesvara became not just whole again but even more capable—anchored in wisdom, expansive in compassion, and committed more than ever to relieving the suffering of all beings.

What does this have to do with those of us living in the reality of the twenty-first century? More than you might think. Compassion is not always easy. It can be fierce and exhausting. We feel pulled in so many directions—toward people we love, causes we care about, strangers we want to help. And yet, we often reach a breaking point. We begin to feel small against the backdrop of so much need. We question whether anything we do really matters.

Avalokitesvara's story reminds us that even the most devoted among us feel doubt. Even pure embodiments of compassion falter. But when that compassion is rooted in belonging—when we remember that we are not alone, that we're held by something greater, whether it's a spiritual path, a teacher, a community, or simply the love of another person—it becomes something we can return to and grow from.

And perhaps most importantly, this story teaches us that our breaking points are not failures. They are often the very moments that give rise to new strength, new understanding, and deeper connection. What shatters can be reshaped—into more arms to help, more eyes to see, more capacity to love.

We begin our journey with this story not because we are expected to become Avalokitesvara but because we, too, are moved by the same impulse: to care, to help, to belong, even when we're not sure how.

As we begin to practice compassion together, you don't need a thousand arms or eyes. What you need is what Avalokitesvara rediscovered—your own deep capacity to care, anchored in connection. And, as you cultivate this capacity, it becomes something you'll return to again and again, even when it feels impossible.

MAKING THE COMPASSION SHIFT: THE SEVEN-STEP MEDITATIVE PROCESS

The stories I've shared in this chapter, of the young man at the cliff and of Avalokitesvara's very human sense of overwhelm, remind us that all it takes is a shift in perspective—seeing something that was always there but has gone unnoticed—to experience the deep gifts of compassion. When this occurs, we steady ourselves in times of despair, reconnect with life, and recognize the invisible threads that bind us to others. I have returned to this lesson again and again, both in my personal journey and in my teaching.

As I mentioned in the Introduction, I grew up in the Himalayas of Northern India. Culturally, our region was Tibetan, but we lived on the Indian side of the border. Unlike those who were forced to flee when the Communist Chinese armies annexed Tibet in 1959, we did not experience the uprooting of our culture firsthand. We did not have to escape the violence of 1959, when His Holiness, many great lamas, and tens of thousands of Tibetans fled to India, where so many have remained in exile.

Yet what has always struck me about Tibetan culture is that, even in the face of unimaginable loss—even when people's families were separated and their homeland was no longer their own—there was very little depression or suicide among the exile community. This does not mean that people weren't scared or sad. But something protected them from falling into despair. I believe that something was compassion. Compassion is not seen as something extra or nice to have—it is a necessity, a way of surviving hardship and making life meaningful. The knowledge that you are not alone, that your suffering is not yours to carry in isolation, changes everything.

Of course, not everyone was raised with compassion woven into daily life the way it is in Tibetan culture. In the West, many of us are taught to value independence, achievement, or emotional toughness over connection and care. Compassion is innate to our humanity, and we can expand its reach in our lives. With the right tools and intention, anyone—regardless of background or belief—can develop it into a steady, guiding presence.

Think back to when you first learned to drive a car or navigate public transportation. At first, every step required conscious effort—checking mirrors, watching for turns, counting stops. Over time, the process became automatic. You could drive to a familiar place or take the same train route without much thought, arriving at your destination as if by instinct.

This is how the brain works. When we practice something repeatedly, our neural pathways strengthen, making it easier and more natural. Neuroscientists call this the default mode network (DMN)—a set of connections in the brain that reinforce habits, whether it's swinging a golf club or determining our own emotional reactions.

What we often don't realize is that the same principle applies to how we relate to ourselves and others. The way we respond to hardship, interpret challenges, view connection and belonging—these are habits shaped by practice. If we have been conditioned to react with fear, self-criticism, or isolation, those patterns will dominate. But just as we can train our bodies for physical skill, we can train our minds and hearts for compassion.

The practice does not require years of study or a lifetime of meditation. It takes as little as fifteen minutes a day. In that time, we can begin to reshape the way we experience our struggles, how we see others, and how we respond to the suffering in the world. With consistency, we become the kind of person who naturally radiates warmth, steadiness, and strength—someone others feel safe around, who brings out the best in people, whose kindness is not performative but deeply rooted in wisdom.

Neuroscientific research now confirms that contemplative practices like compassion training change the brain. I have seen this firsthand in functional MRI scans of meditators practicing compassion training—the brain's joy centers light up, bringing a greater sense of ease and connection to our lives. Compassion strengthens us, grounds us, and makes life more meaningful. It is the key to belonging—to expanding our circle of care until, one day, it includes all beings.

Through CBCT, we have distilled these ancient methods into an accessible, seven-step process:

Finding your sources of nurturance
We begin by recalling a time when we felt deeply loved, safe, or protected—whether by a person, an animal, or even an imagined source of safety. This step activates the nervous system's natural relaxation response, allowing us to settle into a sense of security and care.

Developing a clear and stable attention
From this grounded state, we practice focusing our attention—typically on the breath. Each time the mind wanders, we gently bring it back. Over time, this strengthens our ability to remain present, reducing emotional reactivity and increasing clarity.

Practicing open awareness
With increased attention, we turn our awareness inward. We observe our thoughts and emotions without immediately reacting, creating space between stimulus and response. This step builds resilience by allowing us to experience emotions without being overwhelmed by them.

Making space for self-compassion
Many of us hold ourselves to impossible standards, berating ourselves for mistakes or perceived failures. This step involves shifting

that internal dialogue—recognizing that suffering and imperfection are part of the human experience and offering ourselves the same kindness we would extend to a friend.

Expanding our circle of concern
Compassion starts close to home but is meant to grow outward. In this step, we rehearse the reality that, just like us, every person we encounter faces struggles and vulnerabilities. By intentionally broadening our sense of who is "one of us," we dissolve barriers and increase our capacity for connection.

Nourishing the heart with gratitude and tenderness
When we reflect on how much of our lives depends on the kindness of others—from the food we eat to the knowledge we inherit—we awaken a deep sense of appreciation. This gratitude fosters warmth, empathy, and a sense of belonging.

Easing the suffering of the world
The final step is about action. Compassion is not just a feeling—it is a call to respond. Here, we train ourselves to move from passive empathy to active care, finding meaningful and sustainable ways to help.

With each of these steps, we strengthen the causes of happiness. We rewire our minds so that compassion, clarity, and courage become our default responses to life.

PSYCHOLOGICAL SAFETY AND DEEP BELONGING

We long for a sense of belonging—within our families, our workplaces, our communities, and even in society at large. But despite living in an era of unprecedented connectivity, loneliness and division are at an all-time high. Why?

Part of the answer lies in how we experience safety—not just physical safety but the kind of psychological safety that allows us to exhale, be ourselves, and connect more deeply with others. A sense of inner safety and compassion can shift how we move through the world. But these shifts aren't just inward-facing. They ripple outward—into our relationships, our workplaces, our neighborhoods. Think about a time when you truly felt safe with another person—maybe it was a teacher who made you feel seen or a friend who listened without judgment. Those experiences don't just feel good—they shape how we show up, how willing we are to take risks, to speak honestly, to support others.

I recall reading a story about health care workers in the midst of the COVID-19 pandemic. One nurse, exhausted and on the verge of tears, said that after another day of witnessing loss, all she wanted was to sit in the break room and not feel invisible. "I didn't need a grand gesture," she said. "Just a nod, a smile, someone noticing I existed." That small moment—just being seen—was what she longed for. And in her longing, I saw something universal: This is what safety can look like. Not just the absence of threat but the presence of care. A glance that says, "You matter." A hand on the shoulder that says, "You aren't alone." These moments don't just soothe our nervous systems—they remind us of who we are.

The ability to feel safe, connected, and part of something larger than ourselves is one of our deepest human needs. When we don't have that, we withdraw. We armor up. We stop trusting, stop reaching out, and slowly begin to lose touch—not only with others but with ourselves. But when we feel that kind of safety, we open. We soften. We step in instead of stepping back.

This kind of connection—real, steady, rooted in compassion—isn't a luxury. It's what makes strong families, strong teams, and strong communities possible. We often think change begins with grand plans or sweeping reforms. But more often, it begins in the quiet, human moments where one person chooses to show up with care.

When people feel safe and valued, they show up more fully. One study conducted by Google, known as Project Aristotle, set out to uncover what makes a great team.[3] The researchers expected to find that the most successful teams were composed of people with similar traits—high achievers, extroverts, or those with complementary skill sets. But after years of analyzing data, no single characteristic predicted success. The breakthrough came when they shifted their focus from who was on the team to *how* the team members interacted.

The key factor? Psychological safety. The most successful teams were the ones where people felt safe to speak up, share ideas, take risks, and even make mistakes without fear of judgment. When individuals knew they would be met with respect, empathy, and support, they became more engaged, creative, and productive. This kind of environment doesn't just boost performance. When we feel safe, we feel that we belong. And when we feel we belong, we thrive.

Belonging is a deep evolutionary instinct—one that has allowed humans to form tight-knit communities and survive against overwhelming odds. But like all instincts, it has a shadow side. Throughout history, the same drive that helps us bond with those we consider "our people" has also fueled division, tribalism, and fear of those who are different from us.

Long ago, those outside the tribe could pose a real danger, so our ancestors developed a deep-rooted wariness of the "other." This instinct, once essential for survival, now manifests in ways that divide us—through bias, prejudice, and the tendency to retreat into echo chambers where we engage only with those who think like us. It is an impulse that fuels conflict on every scale, from personal relationships to global politics. No wonder establishing a sense of psychological safety can feel like an impossibility at times.

Human beings have never lived in such large, interconnected societies. Today, we share our cities, workplaces, and online spaces with people with vastly different backgrounds, belief systems, and experiences. Our world is inescapably diverse. It isn't just that we are physically together in massive cities, with more than fifty percent of the earth's population dwelling in urban areas. Our interaction is global. Airplanes and digital communications mean borders are no longer solid. At any moment, whether in person or online, we come face-to-face with people who look different and hold different values. At any moment, that very loud instinct to "other" them, to make them an enemy or to feel disconnected from them, can be triggered. And without actively expanding our sense of kinship beyond our immediate circle, we risk fostering even deeper division, stress, and isolation.

This isn't just an abstract problem—it affects our well-being on a daily basis. When we do not feel a sense of safety and connection with those around us, we experience heightened stress, anxiety, and loneliness. Our nervous system remains on high alert, interpreting difference as danger. In this state, misunderstandings increase, cooperation decreases, and the fabric of society begins to fray.

Without deliberately widening our circle of belonging—without actively choosing to recognize the shared humanity in those we might see as different—we miss one of our greatest opportunities for healing. We miss the chance to not only find connection for ourselves but be a source of belonging and safety for others.

Most animals have some degree of empathy, but what makes human beings unique is our ability to consciously reframe our perspective. We have the capacity to override instinct, to step outside of fear-based reactions, and to deliberately cultivate compassion. This ability comes from our uniquely evolved brain—specifically, the prefrontal cortex, which governs impulse control, judgment, and higher reasoning.

When we practice compassion, we activate this part of the brain in a way that shifts our default responses. Compassion frees us from the wounds of our past, from the fear of how others perceive us, and from the limitations of tribal thinking. It gives us the ability to choose connection over division, to see the humanity in those we might have once dismissed, and to lead with wisdom rather than reactivity.

We cannot afford to wait for leaders, policies, or external forces to fix the fractures in our world. If we want things to change, we must be the changemakers—the ones who model what's possible when we choose compassion over division. We can be firm when necessary, but never cruel. We can refuse to let fear dictate how we see the world.

And it is something we can practice. Every day. In small, simple moments.

REFLECTION QUESTIONS

- Who in your life needs to feel seen and valued? (Consider that the top person on that list might be you.)
- Where can you extend a sense of psychological safety and expand your circle of belonging?
- How might you challenge an assumption about someone who seems different from you?
- What kind of world do you want to live in—and what can you do, today, to help create it?

As a new awareness of our hidden relatedness to others emerges from our meditative inquiry together, how you feel, think, and act will change over time. Warmhearted connection will feel natural, normal. Acting with compassion will become second nature, and you will be a source of care and safety for yourself and others.

CHAPTER TWO

ANCIENT SOURCE, NEW SCIENCE

To grow old is to pass from passion to compassion.
—Albert Camus

Nalanda University—once the crown jewel of Buddhist scholarship in Northern India—was the kind of place that shaped civilizations. Think of it as the ancient world's version of a modern Ivy League institution, where the brightest minds gathered not only to study but to rigorously test and debate ideas that had the power to shape human consciousness. In the eighth century, among the thousands of brilliant monks at Nalanda was a young man named Shantideva.

To most people around him, Shantideva was a disappointment. He didn't engage in scholarly debates. He didn't seem interested in rituals or teaching. In fact, the other monks said he had mastered only three things: eating, sleeping, and defecating. His presence seemed like an embarrassment to the great institution. Eventually, the monastic leadership decided to push him out—not by force but by humiliation.

They called for every monk to give a public teaching from an elevated throne in front of the entire university. When it was Shantideva's turn, they made sure the stairs to the throne were removed—just to make his failure that much more dramatic. But Shantideva surprised everyone. Calmly, without hesitation, he walked to the towering throne, reached out with one hand, and pressed it down until it was low enough for him to step onto. Then, with complete composure, he sat and said: "I have nothing new to share that hasn't already been taught. But perhaps what I say may be of benefit to someone who, like me, is still trying to walk the path."

And then, he delivered what would become one of the most influential spiritual texts in all of Buddhism: *A Guide to the Bodhisattva's Way of Life*—a sweeping, poetic, profoundly practical teaching on how to live with courage, humility, and boundless compassion. It wasn't just a recitation of philosophy; it was an invitation to a way of being. He taught about what it means to be a *bodhisattva*—a person who chooses not only to seek their own freedom from suffering but also to dedicate their life to relieving the suffering of others. He spoke of the power of patience in the face of harm, the strength that comes from humility, and the clarity that arises when we replace self-absorption with concern for others.

One of his verses says:

> May I be an isle for those who yearn for land,
> A lamp for those who long for light;
> For all who need a resting place, a bed;
> For those who need a servant, may I be their slave.
> And therefore I'll dispel the pain of others,
> For it is simply pain, just like my own.[1]

As the story goes, when he reached the final verses—describing the nature of ultimate reality, where compassion and wisdom merge into perfect freedom—his body began to rise into the air. The monks watched, awestruck, as he levitated higher and higher, his voice becoming fainter, until only those with the sharpest inner ears could hear the last lines of his teaching.

But the real miracle wasn't the levitation. It was the depth of what he offered. In that one teaching, Shantideva laid out a complete path—a method for training the mind not only to become calm and focused but to overflow with compassion so powerful it could change the world. His words became a cornerstone of Tibetan Buddhism and the heart of the *lojong* (mind training) tradition.

Shantideva's major insight was that compassion isn't a nice idea or a feel-good emotion. It's a discipline. A skill. A strength we can develop—not to escape life but to engage with it fully, wisely, and with an open heart. Shantideva shared extensively about a capacity known as *bodhichitta*, which you can think of as compassion elevated to its highest expression. It's the desire to live in a way that helps others—not just out of duty but out of genuine love and care. It's what happens when compassion deepens into commitment. In today's world, where loneliness, burnout, and disconnection are so widespread, this mindset matters more than ever. Bodhichitta offers a powerful alternative: Instead of turning inward or shutting down in the face of suffering, we expand our hearts and ask, "How can I help?" Shantideva's teachings are timeless because they speak to something deeply human—the longing to live with meaning, to contribute, and to feel part of something bigger than ourselves.

Centuries later, his text would serve as the inspiration and blueprint for CBCT. Just like Shantideva's teaching, CBCT rests on the truth that our minds are not fixed. We can train our attention, shift our perspectives, and cultivate a sense of care and belonging so deep that it transforms how we live and relate to others.

Without a steady mind, we're easily pulled in every direction—by emails, social media, news alerts, deadlines, and the constant pressure to do more, be more, respond faster. In this reactive state, it's easy to get caught up in anger, anxiety, jealousy, or comparison. We snap at loved ones, judge ourselves harshly, and make decisions we later regret. When our minds are constantly hijacked by stress, anxiety, resentment, or distraction, we lose our center. We might lash out in traffic, scroll past a loved one's quiet distress, or fall into bed each night feeling depleted but not quite sure why. Our choices become reactive. We ghost people instead of having hard conversations. We numb ourselves instead of facing what hurts. And without realizing it, we drift into a quiet loneliness—a life where we're constantly doing, but rarely connecting.

But when we learn to steady the mind, the grip of reactivity loosens. We start to catch ourselves in the pause between feeling and reaction. We notice when we're spiraling—and we come back. We stay present through someone else's pain without trying to fix it. We begin to see others not as problems to solve or threats to manage but as human beings just like us—imperfect, vulnerable, trying their best. Shantideva's teachings remind us of something that feels especially relevant today: We don't have control over most of what happens in the world. (In fact, he explicitly stated this.) We can't stop wars or natural disasters on our own. We can't prevent people from getting sick or guarantee that life will go according to plan. But what we *can* do is shape how we respond. Shantideva didn't pretend that suffering would disappear—he knew life could be painful and unfair. What he offered was a way to face it without falling apart. Even if we can't fix the whole world, we can choose how we show up in it—and that choice has power.

Living with a deep, embodied sense of compassion doesn't mean we're always calm or kind or wise. It means we stay in relationship—with ourselves, with others, with the moment. It means we say "I'm sorry" more easily. It means we ask "What do you need?" instead of jumping to conclusions. It means we set boundaries without shutting people out. It means we begin to trust that our presence matters—that simply being a steady, caring presence in the world is powerful. And from that place, compassion stops being something we try to do. It becomes something we are.

This is what I learned as a young monk studying *A Guide to the Bodhisattva's Way of Life*, listening to His Holiness and other masters expound on its wisdom. It became my personal guide, not just to understanding compassion but to living it. In 1978, when His Holiness traveled to Manali, a small town in the Kullu Valley of Northern India, I was given the honor of translating and summarizing his teachings on this sacred text for my fellow Kinnauris. I was still early in my studies and felt the weight of this responsibility deeply. Determined to prepare as thoroughly as possible, I read and reread the text, committing entire chapters to memory. I recited its verses on long walks and reflected on them during quiet moments.

By the time His Holiness began his teachings, my reverence for Shantideva's wisdom was unshakable. Just as His Holiness had cherished these teachings from his own masters, I tried to absorb them into my very being. That experience convinced me of something that would shape the course of my life.

What Shantideva taught over a thousand years ago is now being confirmed by modern science. Studies in contemplative science show that regular compassion meditation can rewire the brain. Functional MRI scans reveal that compassion training activates the brain's empathy and caregiving networks, increases activity in regions associated with positive emotion and attention regulation, and even dampens activity in areas linked to fear and threat perception.

We're also learning that compassion practice reduces the stress hormone cortisol, lowers inflammation markers like CRP (C-reactive protein), strengthens the immune response, and improves heart rate variability—all physical indicators of greater resilience and emotional regulation.[2]

What's more, the psychological benefits are equally profound. Research participants report higher levels of emotional well-being, less depression and anxiety, and a greater sense of purpose and social connection. One of the most compelling findings is that people become more willing to help others—compassion doesn't just stay inside; it translates into action.[3]

This chapter explores how these ancient teachings at the root of CBCT align with the discoveries of contemporary neuroscience and psychology. What does it mean, scientifically, to train the mind? How does compassion transform not just our inner world but also the world around us? And how can we integrate these timeless insights into our daily lives?

ENCOUNTERING COMPASSION TRAINING

Even though I was raised in a culture steeped in compassion, I still had to train diligently to make those values my own. Growing up with compassionate role models gave me a strong foundation, but that didn't mean I always responded with calm, care, or clarity. Like anyone, I struggled with ego, defensiveness, and emotional reactivity.

Part of how we deepened our understanding in the monastery was through a unique form of meditative debate. Unlike the calm, structured debates of the West, ours were intense, raucous, and physical. A group would challenge a single monk, taking turns pressing their points with the force and energy of a pitcher winding up to strike out a batter. The goal was not just intellectual but transformational—to analyze, question, and penetrate the deepest questions of life, death, existence, and human nature. Debate was a powerful critical-thinking tool to reveal the depth of one's spiritual understanding and how well one had learned to harness emotion.

Take, for example, a debate on whether or not human life is precious. The monk defending his view might face four or five challengers, each trying to dismantle his argument. And if you were the one being challenged, you wanted to win. It was easy to get emotionally invested, to mistake contradiction for personal attack. I certainly did. When I first started debating, I got my feelings hurt all the time. Like most teenagers, my friends and I had thin skins. If we lost a debate, we'd take it personally. We'd get angry, upset, even stop talking to each other for a while. I spent hours ruminating on perceived slights. My mind was unsteady, easily thrown off balance by criticism or loss.

It was then that I encountered the teachings of *A Guide to the Bodhisattva's Way of Life*. I first heard them when His Holiness gave them in Dharamsala. I learned that I could deliberately shift my attention and train my mind to be more resilient, less reactive, more open. The more I practiced, the less preoccupied I became with my own worries, and the more joy I found in cultivating concern for others. It was an unexpected paradox that shifting my focus outward made me happier within.

Through study and practice, my perspective changed. I no longer saw compassion as just a virtue but as a practical, transformative force. I saw how deeply interconnected we all are, how much we depend on one another for survival. That realization dissolved my loneliness, my disconnection, my sense of deprivation. It gave me hope—not just for myself but for humanity.

At the Institute of Buddhist Dialectics (IBD) and later at the much larger Drepung Loseling Monastery in South India, I wasn't lonely, and I wasn't afraid. I belonged, and I thrived. Debate had once been a source of stress, but now I loved it. I discovered I was good at it. My studies were rigorous, my days full, and I was on my way to completing my Geshe degree, the monastic equivalent of a PhD. But in the late 1980s, my path took an unexpected turn.

A massive influx of Tibetan refugees into India meant that our monastery needed resources to grow. We had to build a new temple, and we needed funding. At the time, I spoke only limited English, which I had studied before becoming a monk as well as at the IBD, but I was still one of the few who spoke any at all. That made me the natural choice to serve as a translator and spokesperson for a fundraising initiative: the Mystical Arts of Tibet tour.

This project, organized by the poet and renowned Buddhist scholar Glenn Mullin and the philanthropist Lulu Hamlin, took eight of us across North America. We chanted, created intricate sand mandalas, and shared the richness of Tibetan culture with the world. I was the drummer, playing the percussion instruments. The tour was a success, and when the monastery received a gift of land in Northern Georgia, I was sent back to America in 1989 to help organize a center. If we didn't establish a functioning institution within five years, the land would revert to the donors.

The decision to leave my studies was not mine to make alone. It would delay my Geshe degree, so I sought permission from His Holiness. He granted it, advising me not to simply teach the *dharma* (the teachings of the Buddha that center around liberation from suffering and the path to enlightenment) to a small group of students but to study the Western philosophy of mind, particularly the emerging scientific perspectives on the brain. He wanted me to explore where Buddhism and science might converge. I never expected to come to America, let alone stay. But in 1991,

I enrolled in a PhD program at Emory University, stepping into an entirely new world.

And so, without knowing it, my life had already begun to bridge two worlds—the ancient wisdom of Tibetan Buddhism and the modern insights of Western science. Leaving the monastery, leaving India, stepping into an unfamiliar culture—these are things that many people would find daunting. Change is hard. Many people might have felt out of place moving to a different culture, navigating a new language, building a life from scratch. But I didn't hesitate. I had already learned something invaluable: Belonging isn't about geography. It's something we carry within us. No matter where I went, I found community. I felt comfortable because I brought with me the feeling of belonging. It wasn't tied to a place or a people—it was the natural result of cultivating compassion and connection wherever I was. And that, more than anything, gave me the courage to step into the unknown with an open heart.

THE SCIENCE OF CBCT

Leaving India and stepping into an unfamiliar wider world, I quickly learned how much mystery and mythology surrounded Tibet and its spirituality. People were often more familiar with romanticized versions of Tibet than with the lived reality—versions shaped by fantasy, curiosity, and sometimes misinformation. For example, the belief that singing bowls from Tibet have mystical healing properties. (In reality, those bowls likely originated in Nepal, and there is no long-standing tradition of their use in Tibet.) Yet beneath the myths, there was something real and remarkable that did deserve attention. And some of these stories have been rigorously studied by scientists from institutions like Harvard, Stanford, the University of Wisconsin at Madison, and the Max Planck Institute.

One study, conducted by Dr. Herbert Benson's team at Harvard, documented a remarkable phenomenon. In the Himalayan region of Manali, on the coldest night of the year, a group of monks sat essentially naked in a room with a temperature of 40°F, just a couple of degrees above freezing.

Wrapped in soaking-wet sheets, they began a meditative practice called *tummo*, an advanced technique for generating inner heat. Within forty-five minutes, the sheets—which had been soaked in ice-cold water—were completely dry. The monks themselves showed no signs of discomfort.[4]

But tummo is not about drying sheets or enduring extreme cold. The true purpose of the practice is far more interesting: to awaken the body's subtle energy system, aiding in the expansion of unlimited, unconditional love and compassion—and the wisdom that allows us to see reality clearly.

Naturally, such an astonishing feat captured the imagination of researchers. It seemed that everyone studying biology wanted to measure this heat-generating meditation for themselves. That's how I first met Dr. Charles Raison, a research psychiatrist with an interest in mind-body science. At the time, in 1999, he was leaving UCLA and considering a position at Emory's School of Medicine. A mutual friend introduced us, knowing we shared an interest in meditation and its effects on the brain and body. This was well before the development of CBCT, but several years of discussion with him led to the design of the program when the opportunity arose.

Chuck (as I came to know him) was fascinated by tummo's potential medical applications. He wanted to explore whether this technique could be used to fight infections by raising body temperature without the harmful effects of inflammation. But by then, some things had gone wrong in earlier studies, and many monks had grown wary of participating in Western research. Their reluctance was understandable. Too often, scientific studies attempted to isolate meditation techniques from their broader purpose, reducing them to a mere physiological phenomenon rather than a deep, transformative practice.

Then, something unexpected happened.

At the same time Chuck was interviewing at Emory, we were hosting a program with His Holiness. I was able to invite Chuck to attend a talk by His Holiness. During that visit, Chuck began to see a different opportunity—one that could have an even greater impact. Rather than focusing solely on tummo, what if we studied the role of meditation in preventing and treating depression? His Holiness spoke passionately about the mental suffering he had seen across the world, particularly in the West, where chronic stress was rising. Chuck, already deeply interested in the relationship between stress, inflammation, and mental health, agreed with my proposal that compassion meditation might hold the key.

And so, when Molly Harrington inspired me to create a structured compassion protocol after the class she took with me in 2003, Chuck was the perfect person to help us measure its impact.

We knew that depression and anxiety are connected to high cortisol levels, inflammation, and immune-system impairment—but these aren't just issues for people with diagnosed mental health conditions. Chronic stress affects nearly everyone in today's fast-paced, unpredictable world. And if CBCT could shift people's perspective—helping them experience life through the lens of connection and belonging rather than fear and isolation—then maybe it could also reduce some of the harmful biological effects of stress.

We designed one of the first studies to test this hypothesis. A group of freshmen from Emory were screened for anxiety, depression, and chronic stress levels. Their blood was drawn and tested for key markers: adrenaline, cortisol, inflammation, and immune response. They were then randomly split into two groups:

- **A control group,** where students met twice a week to discuss health-related topics.
- **A CBCT (compassion meditation) group,** where students practiced compassion-based techniques.

For six weeks, both groups followed their assigned practice of meeting twice a week. The control group met without additional encouragement to discuss or practice anything outside of their class. The CBCT group learned about compassion, and they were also encouraged to practice what they learned outside class time as regularly and as long as they could. This was intended to see if there was a dose effect when it came to their meditation practice—that is, if they meditated more often, would that show a greater reduction of their stress markers?

In order to measure their stress levels, all participants across both groups were put in a stressful situation: gathered in a room, called up randomly, and asked to deliver an impromptu speech to a panel that was instructed to remain completely unresponsive—no smiles, no nods, just blank faces.

Before and immediately after their speeches, blood was drawn again to measure the participants' stress levels. Blood was drawn yet again every fifteen minutes for a total of ninety minutes. The results were telling.[5] As a whole, the CBCT group didn't differ from the control group, but as we anticipated, there was a significant difference between the high-practice and low-practice participants in the CBCT group. Not only did the high-practice participants (who engaged in ninety minutes or more of compassion practice a week, on average) show a significant decrease in inflammation markers but they also returned to a baseline state of calm more quickly than the low-practice group (who engaged in less than ninety minutes of practice a week, on average). In other words, their bodies were becoming more resilient to stress.

This was groundbreaking. Researchers had discovered, through functional brain imaging at the University of Wisconsin and Harvard, that advanced meditation practitioners showed heightened activity in brain regions associated with well-being, even joy. Later studies would confirm that compassion meditation triggers the release of oxytocin—the bonding hormone—and activates dopamine, the neurotransmitter linked to motivation and reward.[6]

But now, for the first time, we had proof that even a secular, structured practice like CBCT could have measurable biological benefits—helping people manage stress, improve emotional well-being, and strengthen their immune system.

This was just the beginning of what we would discover. As we came to learn over time, the benefits of practicing CBCT are undeniable. This practice reduces inflammation and calms the body's threat response just as effectively as many other healing modalities.[7]

Mindfulness, as widely taught today, focuses on awareness of the present moment, on noticing sensations, thoughts, and emotions as they arise, without judgment. This is a valuable skill, but it may not address the deeper causes of anxiety and depression—what we have come to recognize as the epidemic of loneliness and disconnection.

Loneliness is more than just an emotional state. It is a profound biological stressor that disrupts the nervous system, weakens the immune response, and, over time, even shortens lifespan. Social scientists have shown that chronic loneliness leads to heightened reactivity to threats, a stunting of social skills, and increased vulnerability to manipulation. A 2025 article in *Philosophy and Social Criticism* explored how this sense of disconnection has fueled the rapid spread of radicalization, extremism, and terrorism.[8] When people feel isolated, they seek belonging anywhere they can find it—even in destructive places. The human need for connection is so strong that it can override rational thinking.

The pain of disconnection isn't just something we feel emotionally—it has real biological consequences. Loneliness has been shown to be as harmful to our health as smoking fifteen cigarettes a day. It raises the risk of heart disease, stroke, depression, anxiety, and even premature death.[9] And these aren't just individual experiences—they ripple out into our families, workplaces, and societies.

That's why the scientific validation of CBCT has been so meaningful. What began as a contemplative tradition rooted in compassion has, over the past two decades, been rigorously studied in medical and academic settings. CBCT has been shown to reduce key biomarkers of stress linked to inflammation and chronic illness. Participants practicing CBCT have reported measurable decreases in depression, anxiety, loneliness, and PTSD symptoms.[10]

But it's not only about reducing suffering. The research also points to real growth and transformation. People who engage with the practice show significant increases in hopefulness, self-compassion, and empathy. Brain imaging studies have even shown enhanced neural activity in regions associated with emotional regulation and connection—meaning that the practice doesn't just feel good, it rewires how we perceive ourselves and others.[11]

The tools for this transformation are already here. The steps of CBCT are designed to expand and restore the natural traits we are endowed with that lead to happiness. These concepts are not new or foreign but hardwired into our neurobiology.

COMPASSION TAKES WING

The growing body of research on CBCT that occurred in the wake of my work with Chuck and other researchers left no doubt: Training in compassion transformed lives—not only in terms of emotional well-being but in terms of physical health, stress reduction, and resilience.

As more evidence emerged that demonstrated the practical benefits of CBCT, we expanded its reach. CBCT was first offered through Emory's counseling services, then as a course for credit, and soon, it found its way into hospitals, schools, and even government programs. One of the first people to see CBCT's potential beyond the university setting was Georgia Commissioner of Human Services BJ Walker, who asked us to deliver CBCT to children in the foster care system. She told us that the agency has no shortage of programs to fix external things, but she was looking for something that could help with change from within. So we created activities for kids that involved role-playing emotions, such as kindness versus meanness, and used empathy-building techniques like Step In, Step Out (i.e., if you have siblings, step in; if you speak more than one language, step in) so that kids could see how much they had in common with each other. A follow-up study with the children showed that CBCT reduced a protein implicated in destructive inflammation (C-reactive protein) in the body. For children who have a high ACE (adverse childhood experiences) score, inflammation from extreme stress indicates a higher risk of heart disease, cancer, and a host of emotional and behavioral problems. In a heartfelt moment, one of the children reported in a court hearing that she wanted her CBCT teacher to continue to be part of her life.

The director of Emory's hospital chaplaincy, Maureen Shelton, took CBCT and immediately began to apply it. She found it helped both the patients with their stress levels and her with exhaustion. Over time, Maureen, my colleague Tim Harrison, and I developed Compassion Centered Spiritual Health Interventions with CBCT-trained spiritual health clinicians. The preliminary findings of a study on this practice supported Maureen's experience that a CBCT-trained chaplain had a stronger and more positive impact on patients. Studies have shown that there is much less distress in the ICUs and among patients who are dying when they come into contact with chaplains and staff trained in CBCT.

We also did research on stress with breast cancer survivors at the University of Arizona with Edgar González, psychologist Sally Dodds, and Tad Pace. Chuck Raison had moved there, so he oversaw the research. CBCT was offered to veterans through the University of California, San Diego, in a study on trauma comparing the stress levels of those treated with exposure therapy and those treated with CBCT. All the results of these studies on the deliberate cultivation of inclusive belonging through compassion training were deeply promising.

In the spring of 2014, the dean of Emory's medical school, Chris Larsen, invited me to offer CBCT instruction to improve the well-being of physicians and hospital staff. In addition to training chaplains, we brought CBCT to Emory's medical school. Research shows that when students enter medical school, they do so motivated by tremendous compassion—higher than the general population, in fact. But by the second or third year of medical school, compassion tanks to levels that correlate with a diagnosis of burnout. In their book *Compassionomics*, doctors Stephen Trzeciak and Anthony Mazzarelli write that patients respond better to doctors with higher compassion levels, and those doctors not only feel better but are more successful by every metric, including how much they earn.[12]

By the second or third year of medical school, when students are dealing with poor sleep, brutal working hours, and profound loneliness, compassion levels become hard to sustain. At Emory's medical school, we separated students into two groups: a control group that had no intervention, and a group that would engage in compassion training for fifteen minutes a day over a ten-week period. Over the ten weeks, the control group continued to show a sharp decline in compassion. But the compassion training group reported that the practice addressed their loneliness and helped with sleep. Their compassion levels actually rose.

The researcher, Jennifer Mascaro, assessed depression levels before the study. She separated high from low, and noticed that even those in the compassion group who had reported high depression levels maintained compassion; in fact, their response to compassion training was greater than those who reported low depression. Those in the control group who reported high depression showed the sharpest decline in compassion. These were individuals who would have a hard time flourishing, as signs of depression and burnout had already emerged. It was a small sample, but the findings were significant.

Bill Eley, who was senior associate dean of the medical school at the time, became a certified CBCT instructor. Today, he teaches the method to faculty and doctors at Emory's medical school and hospital system. CBCT has been taught to the Emory hospital system leadership and administration, medical school students, faculty and staff, and hospital chaplains. According to the Emory medical school leadership, CBCT training has had profound transformative effects on its medical system. Intake forms include questions about life stress and states of well-being. A past-due bill is approached as something to deal with in partnership rather than with punitive harshness. Patients have reported a sense of openness in how they are greeted and the feeling of presence with many of the doctors.

Outside of the United States, the government of the state of Bihar in India, in 2021, in collaboration with Piramal Foundation, rolled out the CBCT protocol at some of their lowest-performing hospitals in Sitamarhi District, which serve 3.42 million people. They trained leadership, doctors, security guards, everyone at every level of contact with patients, in compassionate care. In less than a year and a half, these institutions transformed into award-winning organizations, receiving five awards in 2023, including MusQan certification, the highest certificate for quality child-friendly services, and the NQAS (National Quality Assurance Standards) highest-quality certificate.

In 2015, we were invited by His Holiness in India to develop a framework and age-appropriate curricula for K–12 education—what His Holiness was then referring to as *secular ethics*. We consulted with several pioneers in the social-emotional learning (SEL) field, including renowned author of *Emotional Intelligence* Daniel Goleman, educator Linda Lantieri, researcher Kimberly Schonert-Reichl, and developmental psychologist Rob Roeser. We later named this framework SEE Learning® (Social, Emotional, and Ethical Learning) and launched it in April 2019 in India, in the presence of His Holiness and more than a thousand education experts from thirty-seven countries. Geshe Lobsang Soepa, a Tibetan monk who was visiting Ukraine on a religious tour in May of that year, had a meeting with the then Ukrainian presidential candidate Volodymyr Zelensky. During this meeting, he informed Zelensky about the program, and it was implemented in Ukraine before the war. Finally, we launched a free digital platform that has reached tens of thousands of educators from more than 140 countries to date.

His Holiness has been calling for a compassion revolution since his exile from Tibet. He has asked us to reintroduce an education of the heart into our schools and as a core value in our society in order to bring our human family together, united in caring for our world. Reigniting our biological sense of safety and security is the first step.

What began as a contemplative practice in monastic silence has now touched the lives of veterans, schoolchildren, doctors, hospital patients, and entire health care systems. The ripple effect is real. One child in foster care feels seen and safe for the first time. One doctor on the verge of burnout finds renewed purpose. One classroom of children learns how deeply they depend on one another. And sometimes it's as simple as a parent pausing on a cold morning.

A CBCT instructor named Penny once shared the story of a PhD student in her class. He had been quiet, skeptical, and claimed he couldn't recall a single nurturing moment from his own life. But in the final session, he spoke about walking his five-year-old son to kindergarten in the cold. His son was crying and shivering. Normally, he would have told him to "toughen up"—a script handed down by his own father. But instead, he paused. He unzipped his coat and pulled his son in close. The boy stopped crying. They walked together, sharing warmth. When they arrived at school, his son looked up and said softly, "Thank you." The student smiled as he shared all of this with Penny. "Maybe that was a nurturing moment . . . for him."

This is how compassion begins to work—not as an abstract idea but as a shift in how we relate to one another in the most ordinary moments. Science confirms what this simple act reveals: A shift in compassion calms the body's threat system, heals stress and trauma, and even rewires the brain. But the most profound truth remains the simplest: When one person begins to cultivate compassion, it doesn't stay contained. It spreads. Not all at once but from the inside out.

And now, as we close this section, we turn to the question at the heart of it all: How do we actually do this?

In Part Two of the book, we'll walk together through the step-by-step process of CBCT. You'll learn how to strengthen your attention, deepen self-awareness, shift your perspective, and expand your capacity for compassion in ways that are grounded in ancient wisdom and modern science. Each chapter will offer tools, practices, and reflections to help you not only understand compassion—but live it. This is where your own Compassion Shift truly begins.

REFLECTION QUESTIONS

- What role has science played in shaping what you believe to be true? If something has been practiced for thousands of years—like compassion training—but only recently validated by science, does that change how you see it? Why or why not?
- Have you ever had an experience that science couldn't quite explain? A moment of deep connection, an intuitive insight, or a feeling of profound peace? How do you reconcile those experiences with what you "know" to be true?
- Think about a time when stress or anxiety felt overwhelming. What did your body feel like in that moment? What if you had a tool—not just to calm yourself but to rewire your response over time? How might that change your daily life?
- Many people think of compassion as a soft, emotional trait, but research shows it has real, measurable effects on the brain and body. How does knowing this change your understanding of what compassion is? Does it make you more likely to see it as a skill that can be cultivated?
- Ancient wisdom and traditions often emphasize belonging and interconnection, while modern life can feel isolating and fragmented. What is one small way you can apply both ancient insight and modern science to create more meaningful connection in your own life? (For example, you might start your day with a brief meditation recalling a moment of peace and calm you experienced—a practice rooted in ancient contemplative traditions. Modern science shows that this kind of reflection can activate the calming parasympathetic nervous system, reduce the stress hormone cortisol, and increase oxytocin, the hormone associated with trust and bonding. Carrying that grounded state into your day, you might make it a point to really listen to a loved one, greet a stranger with presence, or offer encouragement to someone who seems discouraged.)

PART TWO

THE SEVEN PRACTICES OF COGNITIVELY BASED COMPASSION TRAINING

CHAPTER THREE

FINDING YOUR SOURCES OF NURTURANCE

All of us, from the cradle to the grave, are happiest when life is organized as a series of excursions, long or short, from the secure base provided by our attachment figure(s).

—John Bowlby[1]

You may never find yourself face-to-face with a murderer, but chances are you've been overwhelmed by someone else's harm—or even your own. Maybe it was the betrayal of a close friend, or the shame of having said something you wish you could take back. Or maybe it's something bigger: injustice that seems beyond repair, violence that tears through the news, wrongs that feel unredeemable. In those moments, we wonder, *Is compassion strong enough to face down real harm?*

A story from the Buddhist tradition might seem far removed from our modern lives, but it reveals something timeless about our human potential.

Angulimala, a notorious mass murderer in ancient India, was feared across the land. His name meant "garland of fingers"—a gruesome reference to the necklace he wore, strung with the severed fingers of those he had killed. He wasn't born violent; he had been misled. A corrupt teacher convinced him that enlightenment could be attained by killing a thousand people. Angulimala believed him.

The Buddha knew of Angulimala's terrorizing acts. And yet, instead of avoiding him, he walked straight into his path; at this point, Angulimala had already taken 999 lives. Angulimala saw him and ran toward him, machete in hand—but no matter how fast he ran, the Buddha remained just out of reach. Out of breath, Angulimala finally shouted, "Stop!"

The Buddha turned to him calmly and said, "I have already stopped. It is you who must stop."

Something shifted. Angulimala had never been looked at like that—not with fear or hatred but with deep love and unshakable presence. In that warm gaze, he saw pure affection, with no trace of judgment, and felt a profound sense of safety. He slowly lowered his weapon. He asked to join the Buddha's community, which the Buddha permitted. The same man who had caused so much harm became a monk.

Of course, not everyone welcomed him. The king himself, who had been hunting Angulimala, came to the Buddha furious: "How could you allow this monster into your community?" But when the king met the quiet monk that Angulimala had become, his anger turned into awe. The Buddha didn't condone the harm Angulimala had caused. But he didn't condemn him as irredeemable, either. He saw the possibility for change. His belief in Angulimala's redemption is what ultimately led to it.

What happened between the Buddha and Angulimala wasn't a miracle. It was a meeting of presence and recognition. A moment of seeing, without judgment, the human being beneath the harm. It's the same recognition that today drives restorative justice—the belief that accountability and healing must go hand in hand.

One CBCT student, Marshall, reflected on this connection during his own training. "After months and years of practicing compassion," he said, "I began to realize just how important compassion is. It is not a fleeting feeling of happiness—it is the removal of the causes of suffering from the world." In his view, compassion wasn't about excusing wrongdoing; it was about preventing future harm and making healing possible. "Being compassionate to a murderer," Marshall continued, "would be to put them in a place where they could no longer hurt others—and to provide the resources for them to become someone who helps society instead: education, medication, therapy." For him, compassion wasn't weakness. It was the only real foundation for peace.

And this is where the story meets our lives. When we respond to harm with compassion—not by excusing it but by refusing to give up on our humanity—we create the conditions for transformation. Compassion doesn't always make headlines, but it can save lives—not just of those who have caused harm but of those who've been harmed, too.

And this is where the first step of CBCT begins: with the possibility of nurturance. Of seeing and being seen. Of feeling a connection so deep it softens our defenses and awakens our capacity to care. If someone like Angulimala could be transformed by compassion, what could that same force awaken in us?

Let's begin here. Take a few deep breaths, settle into your chair, and begin slowly. Now, gently call to mind a time when you felt safe, calm, or deeply cared for. It doesn't need to be dramatic—perhaps it was sitting in the sun, walking beside water, or feeling the warmth of someone's arms around you. Maybe it was a smile from a stranger, or the comfort of a pet who simply wanted to be near you.

If you're alive today, someone cared for you at some point—fed you, held you, comforted you. Even if that memory feels far away, imagine what it might have felt like to be safe and protected, even for just a moment. This care wasn't something you had to earn or deserve—it was a response to a basic truth: Every human being needs comfort, safety, and love. You needed care, and someone responded. That need itself was enough.

If sadness or grief arises, let it be. Let it wash through you like a wave, and gently return to the feeling of nurturance. There is no need to force anything—just rest in whatever comfort you can access now.

Feel how your body responds. The breath deepens. The jaw softens.

The heart opens. If the feeling slips away, come back to the senses. Recall what you saw, heard, felt. Let the memory return.

If it feels possible, let a quiet intention arise—that you, too, can be a source of nurturance for others—not just in grand gestures but in everyday ways.

Know that you can return to this place anytime. This feeling isn't just a memory—it's a resource. A tool you can call upon during hard conversations, anxious moments, sleepless nights.

With practice, it becomes easier to access. And like Angulimala, we can always begin again—with compassion, with presence, and with the simple intention to care.

EVERYTHING IS POSSIBLE WHEN WE FEEL SAFE

Some of my earliest memories are of sitting on my mother's lap, feeling her warmth as she returned from her monthly *puja*, a sacred ceremony where she would receive teachings from a local lama. In her hands, she carried a small offering cake made of barley flour and sweetened with molasses—something she had saved just for me and my youngest sister. I would leap into her arms, savoring the treat as she shared what she had learned that evening.

She told me stories from the Jataka Tales, which recount the past lives of the Buddha before his enlightenment. In many of these stories the Buddha took the form of an animal, each teaching lessons of courage, kindness, generosity, and selflessness. There was the monkey king who stretched his body across a raging river, allowing every member of his tribe to climb across him to safety. The golden mallard, the elephant, the quail—each with their own story of standing up for what was right, of giving selflessly, of refusing to harm even an enemy.

Wrapped in my mother's arms, listening to these stories, I experienced a deep sense of safety, love, and belonging. I didn't yet have words for it, but I *felt* the power of nurturance—how it shapes us, sustains us, and gives us the strength to grow into our fullest selves.

Whether real or imagined, moments of nurturance like these have the power to sustain us, even in the most difficult times. When hardship comes, when we feel isolated or afraid, these moments become something we can call upon. They remind us of our fundamental worth, of our deep connection to others.

Few examples illustrate this better than that of Viktor Frankl. An Austrian psychologist who survived Auschwitz, Frankl found a way to transcend unimaginable suffering by calling upon the love he felt for his wife. Every day, despite the hunger, exhaustion, and cruelty surrounding him, he returned to the sensation of being with her. He summoned the warmth of her presence, the depth of their connection.

In *Man's Search for Meaning*, he describes how this simple act carried him through the darkness:

> More and more I felt that she was present, that she was with me; I had the feeling that I was able to touch her, able to stretch out my hand and grasp hers. The feeling was very strong: she was there. Then, at that very moment, a bird flew down silently and perched just in front of me, on the heap of soil which I had dug up from the ditch, and looked steadily at me.[2]

Even in a concentration camp, surrounded by daily horrors and indignities, Frankl discovered that his mind could become a sanctuary. The love he had experienced was not lost—it was alive within him. By returning to that feeling, he found the strength to endure. This ability—to access a sense of safety and nurturance even in hardship—is something all of us can cultivate. It is a skill that can be strengthened through practice, and it is the very first step in CBCT.

Then, there are stories that touch upon our modern human condition, like that of Dr. LaTonya Goffney.[3] Her early life was marked by chaos—her mother, only a teenager when LaTonya was born, struggled with addiction, and home was often a place of uncertainty. But school felt different. School was where people looked at her and saw something else—potential. "At school, they treated me like I was smart," she said. "And I never heard that I was smart."

That simple, quiet affirmation—being treated as someone worthy, capable—was enough to plant a seed. When she was older, LaTonya went to live with her grandparents Rebecca and Walter McGowan. They had little formal education—neither of them had studied beyond the fifth grade—and yet they became her strongest foundation. Her grandfather couldn't read, but he gave her a vision for what her life could be. "LaTonya," he told her, "if you can read, you can go anywhere."

It was more than a statement—it was a belief in her worth that carried her through college, graduate school, and ultimately to earning a doctorate in education. But more importantly, it gave her a lifelong commitment to being that kind of anchor for others. Now, as the superintendent of Aldine Independent School District in Texas, LaTonya carries that same spirit of nurturance into everything she does. She knows what it's like to be the child sitting quietly in the back of the classroom, unsure if anyone sees her. And she knows what it means to have someone believe in you before you believe in yourself. That's why she's made it her mission to create environments where every child is seen, supported, and given the chance to thrive—just as she was.

She has led initiatives to improve early childhood education, expand dual language programs, and increase equity and opportunity in underserved communities. She understands that academic success isn't just about textbooks and test scores—it begins with belonging. It begins with a child feeling safe enough to learn, confident enough to try, and supported enough to dream.

This need for safety and belonging is not just a human tendency—it is embedded in the very biology of life. Even single-celled organisms, when exposed to a threat, cluster together for protection. For example, when food runs low, tiny organisms called *Dictyostelium discoideum*, a type of social amoebae, send out chemical signals that cause them to come together. Thousands of them join to form a slimy, slug-like group—a slime mold—that can move as one to find a better environment. The drive to come together is also present in more complex organisms. Baby animals instinctively run to their mothers when frightened. When we are children, we do the same, calling out for a parent, a grandparent, a friend, a teacher—someone who will hold us and remind us that we are not alone.

Without this sense of safety, it is difficult to focus, to heal, or to grow. Fear constricts the mind, making it harder to think clearly, to be present, to recover from hardship. But when we feel safe, when we feel connected, everything changes.

In the tradition I was raised in, transformation begins with deliberately resting our attention inside a moment of nurturance and connection. By strengthening our ability to access this feeling—by rehearsing it, making it more vivid, more visceral—we develop a wellspring of resilience that allows us to navigate suffering with greater ease and experience joy with greater depth.

THE ZONE OF WELL-BEING

When we reflect on moments of nurturance—when we felt safe, seen, or truly connected—we are doing more than just reminiscing. We are tapping into something fundamental: our body's natural capacity for regulation and resilience. This is why the first step of CBCT begins with evoking a sense of safety. When we experience even a memory of warmth and connection, our nervous system shifts into balance, and we return to what psychologists call the Zone of Well-Being (ZOW).

Elaine Miller-Karas, director of the Trauma Resource Institute in the San Francisco Bay Area, developed the concept of the ZOW to describe the state where we feel calm, present, and capable.[4] Some refer to it as the "OK Zone" or the "Window of Tolerance." It's that familiar, settled feeling we experience after a good night's sleep, a vacation, an embrace from a loved one, or a walk in nature. When we're in this zone, life feels manageable. We are less irritable, more patient, and able to navigate challenges with flexibility and clarity. Our best selves emerge naturally.

This isn't about being in a constant state of bliss—life will always include highs and lows. In the ZOW, we still experience strong emotions like joy, grief, or anger, but they don't overwhelm us. We can feel deeply without being consumed. We can respond to difficulties without losing ourselves in reaction. This balance is the key to resilience.

At a biological level, the ZOW exists because our nervous system is designed to keep us in balance. We have two main branches of our autonomic nervous system, which maintain homeostasis by working in opposition to regulate the involuntary functions of the body:

> The **sympathetic nervous system,** which activates when we need to react—preparing us to face challenges, fueling motivation, and heightening awareness. It's what helped our ancestors flee predators or fight for survival.
>
> The **parasympathetic nervous system,** which restores calm, allowing us to digest food, heal, and recover. This is the system that allows us to rest after a stressful event and return to equilibrium.

We need both systems. When they work together in harmony, we can shift naturally between states of alertness and relaxation. We can meet challenges with energy and focus, then unwind and recover once the challenge has passed.

But in today's world, our nervous system struggles to tell the difference between real threats and perceived ones. A tense email from a boss, an unpleasant comment online, uncertainty about the future—our body may react to these modern stressors as if we are being chased by a tiger. The result? Chronic stress. Chronic stress quietly wears down the body and mind over time. It weakens the immune system, making us more vulnerable to illness, and increases inflammation, which is linked to serious conditions like heart disease, diabetes, and even cancer. It disrupts sleep, digestion, and hormonal balance, often leading to fatigue, headaches, and long-term exhaustion. Mentally, it fuels anxiety, depression, irritability, and emotional numbness. It can shrink our capacity for joy, connection, and clear thinking—leaving us reactive, withdrawn, or overwhelmed. Over time, chronic stress doesn't just make us feel worse; it makes it harder to care, to connect, and to live fully.[5]

When we live outside of our ZOW for too long, we also begin to experience emotional dysregulation. This can take two forms:

Too high: We get stuck in fight-or-flight mode. Anxiety, irritability, hypervigilance, and reactivity take over. Our bodies flood with stress hormones like cortisol and adrenaline, which can cause inflammation, high blood pressure, heart problems, and depression. We may misinterpret people's words or intentions, feel constantly on edge, and struggle to rest.

Too low: We get stuck in shutdown mode. Exhaustion, numbness, burnout, and lack of motivation take hold. We may feel disconnected from life, withdrawn from relationships, unable to concentrate, or unmotivated to engage in things we once enjoyed.

In both cases, our ability to think clearly, make wise decisions, and connect with others suffers. When we are dysregulated, our attention turns inward to our own distress, making it difficult to be present for others. This is why chronic stress and dysregulation don't just harm our health—they also undermine our ability to cultivate meaningful relationships and a sense of belonging. We are more likely to respond impulsively and even engage in habits that could cause harm to those around us.

This is why CBCT begins with connecting to a moment of kindness—whether real or imagined. The simple act of remembering or visualizing care, protection, or love is a biological reset for our nervous system. It brings us back to a place where we can think clearly, engage with others, and respond to life's challenges from a place of strength rather than fear.

When Shilpa, a faculty member at Emory's medical school, learned CBCT, she didn't set out to change her life. Like many professionals, especially in medicine, her days were packed—filled with urgent decisions, long hours, and the constant balancing act of caring for patients while trying to be present for her own family. Stress, she'd come to accept, was part of the job. Frustration, too. But something shifted when she began practicing compassion meditation.

At first, it was subtle. A deeper breath between tasks. A softening in her voice when a colleague missed a deadline. Over time, though, those small moments added up. "Generally, my emotional state is one that feels calmer and more centered," she reflected. "I find I am more often able to connect to the humanity within others and approach them with kindness, whereas before I might have been more frustrated and angry with someone's actions or inactions."

The biggest surprise, however, came at home. She began a small ritual with her children: a quiet moment of meditation before dinner. Just a few minutes of breathing, letting go of the day's swirl of thoughts and worries. "My children have also enjoyed our little meditation routine," she said, "and it allows us as a family to relax and let go of our busy thoughts and stresses before we sit down together."

These small moments—of pause, of tenderness—started to become routine in her life. She noticed she was more focused at work, more present with the families she met each day. The practices didn't take away the hard parts, but they did give her a way to meet them with more clarity and warmth.

Shilpa's story isn't dramatic. But that's exactly why it matters. It reminds us that transformation doesn't always begin with a grand gesture. Sometimes, it begins in a quiet kitchen, just before dinner, with a breath shared between a mother and her children—a simple moment of kindness that changes everything.

Of course, as Shilpa and many others come to learn, no one stays in the ZOW permanently. Life will always pull us out of balance. We will face setbacks, losses, and moments of dysregulation. But with practice, we can learn to return more quickly. We can train our minds to shift.

Each time we intentionally evoke a sense of safety and connection, we strengthen our ability to regulate our emotions, making it easier to stay openhearted and resilient in difficult moments. Over time, this practice rewires the brain, making compassion—not stress—our default state.

THE POWER OF COGNITION TO PUT OUT THE NERVOUS SYSTEM'S FIRE

Although it may not always feel like it, our biology is wired to respond to warmth and connection. Think about how natural it feels to be comforted by a gentle touch, a reassuring voice, or the presence of someone who cares. As children, many of us had adults who helped us regulate our emotions—whether by picking us up when we fell, drying our tears, soothing us with a soft voice, or even making us laugh to shift our focus away from distress. This kind of social regulation of emotion is how we first learn to feel safe in the world. And it's also a form of cognition. Though often reduced to abstract thinking or problem-solving, cognition isn't just about being conscious—it refers to the way our brain processes, interprets, and responds to experience. It includes perception, emotion, memory, attention, and yes, our ability to attune to others. In fact, connection itself is cognitive. To notice a need, reach out, and co-regulate with another person is one of the most sophisticated forms of intelligent responsiveness we have.

But as adults, we don't always have someone to do this for us. Life gets complicated, and distress doesn't generally come with a comforting hand on the shoulder. Instead, we need to learn how to self-regulate—to find ways to shift our focus, calm our nervous system, and return to a state of clarity and connection. This is where the cognitive regulation of emotion comes in.

Professors of psychology Kevin Ochsner of Columbia University and James Gross of Stanford have extensively studied how we can use our minds to shift our emotional states. Their research explores how our emotions don't arise just from what happens to us but from how we interpret what happens. In other words, external events don't cause emotions on their own—it's the meaning we attach to them, shaped by our past experiences and biases, that determines how we feel.

In a groundbreaking 2005 meta-analysis of brain imaging studies,[6] Ochsner and Gross found something remarkable: When people deliberately shifted their attention or reframed a situation, they could actually change how their brains responded to stress. When a person focused on a calming, positive memory or reinterpreted a distressing event in a different way, the fear and survival networks in the brain became less active, while areas responsible for clear thinking and emotional balance lit up. Ochsner and Gross's research shows that vividly imagining circumstances can elicit the same physiological and emotional response as actually experiencing that moment. A thought that can evoke the feeling of connection, comfort, security, belonging is ideal. Practicing cognitive regulation of emotion through connecting with a moment of nurturance actually leverages the tenderness nature has endowed us with to make the feeling last—to make it more familiar so that, when we need to rely on such feelings in a difficult time, they are more available.

For example, think of a doctor walking into a high-stress emergency room after a difficult conversation at home. Their body is already tense, and their mind is clouded with frustration. But instead of reacting on autopilot, they pause for a moment, take a breath, and recall the feeling of warmth they experienced when their child hugged them that morning. That simple, deliberate shift of attention helps quiet the alarm system in their brain. The emotional heat starts to cool. Their heartbeat slows. They begin to feel more grounded—and as a result, they're able to think more clearly, respond more skillfully, and bring a calmer presence to patients and colleagues.

Perhaps on a more relatable note, you might imagine you're stuck in traffic after a long, exhausting day. You're late picking up your child, your phone is buzzing with messages, and every honk feels like it's directed at you. Your jaw tightens, your chest feels heavy, and you can feel frustration rising. But instead of spiraling, you remember something small but meaningful—like your neighbor surprising you with a plate of food last week when you weren't feeling well. You let that moment sink in for just a few breaths. The kindness, the warmth.

Suddenly, your grip on the steering wheel softens. You exhale. You're still in traffic, but something has shifted. And when you finally pick up your child, you greet them with a tired but genuine smile instead of a sigh.

This is the power of cognitive reappraisal, which doesn't erase the stress but gives us a way to meet it with greater clarity and resilience. We can literally loosen the grip of fear, anxiety, and distress by directing our thoughts in a different way. When we vividly imagine a moment of comfort, security, or love, our brain and body respond as if we are actually experiencing it in real time. This is why connecting with a moment of nurturance is such a powerful first step in CBCT.

RECOGNIZING WHAT YOU'VE RECEIVED

We all come from different backgrounds and experiences. Some of us have vivid memories of being nurtured, while for others, those moments might be harder to recall. But as we reflected on in the opening meditation of this chapter, if we are here today, someone, at some point, cared for us—fed us, comforted us, protected us—whether we remember it or not.

Recognizing these moments of kindness takes practice, especially in a world that values speed over stillness. But these moments are all around us—if we know where to look. A single mother, exhausted from a double shift, comes home to find her teenage son has made dinner without being asked. A cashier, seeing someone short on change, quietly covers the cost. A teacher, pausing after a hard day, remembers the thank-you note a student slipped into their bag months ago. Or someone walking through grief finds comfort in the smell of their late mother's scarf, still holding her warmth.

Nancy, who trained in CBCT, shared how this shift in perspective transformed her way of being—not just in her professional life as a social worker and mediator but in the intimate space of friendship. Her close friend was diagnosed with advanced cancer, and although Nancy had spent years supporting patients through illness and end of life, this felt different. It was personal. But instead of reverting to the tools and strategies she had once relied on, she noticed something quieter emerging—something softer and, in many ways, more powerful. CBCT had taught her not just how to listen but also how to hold space.

"It's not that I allow her to speak," Nancy said. "It's that I hold an open space for her full expression and ask that I be able to hear her feelings—sad, angry, grateful, fearful, uncertain, disappointed—in a space of love."

That simple act—of staying present, quietly attentive, without fixing or offering advice—felt radical. She described the experience as a return to the deep tenderness she had felt holding her babies, "a surrender to love," as she called it. And in that space, she felt connected not only to her friend but to all people who suffer, to the universal longing we each carry—to be seen, heard, and loved.

These aren't dramatic gestures. They're reminders that compassion lives in the ordinary. That connection can appear in small, deliberate acts.

Just as you did at the beginning of the chapter, take a moment to reflect on another specific memory of a time you felt nurtured or cared for. What did that experience mean to you? Did it shape your sense of security, connection, or self-worth? How might things have been different without it?

If no memory comes to mind, imagine what it *would* feel like to be held in that kind of warmth and safety. Picture a moment where you are deeply seen, accepted, and protected. It doesn't have to be grand—the smallest acts of care hold the most power. If nothing comes to mind right away, imagine what it would feel like to receive deep kindness.

As you reflect, notice any physical sensations or emotions that arise. Some people describe warmth in their chest, a sense of relaxation, or even a mix of gratitude and grief. Others feel a deep urge to give back, to offer to others the same care they once received.

When we truly *feel* the impact of being cared for—when we remember how a hand on our shoulder steadied us, or how someone's quiet listening made us feel less alone—it reminds us just how powerful small moments of nurturance can be. And once we've seen that clearly, it becomes almost impossible not to want to offer it to someone else.

Think of the father who, after learning to pay attention to his son's distress, pulled him close under his coat on a cold walk to school instead of telling him to "toughen up." This is how compassion becomes a habit—not through force or obligation but through recognition. The more we notice how good it feels to be on the receiving end of warmth, safety, and care, the more naturally we start to offer those same gifts. One small act of compassion sparks another. And before long, we find ourselves becoming a source of comfort and connection in a world that often feels too rushed, too sharp, too disconnected. That's how the cycle begins. That's how it grows.

IGNITING THE SENSES: BRINGING MOMENTS OF NURTURANCE TO LIFE

By now, we've seen how a moment of nurturance can bring emotional relief—but what's even more powerful is how it builds our capacity over time. Each time we return to that feeling of safety and connection, we reinforce specific neural pathways. The brain's plasticity—its ability to change and adapt—means that these pathways become stronger and more accessible, especially in moments of difficulty. This is not just about momentary comfort; it's about building a foundation.

Research shows that individuals who regularly engage in compassion practices show measurable changes in brain regions associated with empathy, attention, and emotion regulation.[7] Over time, this shapes how we show up in the world.

For example, when we are in a balanced state, we're better able to connect with others, think clearly, and respond with resilience rather than reactivity. Picture yourself in the middle of a high-stakes work project. The deadline is tight, emails are piling up, and your team isn't aligned. In a dysregulated state, a small comment from a colleague might feel like a personal attack. You might shut down, snap back, or descend into self-doubt. But if you've been practicing reconnecting with moments of calm—maybe recalling the feeling of standing under trees during your lunch break or an inspirational passage from the book you're reading—you're more likely to notice your stress rising without being swept away by it. You take a breath, stay grounded, and respond thoughtfully. You ask a clarifying question instead of reacting defensively. That one moment of awareness not only keeps the project moving—it preserves the relationship, too.

The challenge is that, while we experience small moments of kindness all the time, we often don't register them as deeply as we do negative experiences. Meanwhile, moments of stress, conflict, or embarrassment tend to replay in our minds on a loop. One piece of criticism can drown out a dozen words of praise. One frustrating email can color an entire day.

This isn't a personal failing—it's how the human brain evolved. Our nervous systems are wired for survival, and that means keeping a sharp eye out for threats. This built-in system is known as the *negativity bias*. It's an evolutionary mechanism that helped our ancestors detect danger—like a rustle in the bushes that might be a predator—quickly enough to stay alive. For early humans, missing a moment of kindness wasn't life-threatening, but overlooking a threat might have been fatal. So naturally, our brains gave more weight to the negative.

Today, however, this same bias can distort our perception. It causes us to overfocus on what's wrong, what's lacking, or what might go wrong next. We assume someone's silence means judgment, not distraction. We remember the one person who didn't smile, rather than the five who did. We treat minor inconveniences like looming catastrophes. The result? We begin to see the world as colder, harsher, and more isolating than it really is.

And yet, modern neuroscience shows us that this bias isn't fixed. Our brains are plastic—they can be retrained. By deliberately focusing on small, real moments of nurturance and connection, we start to make our internal lens a lot less foggy. Over time, we don't just *think* the world is less hostile—we *feel* it. We start to recognize that connection, cooperation, and care aren't the exceptions—they're the rule. But to experience that reality more fully, we have to train ourselves to see it.

If we don't actively shift the negativity bias, we risk missing the countless moments of nurturance that happen every day. And if we don't feel nurtured, we struggle to offer care to others. No one is suggesting that we ignore real threats or pretend everything is fine when it isn't. But we can begin to notice when our minds assume the worst and gently challenge that assumption.

If you're struggling to recall a moment of nurturance, give yourself permission to start small. Maybe a song lifted your mood, or a breeze against your skin made you feel lighter, or the way your dog snuggled you before you got out of bed gave you a moment of joy. If real memories are difficult, just imagine what a moment of nurturance would feel like. Your mind and body will respond the same way.

Once you feel a sense of ease, ask yourself: In a moment of distress, who would you turn to for comfort and calm? It could be a loved one, a trusted friend, a mentor, or even a figure from your faith or spiritual tradition. Many traditions have prayers and practices that call upon a loving presence—whether that's a deity, the natural world, or a community of support. If your moment of safety comes from a spiritual source, picture that presence. Imagine being in a place of worship, in nature, or among people who bring you peace.

For some, receiving compassion can feel uncomfortable. We may feel undeserving or selfish. If that resonates with you, try shifting the focus. Instead of recalling a time when you received nurturance, consider a time when you gave it. When have you helped calm another person? Maybe you comforted a friend in distress, cared for a child, or simply held space for someone going through a difficult time.

I'm reminded of Erin, who worked in a hospital and often found herself overwhelmed by the suffering around her—patients in pain, families in distress, exhausted staff. Over time, she began internalizing harsh judgments, feeling that no matter what she did, it was never enough. But through her CBCT training, she learned to pause in those moments and reconnect with a feeling of nurturance. One day, while supporting a stressed employee awaiting a high-stakes professional review, Erin quietly accessed calming memories of helping staff members breathe through difficult moments. It grounded her, and from that place, she gently invited him to do the same. In just a few breaths, his face relaxed, his thinking cleared, and they both found more space—more compassion—to meet the moment with steadiness and care.

Perhaps you've offered smaller gestures—holding the door for someone, giving directions to a lost traveler, or making space for another driver on the road. Remember, any act of kindness, no matter how small, can awaken the powerful neurochemical response of oxytocin, the bonding hormone that strengthens connection and trust.

Even as you read this, it might spark memories that bring about a physical response. You may notice a lower heart rate, or perhaps a tightness in your chest or neck has released. Perhaps you are feeling less lethargic. These are physical signs of reentering the Zone of Well-Being. They're also a reminder that the care you think you're missing has always been there, waiting for you to remember it.

The story of Liam, who trained in CBCT, comes to mind here. One morning, he was running late. He'd hit snooze one too many times, skipped breakfast, and had just spilled coffee on his shirt. As he rushed out the door and slid into his car, he was mentally rehearsing the presentation he had to deliver that morning—one he didn't feel fully prepared for. He turned the key. Click. Nothing. He tried again. Still nothing. His heart rate spiked.

"You've got to be kidding me," he muttered, slamming his hands on the steering wheel.

The stress started to snowball. Late to work. A boss who already seemed on edge. Deadlines piling up. A presentation that might tank. He could feel himself spiraling—his thoughts racing, his jaw tightening, his mind feeding him worst-case scenarios one after another.

But then, something from his CBCT class flickered into his awareness: the Zone of Well-Being. He remembered the conversation from class just the week before—about how stress hijacks our bodies and minds, and how we can deliberately shift our attention to find balance again. He didn't have much time, but he didn't need much.

He closed his eyes for a moment and took a deep breath. He brought to mind a recent evening with his girlfriend—curled up on the couch under a shared blanket, a bowl of popcorn between them, watching an old comedy they both loved. He remembered the warmth of her hand in his, the sound of her laughter, the soft glow of the lamp in the corner. In that moment, there was no pressure, no deadlines. Just comfort. Love. Safety.

Liam stayed with that memory for a minute or two, letting the calm wash over him. When he opened his eyes again, the situation hadn't changed—his car still wouldn't start—but *he* had. The tightness in his chest had eased. His jaw had unclenched. And suddenly, the problem in front of him felt solvable, not catastrophic. He called a rideshare and made it to work just in time. The presentation? Not perfect, but not a disaster, either.

Later that week, he found himself once more snuggled on the couch with his girlfriend, the movie flickering on the screen. But this time, he did something different. He took a moment to fully *feel* it—the comfort, the connection, the safety—and to lock it into his memory. He knew he'd return to this moment the next time life threw something unexpected his way. CBCT had taught him that nurturance isn't just something that happens to you. It's something you can return to, build from, and eventually offer to others.

THE PRACTICE OF CULTIVATING SAFETY BY CONNECTING WITH A MOMENT OF NURTURANCE

This practice is a more extended meditation than the one I walked you through in the beginning of the chapter. Here, you'll fully immerse yourself in the experience of nurturance, connection, and belonging. Before beginning, choose a simple memory of a time when you felt nurtured and safe. Begin with considering where you are happiest alone, and what helps you reenter the Zone of Well-Being most easily. A favorite chair, blanket, room, or sweater? Deep breaths? Giving yourself a hug? Turning up the corners of your mouth into a smile? This activation of facial muscles has a proven impact on mood that may help open the door to a feeling of comfort.[8]

If it feels helpful, you might record yourself reading the meditation, and then use the recording to guide you through the practice. (You can do this for all subsequent practices in the book.) This can help you to relax more fully and focus on the experience without needing to recall each step. However, whether guided or self-led, the key is to approach this with curiosity and openness, giving yourself time and space to truly absorb its benefits.

Settling (3 minutes)

Please take a moment to find a comfortable posture and connect with your body and current feelings. If you notice tension in any part of the body, feel free to stretch or move gently to help yourself relax. You may close your eyes or keep them slightly open. Feel your body in your seat, and allow yourself to settle into the present experience.

When you're ready, take a few deep breaths. Gently inhale, having the sense that nourishing air, rich with oxygen, is infusing your entire being. As you breathe out, see if you can release tensions and worries to some degree.

Take time to connect with your moment of nurturance in order to introduce safety, remind yourself of the benefits of kindness, and enliven the motivation to become a source of nurturance through the practice of inclusive belonging and compassion. If settling is hard today, spend some extra time here.

Going forward, you should settle in for a couple minutes before moving into the meditations in the next several chapters.

Nurturing Moment Meditation (6–8 minutes)

Now, let's gently bring to mind the nurturing moment you have chosen—a memory, an experience, or an imagined scene that brings a sense of comfort, safety, or joy. Let it come to life as vividly as possible, as if it is happening right now.

Awaken your senses. Where are you? What do you see—the colors, the textures, the light? Are there sounds? Maybe a voice, the rustling of leaves, the hum of a familiar space? Are there any scents in the air, perhaps something warm and familiar? If this is a moment of shared kindness with another person, notice their presence. Do you recall the warmth of their touch, the gentle reassurance in their voice, the expression on their face? Can you feel the deep sense of connection that comes from being cared for?

Let yourself fully absorb the feeling of this moment. Allow it to wash over you and through you, letting it fill every part of your being.

Now, gently shift your attention back to your body in the present moment. What sensations do you notice? Has anything shifted? Perhaps there is warmth in your chest, a lightness in your breath, a softening of tension in your shoulders. If there's any discomfort, take a few deep breaths to settle your body and mind. If it helps, return to your nurturing moment for a little longer or focus on a part of your body that feels at ease.

As you reconnect with the feelings of calm, safety, and belonging, take a moment to reflect: How does it feel to receive kindness, safety, and care? How do these moments shape your sense of well-being? And how might embracing this awareness change how you move through life and connect with others? Let these reflections unfold naturally. There is no need to rush. Simply rest in the experience, allowing it to deepen and settle within you.

As you reflect on the comfort that comes from connecting with moments of nurturance, take a moment to imagine how others might feel if they had the same experience. Picture someone you care about—perhaps a friend, a family member, or even a wider group of people. See them as they tap into a moment of warmth, kindness, or safety. How does it change them? How does it make you feel to see them experience that kind of peace and connection?

While you hold that feeling, consider the possibility that one day, you might become a source of nurturance for others. What would it be like to bring comfort and kindness into someone else's life? Let that thought settle and grow within you.

Now, as we begin to close this practice, take a moment to send well wishes to those who may be in need of care and healing. If it feels natural, expand that circle of goodwill—starting with those closest to you, then your community, then beyond, until it includes all living beings. You can set an intention to carry the insights from this practice into your daily life, becoming someone who brings a sense of warmth, connection, and belonging to those around you.

BRINGING THE SKILLS TO LIFE: PRACTICE BETWEEN SESSIONS

This is not a practice reserved for quiet meditation sessions. It is meant to be woven into your everyday life. Whether you are waiting in line at the grocery store, sitting in traffic, feeling anxious before a difficult conversation, or struggling with sleeplessness, you can take a moment to return to that feeling of warmth and safety. There is no special or sacred space required—any moment, anywhere, is an opportunity to reconnect.

Perhaps set an intention to check in with yourself throughout the day, at least once a day for the next week. When you feel tense, anxious, or overwhelmed, see if you can pause and recall a moment of nurturance. Notice any shifts, however subtle. Maybe at the end of the day, take a moment to write down or reflect on acts of kindness you witnessed or received.

Throughout history, people have sought comfort and strength in times of uncertainty. Many spiritual and cultural traditions offer built-in sources of nurturance, whether through faith, sacred texts, or supportive communities. In my tradition, we take refuge in the three jewels—the Buddha, the dharma (his teachings), and the sangha (community of practitioners). The Buddha represents the possibility of freeing oneself from suffering, the teachings offer a path forward, and the community provides support and encouragement. Simply knowing that these sources of guidance are available can offer a profound sense of stability and reassurance.

Another practice in my tradition is guru devotion—connecting with a teacher who embodies the qualities we wish to cultivate. This teacher might be someone we have studied with directly or a figure from history whose wisdom continues to inspire us. Much like a mentor who sees our potential, a great teacher's presence—even in memory—can remind us of what we are capable of. Over time, this connection deepens, and we realize that the best way to honor the kindness we have received is to extend it to others.

These practices are not exclusive to Buddhism—they are universally human.

Before we can extend genuine compassion to others, though, we need to be able to handle our own emotions. If we don't notice sparks before they become fires, we risk reacting in ways that cause harm rather than healing. That's why our next step is to turn our attention to attention itself—the skill that allows us to remain steady, present, and truly open to others.

CHAPTER FOUR

DEVELOPING A CLEAR AND STABLE ATTENTION

The faculty of voluntarily bringing back a wandering attention, over and over again, is the very root of judgment, character, and will. . . . An education which should improve this faculty would be the education par excellence.

—William James

One of the most difficult and important things we can possibly do is train our minds to remain present. We've all had moments when we lose ourselves—when a memory or distraction sweeps in and pulls us off course. You're in the middle of writing an email, and suddenly you're replaying an argument from last week. Or you're trying to fall asleep, and your mind won't stop scrolling through tomorrow's to-do list. It happens to all of us. And it's not because we're lazy or undisciplined—it's because the untrained mind is like an unruly horse. It moves fast, often without direction, easily startled by habit, memory, or mood.

There's an old story from Tibet about this very tendency. A soldier, once hardened by years of war, eventually turned away from violence and sought a new life. He became a hermit and retreated to the mountains to meditate in solitude. For years, he worked diligently to transform his anger into compassion. But one day, while he was sitting in his cave, a small line of pigeons landed outside and began to march across the snow in single file. The sight reminded him of his days in the army—of drills and marches, of rage and revenge. Before he even realized what was happening, the memory pulled him out of meditation. His breath quickened. His chest tightened. Fueled by a wave of agitation, he left his cave and rejoined the army.

All this, from a few pigeons!

This story may sound extreme, but the lesson is deeply human. It shows us how easily our past patterns can take over if our attention isn't stable and we fail to notice our unconscious associations and impulses. When left untrained, the mind will chase anything: a sound, a thought, a mood, a memory. And in doing so, it can lead us right back into behaviors and emotions we thought we had left behind.

Attention is at the center of everything we do. And when we learn to steady it—to return it, gently, again and again—we reclaim the freedom to choose how we respond to life.

Imagine this: You're working on a deadline—maybe it's a report for work, a presentation, or even a thoughtful email you've been meaning to send. You sit down with your coffee, clear your desk, and get started. At first, your focus is sharp. Your fingers move easily over the keyboard. One sentence flows into the next—you're in the zone. Then, a distraction: A phone buzzes, a song lyric loops in your head, or you suddenly remember a bill you forgot to pay. Just like that, your concentration slips. You reread the same paragraph three times, but you can't find your rhythm again. You're frustrated now. It's harder to return.

It wasn't your laptop, your schedule, or even the task itself that made the difference. It was your attention.

When our attention is steady, even hard tasks feel smoother. The experience of being fully engaged in something—whether it's chopping wood, writing, painting, listening to a friend, or cooking a meal—can bring us into a state of quiet joy. Neuroscientists call it *flow*, and it's one of the most restorative states our minds can enter. It calms the nervous system, quiets the mental chatter, and awakens a sense of purpose and connection.

Think back to a time when you felt that kind of engagement. Maybe it was during a hike, or while playing an instrument, gardening, working on a project, or getting lost in a good book. Maybe it was a moment of being completely present with someone you love. That feeling of alert stillness, of being both relaxed and clear—that's the mind in balance. That's the foundation of compassion—because without stability, we can't truly see ourselves or others.

When the mind is scattered—racing with stress about a looming deadline, clouded by anxiety after a tense conversation, or overwhelmed by the emotional weight of caregiving—it's nearly impossible to notice someone else's suffering, much less respond to it skillfully. We might snap at a coworker who's simply asking a question, withdraw from a friend who's trying to connect, or assume someone's bad mood is about us. But when the mind is steady—settled after a walk in nature, grounded after a few deep breaths, or calmed by recalling a moment of nurturance—we become more attuned. We can hold space for different experiences: a child's meltdown (without absorbing it as failure), a colleague's silence (without assuming rejection), a loved one's fear (without rushing to fix it). We can respond with clarity and care instead of reacting in accordance with old patterns.

In this balanced state, our nervous system shifts out of survival mode. The threat system quiets. Our heart rate slows, breath deepens, and the brain's social engagement circuits come back online. We can read facial expressions more accurately. We can feel empathy, and we have the inner resources to offer care. From that ground of inner safety, compassion arises naturally. It's not forced or abstract. It flows from a regulated body and a clear mind.

With a little practice, we begin to see how powerful attention really is. It's what allows us to notice our thoughts without becoming them. It's what gives us the space to pause before reacting. And it's what makes it possible to choose a compassionate response, even in the heat of difficulty.

Before we move forward, take a moment to reflect. Can you recall a time when your attention felt steady and joyful? A time when you felt present, absorbed, and alive? What did that feel like in your body? In your mind? Was your breathing slower? Did you feel open, calm, clear?

Let this be your entry point. Not some lofty idea of meditation but your own lived experience of presence. Begin here, with what you already know. And just like the soldier who found his way to the cave, we, too, can learn to return—not just once but again and again—to the steady, grounded clarity within us. Because while the mind will wander, we can train it to come home.

Of course, this raises the question: What exactly are we training our attention *for*? What are we meant to focus *on*? In this chapter, attention doesn't just mean the ability to concentrate on a task—it means the capacity to return, again and again, to what matters most. We are learning to steady our minds so that we can be present with life as it is: with the emotions that arise in us, with the people who need us, with the values we want to live by. Attention, in this context, becomes a stabilizing force that allows us to stay grounded in clarity and care. It's the foundation that makes every other step in the Compassion Shift possible. Without attention, we are swept away by habit, by reactivity, by the momentum of stress or memory. With it, we can notice suffering—our own and others'—and choose to meet it with presence instead of avoidance, with warmth instead of judgment.

This chapter will guide you in cultivating attention that's both focused and spacious, deliberate and kind. An attention that clears the fog so the heart can see.

FANNING OUR MIND WITH THE WINDS OF PROJECTIONS

I first began learning to train my attention in the form of *shamatha*—placing awareness on an object like the breath—then later, I was introduced to a deeper form of meditative awareness known as *mahamudra*. In 1990, while serving as a translator for His Eminence Rizong Rinpoche, I learned this extraordinary practice. Mahamudra means "great seal"—a way of resting the mind in itself. No object, no story, no distraction. Just the raw awareness of awareness. When the mind no longer stirs the murky waters, the sediment settles, and clarity returns.

Western science is beginning to echo what these contemplative traditions have taught for centuries: that so much of our experience—our emotions, our judgments, our decisions, our reactions—remains unconscious to us. A study in the *Harvard Business Review* suggested that as much as 95 percent of cognition happens beneath our conscious awareness.[1] That's why cultivating clear and stable attention is so important. It gives us access to what is otherwise hidden. It lets us see.

Of course, this doesn't mean it's easy. When you sit down to practice, the mind rarely stays still. It's like trying to rest a glass of water on a shaky table. At first, it wobbles. But each time you return your attention to your chosen object—your breath, a sound, the feeling of your feet on the ground—you are strengthening the muscle of attention. You are learning to stay.

I often return to the image we use in Tibetan teachings: The mind is like the sky. Thoughts, emotions, and sensations are like clouds—sometimes light, sometimes stormy, sometimes dense. But clouds are not the sky. The sky remains vast, open, unchanged by the passing winds and storms. We don't try to catch the clouds. We simply let them pass.

When we develop this kind of awareness, we begin to relate to our thoughts differently. We stop believing every story the mind tells us. "I am a failure" is just a thought. "I'll never be enough" is just a pattern. These thoughts seem solid—until we look closely. And then we see: They are like dust motes, drifting. They arise. They pass. And we do not have to be ruled by them.

This shift in perspective—seeing thoughts as fleeting rather than fixed—begins to soften our internal landscape. And as our relationship to our own thoughts changes, so does our relationship to the world around us. We start to notice how quickly the mind forms opinions, how subtly it labels and reacts. Often, we don't even realize we're doing it. But the more aware we become, the more we can catch ourselves in the act of interpreting reality through old filters. And that brings us to another layer of attention: the judgments we carry—not just about ourselves but about everyone and everything we encounter.

We all walk through life constantly making judgments—about situations, people, ourselves. It's natural. Our preferences and reactions help us navigate the world. Sometimes they even protect us. But other times, especially when we're stressed or triggered, those snap judgments can backfire.

Imagine you're having a stressful day at work, and a colleague says something that hits a nerve. Before you even realize it, you're spiraling—annoyed, defensive, maybe even angry. It's not just what they said. It's what you *think* it means, what it reminds you of, what it *feels* like it's really about. This is how the mind works: It doesn't just respond to what's in front of us—it reacts to everything we've carried with us from the past.

That's the problem with projections. We take a present moment and overlay it with old stories. Like Paul Ekman, a psychologist who worked closely with His Holiness, describes: His wife asks him to take the plates to the sink. A simple request. But it triggers something from his childhood—his mother's constant judgment. His brain confuses the present with the past, and he gets angry. Not because of the chore but because of the script playing in his head.[2]

We all do this. And when we don't catch it, the emotional reaction that follows can grow—like a spark catching fire in dry grass. More than 1,500 years ago, the Buddhist philosopher Vasubandhu wrote, "When we haven't cleared away our emotional dispositions, and when the stimulus is in proximity, and if we engage with distorted judgment, then all the conditions for afflictive emotions are complete."[3] He saw this distorted judgment as the wind that could fan a spark into flames. A single unexamined thought can ignite anger, anxiety, or shame that spreads through our relationships, our bodies, and our lives.

But the goal isn't to get rid of our emotions. Anger can fuel justice. Sadness connects us to what matters. Even fear can protect us from danger.

The problem arises when the story we're telling ourselves about what's happening isn't actually true.

We can't always stop the spark from forming. But we *can* stop fanning it into a fire. That's where awareness comes in. If we can pause, even briefly, and ask: "Is this reaction really about what's happening right now?"—we create a sense of spaciousness. A chance to respond with clarity instead of reactivity.

That space, Viktor Frankl wrote, is where our freedom lies. It's the space between stimulus and response—and in it lives the power to choose something different. In that space, even the old stories can begin to change.

CHANGING THE DEFAULT

Attention is hard to come by these days. Notifications buzz, thoughts spiral, the to-do list never ends. We're pulled in a dozen directions at once, and often we don't realize how much this scattered attention is draining our energy, muddying our emotions, and blurring our sense of what matters. It's easy to go through an entire day without feeling truly present.

But presence is a biological necessity. In 2010, researchers at Harvard found that people who were focused on what they were doing, regardless of what it was, reported feeling significantly happier.[4] In fact, they concluded that "a wandering mind is an unhappy mind." Why? Because when our attention drifts, it doesn't usually float toward pleasant daydreams. Thanks to our brain's negativity bias, it tends to land on worry, self-doubt, rumination, or regret.

This pattern is deeply tied to the default mode network (DMN), a part of the brain you'll recall from earlier in the book. The DMN activates when our minds aren't focused on a particular task—like when we're driving on autopilot or brushing our teeth. While this network is essential for imagination, memory, and creativity, it can also become a breeding ground for rumination if left unsupervised. That's when we start replaying an argument from last week or spiraling through every possible "what if" about something that hasn't even happened.

Mindfulness, then, isn't about "never thinking"—it's about gently returning to the present so that we can step out of those loops when they're no longer helpful. It's not that the default mode is bad—it's just that it needs a little guidance. With practice, we can learn to notice when the mind has wandered and come back to what's actually happening, here and now, where we have the power to respond with clarity and care.

And that's where attention becomes powerful. Neuroscientists have shown that attention training, including focusing on the breath or redirecting attention to positive sensations, not only calms the nervous system but actually changes the brain. Pain patients have found real relief, not through medication but by learning how to shift their focus. The mind, it turns out, is incredibly adaptable.

This ability to redirect attention isn't just for monks in mountain caves or patients in clinical trials—it's for all of us, in the mess and momentum of everyday life. When we're overwhelmed, pulled in too many directions, or caught in a loop of worry, the simple act of returning our attention can shift everything. Not because the chaos disappears but because we begin to meet it with a steadier mind. That's what happened for Layla, a young professional who trained in CBCT.

Layla had always been the go-to person at work—the one who kept everything running, who never missed a deadline, who carried not just her own weight but often everyone else's, too. But lately, the pressure had started to wear her down. The meetings never seemed to end, her inbox was overflowing, and even small tasks felt like mountains. One Monday morning, after a weekend that had offered no real rest, she sat in her car outside the office, hands gripping the steering wheel, chest tight, heart racing. She thought, *I can't do this again. Not like this.*

Her usual ways of coping—grabbing coffee, powering through, distracting herself with a podcast—felt like patchwork. What she wanted, more than anything, was to feel grounded again.

Then, something she'd learned in a CBCT session floated into her mind: Just start with the breath.

She turned off the ignition, placed her feet flat on the floor, and closed her eyes. One inhale. One exhale. Slowly. Again. And again. It wasn't dramatic. The weight didn't lift all at once. But in those quiet moments, something shifted. Her thoughts, once a blur of panic and pressure, began to settle. The tension in her shoulders eased slightly. She didn't suddenly have all the answers. But she had enough space to remember that she could take things one step at a time.

Later that day, when a colleague snapped at her during a meeting, she felt the sting—but it didn't knock her off center. She paused, breathed, and responded with calm. That moment, she realized later, was the ripple effect of that morning's breath. Layla hadn't expected so much to come from something so small. But in a world that pulled her in every direction, learning how to steady her mind—just enough—was a way of reclaiming herself. She didn't have to fix everything, but she did have to come back to what mattered.

As Layla discovered, even automatic patterns can be rewritten. These mental habits—especially the ones that hijack our attention—aren't fixed. Just as we once learned to walk, drive, or tie our shoes, we can also train the mind to stay present and clear. What starts as effortful and awkward can, with practice, become second nature. Even the DMN, that part of the brain responsible for mind-wandering and rumination, can be reshaped.

Everyone gets caught in mental loops sometimes—replaying an awkward conversation, stressing about something that hasn't even happened, spiraling over a small annoyance. You're not alone. Take a moment and think of a time when your mind got stuck. Not a traumatic moment—just something mildly irritating or distracting. Maybe you couldn't sleep because you were worried about a looming deadline. Maybe you snapped at someone because your brain was still replaying a fight. Maybe a negative interaction on the road left you fuming.

What did that mental loop feel like in your body? Were your shoulders tense? Did your breathing get shallow? Did you withdraw from others or become short with them? And—if you managed to shift out of it—how did you do it? What brought you back?

KNOWING WHAT'S AT STAKE

Mike, a high school science teacher in his early forties, had always loved the feeling of freedom that came with riding his motorcycle. Every Saturday morning, he'd take the same winding road outside town, a stretch lined with trees and glimpses of water that made him feel like he could breathe again after a long week. It was his ritual, his reset button.

But on this particular morning, something felt off. His mind was still buzzing from a difficult parent-teacher conference the day before, where a student's father had accused him of being unfair. The tension lingered, unspoken but heavy. He thought the ride would clear his head. Instead, it only took five minutes on the road before he found himself stuck behind a car going twenty miles under the speed limit. An elderly man at the wheel.

The frustration flared instantly. "Of all mornings," Mike muttered under his breath, gripping the handlebars tighter. His chest clenched, and a familiar, seething energy began to build. The old Mike—before CBCT—might have revved the engine, tailgated, passed recklessly, fumed the whole way home. But this time, he caught himself. Something he'd practiced over the last few months kicked in. He heard the warning in his thoughts: *You're spiraling out of your Zone of Well-Being.*

He said it out loud. "Stop." He let his shoulders drop and softened his grip. As he exhaled, he widened his vision—literally. Instead of locking onto the back of the car, he glanced left. That's when he saw it: the lake. Quiet, still, almost silver in the morning light. He realized he'd driven down this road dozens of times, but he'd never really seen it or noticed how beautiful it was. The anger melted, replaced by something else.

"I'm rewiring my brain," he'd later tell a friend. "I didn't think that was possible in my forties. But it is. And I'm here to be present and grateful."

It's in these small, everyday moments that attention becomes powerful. The ability to pause, notice, breathe, and choose—rather than be hijacked by emotion—is what allows us to stay connected, to ourselves and others.

How many other things have I been missing, Mike later wondered, *just because I wasn't paying attention?*

In that one moment, Mike practiced all three components of a trained attention:

Monitoring awareness: He noticed his mind had wandered into frustration.

Mindfulness: He remembered to come back, to pause, and to breathe.

Heedfulness: He knew what was at stake. He understood that losing his attention would mean losing his peace, his joy, even his connection to the world around him.

That lake, quiet and unnoticed until now, became more than scenery. It became a turning point. He realized what was at stake—not just a nice motorcycle ride but the kind of person he was becoming.

Attention doesn't operate on sheer willpower alone. It works because we understand *why* it matters. That's what motivates us to bring our focus back, again and again. In small moments, we're asked to hold our attention steady. Because if we don't, we know what can happen: We snap, we spiral, and we hurt ourselves and the people we care about.

When we remember what's at stake—not just the task at hand but our well-being, our relationships, our integrity—we gain the motivation to stay present. That's the third and perhaps most powerful component of attention: knowing what it costs us if we don't return. But the first two steps are what make the return possible. We begin by simply noticing that we've drifted—this is monitoring awareness—catching ourselves mid-spiral, mid-frustration, mid-distraction. And then we *remember* to come back—this is *mindfulness*, the moment of return.

When our attention is clear, so is our path. And when we're steady, others feel it. They lean in. They feel seen. That's how compassion begins to grow—from attention that's not just trained but deeply human.

PERSONALIZING WHAT'S AT STAKE

We've explored how the mind wanders, how quickly it can spin out in fear, stress, or frustration—and how powerful it is when we can bring it back. But sometimes we don't fully understand just how high the stakes are until we've seen the consequences for ourselves—missed opportunities, ruptured relationships, words we wish we could take back. And sometimes, we need a story that makes that truth impossible to ignore.

There's an ancient tale that offers just that—a story meant to jolt us into remembering what balance really demands of us.

A monk was once invited to a grand celebration hosted by a local king. Along the path to the palace, the king had arranged a stunning display: parades, food offerings, musicians, and artists showcasing their finest work. But the monk, absorbed in his meditation, walked to the castle without so much as glancing at them. When the king asked him afterward what he thought of the spectacle, the monk simply replied, "I saw nothing."

The king was furious. "How could you not see the celebration I arranged in your honor?" he demanded.

The monk remained calm. "If you were as fully absorbed in attention as I was," he said, "you wouldn't have seen them, either."

To prove his point, he offered a challenge. A servant would be made to carry a bowl of oil, filled to the absolute brim, through a bustling marketplace. A guard would walk beside him with a sword pressed lightly against his ribs, with one instruction: "If you spill a single drop, you die."

The servant walked slowly, carefully, with every muscle and nerve tuned to the task. When he finally returned, the king asked him what he had seen in the market—what vendors, what sights, what smells.

The man shook his head. "What vendors?" he replied.

That's the kind of attention we're cultivating. Not out of fear—but out of care. Care for what matters. Care for what might be lost when we let our minds wander too far from the present moment.

Certainly, you might read this story and think, *Seriously? The monk ignored all that beauty and generosity and called it wisdom?* That's a fair reaction. In today's world, presence isn't about turning away from life but about turning toward it with clarity. The monk's level of focus might seem extreme, even self-absorbed, but the deeper message isn't about shutting out the world. It's about the power of undivided attention in moments that truly matter.

We may not be carrying bowls of oil with swords at our ribs, but we're still being asked to walk through crowded, noisy, overwhelming worlds while holding something precious: our own presence. And when the stakes are high—when someone needs us, when we're on the edge of burnout, when a single reaction can shift a relationship—we need the kind of attention that isn't easily pulled away by habit, anxiety, or distraction.

In our compassion workshops, we use a much gentler version of this lesson. We give participants plastic cups, filled to the brim with water—so full that even a grain of rice could send a ripple over the edge. Their task is to walk across the room without spilling a drop. The group watches, holding its breath, cheering them on. What's so beautiful is not just the effort—but the energy in the room. The participants become present. They feel the high-stakes intimacy of caring. Not for oil or water or polished floors—but for the feeling of attentiveness itself.

You can try this at home. Take a small, lightweight cup, fill it to the very top with water, and try walking across the room. Imagine the carpet beneath you is antique silk, or your child's painting is drying on the floor. Suddenly, your steps slow. You feel your fingers tense and soften. Your breath adjusts. You are *here*.

When you're finished, take a moment. What was the texture of your attention? Did the world quiet down? Did your senses come alive? Did you notice how a small shift—just a breath of distraction—could have caused a spill?

That's the kind of attention we train through CBCT. Because, in real life, what we're holding isn't water—it's the integrity of a conversation, the fragile trust in a relationship, the opportunity to respond instead of react. When we stay focused, we keep from spilling over into frustration, judgment, or regret. When we know what's at stake, we choose presence, which is where compassion begins.

DEFUSING THE THREAT SYSTEM

In the last section, we saw how attention isn't just about getting through a to-do list. It's about staying connected—to the moment, to ourselves, and to others. When we lose that connection, the consequences ripple outward: a cutting comment, a missed signal, a moment of care that passes us by. Training our attention is the first step in learning how to respond with clarity, presence, and care—especially when emotions run high.

Neuroscientist Antonio Damasio explains that emotion begins as sensation in the body. Our systems are wired to respond quickly to the world around us with a basic question: *Is this good for me, or bad for me?* When something feels safe, we soften. Muscles relax, warmth spreads through the chest or belly, our breath deepens. When something feels threatening, we contract. Our jaw tightens. Shoulders rise. The body prepares to defend.

Most of us don't notice these signals until our emotions are already in full bloom. But with a steady attention, we can begin to catch them in their earliest stages. That's the power of stable attention—it helps us notice the moment *before* we lose control.

Cassy learned this the hard way. "There was a time in my life when I was an emotional mess," she said. "I was explosive at work, and when I came home alone to my apartment, I couldn't stop replaying everything. Imaginary arguments, worst-case scenarios—it was like my mind was punishing me on a loop. It was torture."

She tried playing the flute again, something she had loved as a child, but even that was too much. Her mind couldn't settle. Nothing could quiet the storm. Then, during therapy, her practitioner—who'd meditated for decades—gently suggested she try a simple practice: to just sit and count her breath up to ten. She resisted. For weeks, maybe longer. But eventually, she gave it a shot.

"The first time I tried, it felt like it made everything worse," she admitted. "But then I realized—it wasn't that anything had changed. I was just finally noticing what was already there. That storm I kept blaming on other people? It was inside me."

So, she kept at it. Ten breaths. One minute. Then two. It wasn't easy. Her thoughts still surged. Her body still reacted. But slowly, something began to shift. She could sit a little longer. The spiral slowed. She picked up her flute again.

"I started to find some relief," she said. "Not because the world changed but because *I* was learning how to stay with myself."

In *A Guide to the Bodhisattva's Way of Life*, Shantideva compared the untrained mind to a wild elephant. In other traditions, it's a bull in a china shop, a monkey in a museum. We all know what it's like to be knocked around by our own emotions, to say or do something we regret, to feel the damage we can cause when we're reactive. But what we forget is that we are also the ones being trampled—our own peace, our own relationships, our own sense of who we want to be.

And that's why the stakes are so high. The emotions that come with our threat system—anger, fear, panic—aren't bad. They're deeply wired survival tools. But the problem is that our brains don't always know the difference between an actual lion and a stressful email, so we react with the same fight-or-flight urgency. Our heart races. Our thinking narrows. And we lash out or shut down.

This doesn't mean we should become passive or permissive. True compassion is clear-eyed. It's not about letting harm continue. It's about developing the stability and clarity to face strong emotions without being overtaken by them—and to use that energy in ways that protect and connect.

The ability to pause, to notice a clenched jaw or a rising heat in the chest, and choose to redirect that energy toward wisdom and care? That's what makes the difference between escalation and healing. Between reactivity and responsiveness. Between disconnection and belonging.

What's at stake when we lose attention isn't just a missed deadline or a forgotten task. It's our relationships. Our sense of integrity. Our ability to be a force for care in a world that desperately needs it. That's why this step matters.

Cognitive regulation of emotions relies on strength of attention. In the previous chapter, we learned to shift from distress to a feeling of safety, warmth, and belonging. Now, we stabilize attention and clarify it so that we have a choice not to react in a way that has caused or can cause us and others suffering. Attention training becomes a compassionate act.

The Sanskrit word for meditation is *bhavana*—to cultivate. In Tibetan, it's *gom*—to become familiar. This is what we're doing in this second step: becoming familiar with our own mind, so that we can stop being surprised by the storms and start learning how to ride them out with steadiness, wisdom, and care.

THE NECESSITY OF NONJUDGMENTAL AWARENESS

Using mindfulness to train attention has its roots in an ethical commitment thousands of years old: the commitment to avoid causing harm to ourselves and others. That ancient system of ethics required extraordinary presence. It asked us to observe our circumstances closely, to anticipate the consequences of our actions, and to take full responsibility—not just for our intentions but for the actual impact of our words and choices.

Today, we talk a lot about the difference between intention and impact. You may not *mean* to dismiss someone, to speak harshly, or to ignore what they're going through—but if your mind is scattered or your emotions are running high, your impact can still cause harm. In a distracted, fast-moving world, good intentions are not enough. What matters is how others experience us. Are we present with them? Do we really hear what they're saying? Do our actions reflect care, or just reactivity?

When we train attention, we strengthen our capacity to respond—not react. We can notice our impulses before they take over, and we can choose a wiser course. This is the foundation of emotional regulation, ethical decision-making, and real connection. It's how we move from simply wanting to be kind to actually being a source of kindness. It's how we close the gap between our values and our impact. This doesn't require perfection; it requires practice—a lot of practice. Attention is a skill, not a trait. It also requires self-awareness: the ability to notice our impulses as they arise, and to relate to them by observing them without immediately reacting.[5]

This is where attention meets awareness. In fact, the two are inseparable. If attention is our ability to direct the mind—to choose what we focus on—then awareness is our capacity to see what we're focusing on with clarity, curiosity, and care. While attention trains our ability to stay focused, awareness trains our ability to see clearly—without judgment, without contraction, and without getting swept away. First we learn to stabilize attention, then we learn to open it. This is how we begin to transform reactivity into resilience, and presence into compassion.

This isn't just theory. In one study, researchers used mindfulness-based cognitive therapy (MBCT) to help people with recurrent depression learn how to recognize a deteriorating mood before it spiraled into full-blown relapse. Originally designed to prevent depression from returning in people with a history of multiple episodes, MBCT has since been found to benefit those currently experiencing depression, too. For individuals with a history of three or more depressive episodes, MBCT cut the risk of relapse nearly in half. The evidence now suggests it's just as effective as antidepressants and, in some cases, more enduring.[6]

One particularly striking experiment, led by neuroscientist Richard Davidson, explored how meditation affects the brain's response to physical pain.[7] Using a thermal stimulator, researchers delivered painful heat to a group of novice meditators and a group of advanced meditators trained in open-monitoring awareness—the practice of staying present with whatever arises without judging it. Participants were warned ten seconds before the pain would begin.

Here's what happened: The novice meditators showed brain activity in the pain centers even before the stimulus began. Their anticipation of the pain activated the same brain regions as the pain itself. And even after the heat was removed, their brains stayed lit up—as though the pain were still happening. The experienced meditators, by contrast, showed minimal reactivity in advance and recovered quickly afterward. All because they could distinguish between the thought "pain is coming" and the actual experience of pain. That self-awareness gave them space. It gave them choice. It gave them resilience.

When we treat our thoughts as concrete facts, we suffer more acutely. But when we relate to them as passing events—fluid, changing, often inaccurate—we reclaim agency. We stop rehearsing pain before it happens. We stop clinging to it after it ends.

There's no fundamental difference between novice meditators and experienced ones. The brain is plastic. It adapts. The difference is training. We can all strengthen our capacity to observe rather than react—to catch the spark before it becomes a forest fire.

Today, this kind of attention training is often called mindfulness or *vipassana* meditation. It has existed for centuries in multiple traditions, but only in recent decades has it been rigorously studied. A 2021 review of more than a thousand studies on mindfulness-based interventions found compelling evidence that mindfulness helps improve conditions as varied as depression, anxiety, stress, insomnia, chronic pain, hypertension, and cancer-related symptoms. Early studies also suggest benefits for attention deficit hyperactivity disorder (ADHD), post-traumatic stress disorder (PTSD), and eating disorders.[8] That one practice could touch such a wide range of conditions may seem surprising—until you remember that attention shapes everything. How we attend to our experience changes how we feel, how we think, and how we behave.

It helps us in everyday life, too. In one study, participants were shown rapid sequences of letters with occasional numbers thrown in. Everyone noticed the first number. But novice meditators often missed the second—

because their attention got hijacked. Experienced meditators, by contrast, stayed with the task. They saw both.

This kind of focus can change the smallest habits. Imagine you've always reached for candy when you're stressed. You barely notice the impulse—it just happens. But with trained self-awareness, you begin to see the impulse arise. You pause. You notice the craving. And then, maybe for the first time, you make a different choice. This might seem minor, but it's not. That moment of awareness holds freedom. Freedom from compulsion. Freedom from patterns you've spent years trying to break.

Talia, a mother of two energetic kids and a boisterous Labrador, used to think of weekday mornings as a kind of domestic battlefield. "It was like a storm," she said. "Everyone needed something at the exact same time. 'Mom, where's my homework?' 'Can you zip my jacket?' The dog's barking to go out, the toast is burning—and I haven't even had coffee yet." By the time she got the kids out the door, she was spent. "It felt like I'd already lived an entire day by nine a.m."

The chaos wasn't new, but what had changed was her awareness of just how depleted it left her. "I was snapping more, feeling more anxious, and I didn't like the way I sounded—especially not first thing in the morning. I didn't want that to be the tone I set for the day."

When she began practicing stable attention through compassion training, something shifted. She started to notice the early warning signs—"the sparks," as she put it—of rising frustration. "Just that slight tightness in my chest, the rush to do ten things at once. I used to ignore it. But now I catch it." That tiny window of awareness changed everything.

"I realized that multitasking was the problem, not the solution. So I stopped trying to do it all at once." She began to approach her mornings differently: one request, one task, one breath at a time. "I started saying to my kids, 'I'll help you as soon as I'm done with your brother.' And to my surprise, they got it. They started waiting their turn."

Her mornings didn't become magically serene, but they did become more humane. "They were calmer—not perfect, but manageable. And I felt more present. More like the mom I wanted to be." What surprised her most? "The kids noticed, too."

This is the power of stable attention. Beyond mere stress relief, it helps you show up for your life with greater clarity, kindness, and wisdom. And it's not something reserved for monks and nuns in mountain caves. It's for all of us: the parent rushing through breakfast, the teacher trying to reach a restless classroom, the nurse overwhelmed by alarms, the employee trying not to break down before the next Zoom meeting.

LIGHTLY ANCHORED: CHANGING OUR ATTENTION HABIT

In ancient times, a trained elephant was one of the most powerful forces in the world. With its strength directed and its attention steady, it could clear forests, carry massive loads, and build entire villages. When its mind was tamed, it became a source of immense good. But left to its own wild impulses, that same elephant could trample crops, crush homes, and injure anyone in its path.

This is exactly how Shantideva spoke of the human mind. In *A Guide to the Bodhisattva's Way of Life*—the text he famously delivered in his single soaring speech—he notes the similarities between an untrained mind and a wild elephant, in that both are unpredictable and can be dangerous. But he didn't leave us there. He also gave us the tools to gently tether that wildness. To guide the mind—not through force but through care, consistency, and a clear ethical vision.

A wild elephant isn't evil. It's just untrained. And the same is true of our minds. We all have the capacity to embody deep compassion and inclusive belonging. But we can't access that power if we're constantly being tossed around by reactivity, distraction, or old emotional patterns. We need a way to guide the mind gently, to help it become steady, strong, and wise.

In ancient India, elephant trainers would tie a young elephant to a post with a strong rope—not to imprison it but to help it stay still long enough to begin learning. For the mind, we need a similar tether: a gentle, steady point of focus that helps anchor our attention. Like the feeling of safety, a stable and clear attention can be cultivated. Flow and focus don't have to be left to chance. We can learn to create the inner conditions that allow steadiness to grow.

Attention is like a muscle. The more we work with it, the stronger and more natural it becomes. With practice, we get better at noticing when the mind wanders—and gently returning it to where we want it to be. But meditation isn't a mental jail. The stable mind is not locked or frozen. Instead, well-developed attention is powerful, discerning, and flexible, and can both unlock the mind's gifts and guide them toward what matters most.

Maybe you've already tried a meditation practice before. You sit down, close your eyes, rest your attention on your breath—and expect to drop into peace. But what often happens? Distraction. Restlessness. Sleepiness. Doubt. The mind wobbles, just like a beginner on a balance beam. We fall off, again and again. But every time we get back on, we grow stronger. Balance isn't built by staying perfectly upright. It's built by wobbling and returning, over and over again.

That's how it works with the mind. You place your attention, it wanders, you notice (that's monitoring awareness), you remember to come back (that's mindfulness), and you return. The act of returning is the practice. Each return is a rep at the gym that strengthens your attention. And that's what builds stability.

Zack, a thirty-five-year-old veteran, used to feel like his attention was a wild horse—racing ahead, dragging him into ruminations, flashbacks, or shutdowns. "I had a history of trauma, depression, and a traumatic brain injury," he shared. "Focusing on anything—work tasks, conversations, even dinner with my family—was a struggle."

But after thirty weeks of CBCT training, he said, "I can meditate anywhere now. I don't lose my cool the way I used to. At work, I can stay with what matters. At home, I don't react in ways that escalate conflict. People close to me have noticed the shift—and honestly, so have I." The horse wasn't gone, but it was no longer wild. It had learned to listen.

How do we begin to teach the wild elephant to listen and stay? First, we need to find an object of focus—a gentle anchor for our attention. This is your tether, your training post. It doesn't need to be dramatic. It just needs to be steady and grounding.

Try experimenting with what works best for you:

The breath: You might focus on the sensation at your nostrils, chest, or belly. If that feels tight or difficult, try opening your awareness to the whole body or the sensation of air on your skin. You can even count breaths—first, one cycle of inhalation and exhalation, all the way up to ten. If you lose track (most of us do by three), start again.

Soundscape: Tune into the sounds around you—traffic, birds, distant conversations, a hum from the fridge. Let them come and go without grabbing or pushing away.

Body sensations: Feel the weight of your feet on the floor, the contact between your body and the chair, the sensation of your clothing. Choose one area and let your attention rest there. If it's uncomfortable, shift your focus to a more neutral or pleasant area.

A small object: A pebble, a candle flame, a flower—something to rest your attention on gently.

Spiritual focus: If you have a devotional or spiritual practice, use an image or mantra that holds meaning.

Movement: Slow, mindful movements like raising and lowering your hands with your breath.

What matters isn't what you choose. It's that you choose *something* and that you stay with it. Over time, your attention will become steadier, clearer, and more responsive. And when it does, you'll begin to feel what Shantideva knew so many centuries ago: The untamed mind is raw power, waiting to be harnessed. And once it's trained, it becomes a force strong enough to move mountains, reshape relationships, and transform the course of a life.

THE PRACTICE OF DEVELOPING A CLEAR AND STABLE ATTENTION

This practice is a longer meditation than the brief exercises we've done earlier in the chapter. Here, you'll have the chance to deepen your ability to cultivate a clear and stable attention—one that anchors you in the present moment and helps quiet the internal noise that pulls you away from ease, clarity, and connection.

Before you begin, take a moment to get comfortable. Find a position that feels relaxed but alert. You might gently stretch or take a few deep breaths to help settle your nervous system. Choose something simple to rest your attention on—your breath, a sensation in your body, a sound in your environment, or an image that brings you a sense of calm. There's no perfect object, only what feels workable to you.

If it helps, you may wish to listen to an audio guide so you can fully immerse yourself in the experience without needing to remember each instruction. But whether guided or practiced on your own, this is your time. Let the experience unfold gently. Your only task is to return, again and again, to the place where your attention can rest.

Training attention can feel especially hard when we're emotionally activated—anxious, uncertain, or overwhelmed. Maybe you've just opened your inbox and found three urgent requests from your boss, your child is home sick, and the news cycle is relentless. Or maybe you've had a falling out with someone you care about, and the ache of that conflict is still sitting heavy in your chest. In those moments, it's nearly impossible to just "focus."

That's why we don't begin by forcing concentration. We begin by calling up a sense of safety and nurturance (step one). We remember the moments of kindness we've experienced. We reconnect with the reasons we chose this path—the reasons we care. Maybe it's because we want to show up more patiently with our children, or be less reactive in high-pressure meetings, or feel less exhausted by constant internal noise.

The goal is to build a foundation of care so that, over time, attention becomes something we can rest into. That's why we practice when things are relatively calm—so we can access the strength of that practice when life is not.

Before we begin the meditation practice of training attention, we ease ourselves into a more neutral state of mind. Trying to settle a mind that's spinning with daily stress is like trying to slam the brakes on a massive cargo ship—it doesn't stop on a dime. It takes effort to slow down. And that's OK.

We start with the small things. Creating a dedicated spot for practice can help—somewhere you feel comfortable. Maybe a favorite chair or cushion, a quiet corner with a candle, a photo of someone you love, or something beautiful that makes you feel grounded. These small touches help signal the brain: Now is the time to soften, to center. But even with the most peaceful surroundings, there's no guarantee the mind will settle right away. That, too, is part of the process.

Please be gentle with yourself. If you feel too agitated to sit still, move around first. Go for a walk. Shake it out. Call a friend. Sometimes, we need to clear some space before we can settle. And if your posture causes discomfort, don't hesitate to adjust. This isn't a test of endurance. We're not trying to "push through." Meditation is about learning to listen and respond to your inner world with kindness.

It's natural for the mind to wander. Getting upset about it is like being angry with a toddler for squirming in a chair—it misses the point. The mind is lively and full of momentum, and it needs guidance, not punishment. Think of your early sessions as playfully short: thirty seconds, one minute, maybe three. That's enough. Do a few each day if you like. Try to end each one while you're still enjoying it, so that meditation remains something you look forward to—not another task to check off a list.

Most importantly, redefine what success looks like. Success isn't about perfect focus or instant calm. Success is remembering why this matters. It's noticing when your mind drifts. It's the moment you return. That moment is everything. That moment is the muscle being built. Each time you gently bring your attention back to your chosen focus, you're strengthening three powerful capacities: your monitoring awareness, your mindfulness, and your attention itself. And each time you do that, you're making progress worth celebrating.

At first, you might want to use guided meditations to walk you through the steps—you can find recordings at compassionshift.emory.edu. They're there to support you. But over time, it's worth trying the practice on your own. You'll start to develop your own rhythm, and that deepens the training even more. Returning to the original instructions now and then can be a helpful reminder—you may hear something differently after a few weeks or months of practice.

If strong feelings or memories arise during meditation, be especially kind to yourself. Sometimes the stillness of practice shines a light on places we've kept tucked away. That can feel intense or disorienting. Please listen to your inner wisdom. You don't need to force anything, and you never have to sit through distress alone. If old wounds or trauma surface, know that meditation isn't about pushing through. It's about learning how to make choices within your mind—what to open to, and when to rest. If anything feels too big to handle alone, that's a signal to reach out—to a friend, a teacher, or a trusted therapist. Working through deep emotional pain is important, but it's not the work of this particular practice. Compassion training is not about retraumatizing yourself but rather about learning, slowly and steadily, how to live with greater clarity, stability, and kindness—toward yourself and toward the world.

Clear and Stable Attention Meditation (5–7 minutes)

Once you've spent a couple of minutes settling in, lightly direct your attention to your object of focus; rest it on a lotus flower floating on a smooth pond, or a butterfly landing on a flower petal. See if you can sustain it moment by moment.

Out of the corner of the mind's eye, observe if you can catch your attention wandering to another object, getting stuck on a particular thought, planning what to do after you finish practice, and any other emotions, memories, etc. If you find yourself thinking of something else, gently disengage and redirect your attention back to your object of focus. Each time you reconnect, notice if you can sustain the attention for even a bit longer. For the majority of us, the repetition of this pattern of wandering, noticing, and redirecting could happen dozens of times in a minute. By remembering what's at stake if we allow the attention to remain untrained, we can counter feelings of frustration or tedium.

If the object of focus becomes fuzzy or your energy feels like it's sinking, try sitting up a little straighter, opening the eyes a bit wider, looking up, or taking a deep breath and exhaling fully to clear the drowsiness. Then, reset the focus on your chosen object, sustaining it in the present moment once again. Each time you notice that your attention has wandered, you can see it as an opportunity to exercise your choice to bring your attention back to the object.

When you feel ready, release your attention from your object of focus and attune to your current feelings and sensations. What shifts do you notice that arise from this practice? Take a moment to reflect on the importance of cultivating attentional clarity and stability. How helpful is it to have the choice to redirect your attention when needed and to sustain it where you want it to be? How might this practice help you build resilience and remain in the Zone of Well-Being? How might it impact your relationships with others?

Let's dedicate our practice today to those we know to be in need of health and well-being and, as we are able, expand this dedication to include a widening circle of beings on this planet.

And let's conclude by setting an intention to extend the skills and insights from this practice into everyday life.

BRINGING THE SKILLS TO LIFE: PRACTICE BETWEEN SESSIONS

As you move through your day, try building in simple check-ins with your attention. Maybe it's three times, maybe six—whatever feels realistic. Set a gentle timer or use natural pauses as your cue: when you finish a task, pour a cup of tea, walk from one room to another. When the reminder comes, pause. Ask yourself, *Where is my mind right now?* Is it here, in the texture of this moment—your feet on the floor, the sound of your breath, the words you're speaking or hearing? Or has it wandered off, pulled into planning, worry, distraction?

If you find your attention has strayed, don't judge. Just gently guide it back. Try redirecting your focus to something neutral, like the sensation of your hand resting on your leg, or the sound of birds outside your window. Or something pleasant—the comfort of your clothes, the breeze on your skin, the memory of someone who's been kind to you. You can even call up your moment of nurturance and rest there for a breath or two. Over time, this small shift can change the way you relate to stress.

That's exactly what happened for Maya. One afternoon, she found herself in what she called "a total meltdown." Her toilet had overflowed, the bathroom reeked, and every plumber she called was booked for days. "I was freaking out," she said. "The smell was unbearable, and the feeling of being stuck just sent me over the edge."

But then, she looked outside. The sun was streaming through the trees, and the air felt crisp and clear. "I stepped out onto the balcony," she said, "and just stood there in the light. I focused on the sun warming my skin, the little chill in the breeze, the sound of the leaves rustling. And something in me started to soften."

That moment helped her reconnect—not just with the present but with herself. "I realized I didn't need to lose my mind over this. It was awful, yes, but it wasn't everything. I could take one step at a time. I made more calls. I asked a friend if I could crash with them for a night. And somehow, I got through it."

What helped her shift wasn't willpower or problem-solving—it was attention. And that's important to name, because in the modern world, we're taught to push through. To fix. To muscle our way out of discomfort with logic, productivity, or a to-do list. But sometimes, problem-solving isn't what's needed—especially when the problem can't be solved right away. In those moments, what helps is learning how to be with the experience without being overtaken by it. It's remembering that even when the bathroom floods, the sun still rises. That we can choose where to rest the mind, even when the world feels like it's falling apart.

With this practice, try keeping a meditation journal if it helps—jotting down the moments you were able to catch yourself, shift your focus, or simply return to the present. Over time, these small moments add up to the ability to meet life with presence and grace, no matter what's overflowing.

When we stabilize the mind, we can begin to see the emotional weather that keeps us locked in cycles of disconnection: anxiety, reactivity, defensiveness. With a steady mind, we become more open to connection. We can notice when someone is hurting. We can pause before snapping. We can remember the people we love, even in the midst of conflict.

Zack, whom I mentioned above, told me, "This training gave me my life back." He had lived through trauma, battled depression, and suffered from a traumatic brain injury. "But now," he said, "I meditate every day. I don't lash out anymore. My coworkers have noticed. My family has noticed. I'm just . . . more present."

This is what training the mind can do. It's not about escaping life. It's about showing up for it—fully.

In the next chapter, we take this clarity and turn it inward. We start to become even more aware of the subtle patterns that drive our behavior—our habits of mind, our conditioned reactions, our unseen stories. And with each moment of mindfulness, we build the foundation for meaningful connection, the spark of the Compassion Shift.

CHAPTER FIVE

PRACTICING OPEN AWARENESS

It isn't the events themselves that disturb people, but only their judgments about them.

—Epictetus

Life doesn't always give us space to be our best selves. Sometimes it pushes us right to the edge—and it's in those moments, when we're overwhelmed or exhausted, that old patterns that don't work for us tend to take over. That's exactly where John found himself one Saturday morning, caught between the weight of caregiving, the demands of fatherhood, and the crushing disappointment of being let down—again—by someone he was counting on.

John was furious. It wasn't the first time that his brother Anthony had left him in the lurch with a family mess. Caring for a father with dementia while raising two kids and working full-time, he was already at the brink. He'd asked Anthony to stay with their father for just one day—John had covered every day that week due to a gap in the shifts of caretakers, and he was counting on this Saturday off to attend a compassion workshop. He'd just begun practicing daily moments of nurturance and stabilizing attention, and he was looking forward to the group. But now Anthony had called to cancel, and John was crushed.

A nurse had just arrived to help his father bathe and administer medications, so John grabbed his coffee and headed across the street to the park, hoping to salvage at least an hour of calm. But by the time the elevator doors opened, John's thoughts had already spiraled into resentment. Eyes fixed on the floor, his mind flooded with every instance of Anthony's unreliability, every unmet promise.

And then—BAM. John walked straight into another resident, spilling hot coffee all over both of them. Flustered, humiliated, and already on edge, John snapped: "What, are you blind?"

The quiet lobby went still. The man he'd bumped into paused and calmly said, "Actually, I am blind. I'm so sorry. This happens sometimes. Please let me pay to clean your clothes."

Around them, a dozen neighbors stood watching—some of them friends of John's father. John felt the eyes, the judgment, the shame rising in his chest like heat. He clenched his fists, breath short, then turned and walked out in silence.

At the park, the shame gave way to self-recrimination: *If only Anthony had helped. If only I hadn't been so stressed. If only I could control my mood. If only people were more careful. If only I weren't this way. I'm angry when I'm overwhelmed—and I'm always overwhelmed. There's nothing I can do.*

Because of the compassion training he'd begun, John had just enough presence of mind to notice. He saw the thought spirals as they arose. He saw how one assumption led to another. He wasn't free yet—but he was aware. And awareness changes everything.

John couldn't control Anthony. He couldn't fix the stress of his life. But for the first time, he glimpsed the possibility of changing how he related to it. Stabilizing attention had given him a foothold—a way to step back, to interrupt the flood, to glimpse the space between the trigger and the reaction. It wasn't perfect. But it was something. And that something—that space—is where this chapter begins.

In the last chapter, we explored how training attention gives us a lever to return to the present. Our minds, untethered, will leap to assumptions, to blame, to fear. But with attention comes the space to pause. To choose. And now, in this chapter, we expand that space.

We begin to work not just with where we place our attention but with how we relate to what we find. This is the practice of open awareness—the skill of observing our thoughts, emotions, and inner experiences as they arise, without getting swept away by them.

In the previous chapter, we trained our attention to find that space. Now, we learn how to dwell within it. We learn to use it—not to escape ourselves but to understand ourselves more clearly, more compassionately. Whereas the previous practice taught us to rest the mind, this one teaches us to *see*—to notice the thoughts, judgments, assumptions, and emotional patterns that fill the mind moment by moment. Not to believe them blindly. Not to wrestle with them. But to observe them with clarity, and in doing so, begin to unlearn the habits that keep us stuck.

Before we begin, take a moment to check in. Close your eyes, if it's comfortable. Take a few deep breaths. What thoughts are arising right now? What emotions are present? Is there a story playing in the background? A loop of worry? A judgment? Just name it silently—"thinking," "judging," "remembering"—and return to noticing.

Now, gently shift your awareness to your breath. Feel the inhale. The exhale. Let this rhythm ground you in the present. When your mind wanders—and it will—just bring it back. No force. No shame. Just return.

This is the practice of open awareness. We'll explore how it works, why it matters, and how it helps us uncover the patterns, assumptions, and stories that shape our lives—and sometimes keep us from love. Let's begin.

"THIS IS WHO I AM"

After developing stable attention, many people begin to notice something surprising: The thoughts and emotions that once felt so defining—so real—begin to lose their grip. But that doesn't mean the work is done. If anything, this is where the next layer begins. Because without awareness, even a well-trained attention can be hijacked. One distressing thought can trigger a cascade of assumptions, and before we know it, we've been swept up into a whole narrative about who we are, how the world works, and what's going to go wrong next. This chapter is about catching that cascade. About turning our steady attention inward and shining it—gently, courageously—on the stories we tell ourselves. This is where open awareness begins.

When we say *This is who I am*, what do we mean? What is the feeling beneath that statement? Maybe it's a little like John thinking and believing, *I am a stressed and reactive person.* Or those moments when we live a lifetime of what-ifs in an instant, certain a headache is a brain tumor—only to discover it was dehydration, cured by two glasses of water. The minute our thoughts and emotions emerge, we believe, *That's me.* And without giving it much thought, we are carried off by the mind's latest scenario: convinced of an illness, an impending conflict, or that a text is more important than the safety of ourselves and others while we're behind the wheel of a car.

If you've ever spent the night wide awake, spiraling through something that happened earlier in the day—or obsessively worrying about something that hasn't happened yet—then you know what it feels like to have no gap between yourself and your thoughts. Worse, we can feel bad about feeling bad: *I shouldn't be so worried about this. I shouldn't be feeling this way. I meditate. I do yoga. I practice mindfulness. Why can't I get it together?*

We can feel trapped in a running commentary that persistently and unconsciously shines a negative light on everything we think and feel. We become so completely locked in by our thoughts and emotions—and by our assumptions about the world—that we lose our internal optionality. We are left with little control over our attention and little control over our reactions.

But consider another approach.

Ravi, a father of three with a demanding job and a lifelong habit of road rage, used to believe his outbursts were just part of who he was. "I'm impatient. It's just how I am," he would say. But one day, as he was driving home after a difficult meeting, another driver cut him off on the highway. He felt the surge of anger almost immediately—his face flushed, breath shortened, and that sharp spike of judgment arrived right on cue. *What a jerk. Learn to drive!*

But just as he was about to lay on the horn, Ravi paused. He noticed the feeling rising. He didn't try to push it away or scold himself for having it—he simply noticed. He took a breath. And in that space, the feeling shifted. "I acknowledged my impulse to judge the other person and to feel annoyed," he said later, "but then I let it go. I stayed calm and kept driving."

This is the power of open awareness: It doesn't eliminate our reactions, but it does allow us to see them clearly enough that we're no longer ruled by them. It allows us to remember a thought is just a thought. A feeling is just a feeling. And *we* are something more spacious, more free.

THE SNAP JUDGMENTS THAT CONTROL US

John's emotional misfire in the lobby—the hot coffee, the blind man, the public outburst—wasn't just about stress. It was a result of the hidden patterns that influence how we see and react to the world. When we've been overwhelmed, disappointed, or burned out again and again, our brains begin to draw connections that may not exist. We react not just to the moment itself but to every unresolved moment that came before it. Psychologist Paul Ekman calls these reactions *emotional scripts*—patterns of appraisal shaped by past roles and experiences.[1] When they're triggered, we may not respond to the truth in front of us. We respond to a ghost from our past.

In that moment, John didn't see a stranger in the lobby. He saw his brother—careless, absent, impossible to count on. It was a projection, born of exhaustion and frustration, but it felt real. When the mind is hijacked by an emotional script, it will snap to conclusions. Ekman describes this appraisal system as one that can save our lives *or* make us miserable, depending on how much awareness we bring to it. The problem isn't the emotions themselves—it's the lack of recognition that we're being carried by them, blindly. As Ekman puts it, if we want to improve our emotional lives, we must become aware that the impulse has arisen, and then choose whether to engage—or to let it pass.

That choice only becomes possible when we have enough attention to *notice* the impulse before we act on it. Otherwise, our nervous system gets swept into action. The brain's threat circuitry lights up. We get defensive, impulsive, angry. And afterward, we wonder why things went sideways—why we keep playing out the same emotional dramas again and again.

But we can learn to pause. To notice the spark before it becomes a fire. And to see our thoughts for what they are: weather patterns in the mind. Temporary. Shiftable. Not always true.

Daniel, a senior manager at a fast-paced tech company, had spent years running on adrenaline. "Every day, my staff would come to me with problems—and they were usually stressed, which made me stressed," he said. "I felt like I was putting out fires from the moment I walked in." He started practicing open awareness—just a few minutes each morning to check in with his body, his breath, the moment. "At first, it didn't seem like much. But one day I realized I was responding differently. A team member came in upset, and instead of snapping or shutting down, I took a breath. I waited. I let her speak. That pause changed everything. I was no longer absorbing everyone's panic. I felt steady, like I had space to choose how I wanted to show up."

That space between stimulus and response is where open awareness begins. Stabilizing attention, as we explored in the previous chapter, gave us the capacity to focus the mind. But open awareness teaches us what to do with that focus: to observe the mind itself with kindness and clarity. To recognize when our appraisals are out of sync with reality, when we're acting from scripts rather than presence.

Before moving on, try this short reflection. Sit quietly for a few moments. Bring to mind a recent situation where you felt reactive or overwhelmed. Try to recall it without judgment. What were the thoughts running through your mind? Were they based on what was actually happening—or what you feared, assumed, or believed based on past experience?

Now imagine that same situation with a little more space. Could you have paused before responding? Could you have checked the facts more gently, more openly?

Open awareness allows you to see clearly—not just the world around you but the mental filters that shape this view. And through this clarity, you'll find the freedom to respond with compassion rather than compulsion.

IF I COULD COVER THE EARTH WITH LEATHER

The Stoic philosopher Marcus Aurelius once wrote, "If you are distressed by anything external, the pain is not due to the thing itself but to your estimate of it; and this you have the power to revoke at any moment."

It's a seductive belief that if the world would just behave, we'd be fine. If the commute were smoother, if our partner didn't forget again, if the people we worked with could just manage their emotions better, we'd stay calm, steady, centered. And when we're under strain, as John was, it can feel not only justified but obvious to blame our inner turmoil on outer events. His brother bailed. His father was sick. His Saturday—his one small hope for respite—was gone.

We've all been there. And yet, as Marcus Aurelius reminds us, what distresses us most isn't always the situation itself. It's how we interpret it. It's our estimate of it. The meanings we assign, often without even realizing. *He never shows up for me. I'll never get a break. This always happens to me.* These aren't just passing thoughts. They're sweeping stories our minds generate in the heat of stress, written in the stark ink of *always* and *never.* Such black-and-white thinking can feel definitive, but it rarely reflects the full truth. Still, we live them as fact. And the more we rehearse them, the more real they seem—until we forget there's another way to see.

This is not to say life doesn't bring genuine hardship. It does. Sometimes people do let us down. Sometimes things really are unfair. But if our only strategy is to manage or rearrange external conditions, we won't get very far. More than a thousand years ago, Shantideva had a practical image for understanding why the strategy of defeating outer enemies of inner peace is an unending task. He likened it to trying to cover the entire Earth with leather to avoid hurting our feet. There would never be enough—and we would smother the beautiful grass, flowers, trees, and fields in the process. The more efficient solution is to cover our own feet with leather—or the best vegan and sustainable alternative—in order to create a barrier between ourselves and that which might cause harm. The Norwegians have a similar philosophy toward their freezing winters: If you're cold, they say, it's because you don't have enough clothes on. In the same way, the most efficient solution to finding happiness is to address our own difficult reactions. Learning these tools is like creating shoes for the heart.

Courtney came to this realization during one of the most difficult periods of her life. She was a senior manager at a large company and responsible for a growing team. But at home, everything was falling apart—her mother had been hospitalized unexpectedly, and Courtney was the one who had to juggle the care, the bills, and the emotional fallout. "I felt like I was the hub of a wheel with everyone spinning around me in panic," she said. "My phone was constantly buzzing, and everyone needed me to fix something. I was angry, overwhelmed, and more than anything, exhausted."

At first, she focused on trying to get everyone else to calm down—managing schedules, making contingency plans, trying to control each spinning spoke. But the relief never lasted. And then something shifted. "It was this one idea that landed: Maybe it's not the chaos, maybe it's how I'm relating to it. That became my turning point."

She began to work with her attention. She noticed when a reactive emotion arose, and instead of immediately acting on it, she would pause. Breathe. Step back. "It wasn't about ignoring the people around me or pretending I was fine," she said. "It was about giving myself the space to respond from clarity, not reactivity. That tiny gap saved me."

And it didn't just help her—her relationships changed, too. People started coming to her with less panic, less defensiveness. "They felt the difference. I wasn't bracing all the time. I had the energy to walk my dog at the end of the day again. I could enjoy my life a little, even in the middle of the mess."

What if, like Courtney, we stopped trying to control every variable in our lives, and started cultivating the capacity to meet life as it is—with awareness, steadiness, and care?

That's what this practice is for. To help us slip on shoes for the heart, so we can move through the world not armored but prepared—and with enough clarity to remember that pain is real, but so is the freedom to choose how we meet it.

ENTERING THE GAP

In the practice of stabilizing attention by anchoring it to the breath, we began strengthening our ability to place the mind where we want it to be. That was our entry point into what Viktor Frankl called "the space"—the gap between stimulus and response where the freedom to choose lives. A weak attention is like a leaf in the wind, tossed by every passing thought, sensation, or emotion. When we learn to anchor attention, we begin to steady ourselves. But that's only the beginning. If attention is the doorway to freedom, open awareness is the path we walk once we're inside.

With open awareness, we learn how the mind actually comes into contact with, and responds to, everything around and within us. This includes our preferences—what we're drawn to, what we avoid—and the snap appraisals that happen beneath conscious awareness: what's good or bad, safe or dangerous, lovable or not, possible or impossible. It includes the quiet assumptions that govern how we interpret others' behavior, what we believe about ourselves, what we think we deserve.

One of the easiest ways into open awareness is by attuning to sensation. This is not about zoning out or rising above discomfort. It's about the exact opposite: an unconditional kind of listening, a willingness to show up for what's real right now. Mindfulness-Based Stress Reduction (MBSR) and other body-scan techniques have long demonstrated that when we pay kind, nonjudgmental attention to the body, it can reduce stress, soothe the nervous system, and even ease chronic pain.[2] And with each moment of honest observation, we loosen the grip of unconscious reactivity and reclaim the capacity to choose.

But attuning to sensation does more than calm the system. It initiates a different kind of knowing. While focused attention helps us build stability by anchoring the mind, somatic awareness begins to widen the field. In that widening, we begin to notice not just the object of focus but our relationship to it—how we interpret it, how we want to grasp or push it away, what memories or judgments are linked to it. The body becomes a map of our inner life: the clenched jaw, the fluttering in the chest, the numbness in the limbs—all of it is information. And when we meet that information with curiosity instead of critique, something profound begins to shift.

This is where open awareness begins to diverge from selective attention. Remember, attention is about placing the mind. Open awareness is about widening the lens—inviting in what we didn't even know we were bracing against. Somatic practices like body scanning cultivate the capacity to witness without interfering. They expand our field of perception so that we can begin to notice not just what is happening but how we are relating to it. Are we resisting? Bracing? Dissociating? Attuning to sensation in this way reveals not just what's present in the body but how the heart and mind are meeting it. And that is what opens the door to insight, to compassion, and to freedom.

Begin by taking a few deep breaths. Stretch if needed. Let your body settle. Then, gently bring awareness to your toes. What do you notice? Tingling? Warmth? Nothing? Let that be enough. See if any thoughts or stories arise around the sensation—*I stubbed that toe yesterday*, or *I wish I were walking barefoot on a beach right now.* Let the stories come, and let them go. Release the judgment of *good* or *bad*, *pleasant* or *unpleasant*. Instead, meet each sensation with openness, letting it arise and fade naturally.

From there, continue scanning upward—feet, legs, belly, chest, arms, neck, face, scalp—pausing for ten to fifteen seconds in each area. When memories or associations surface—*That's where my surgery scar is*; *That's the spot my mom used to stroke when I was upset*—acknowledge them. Let them drift like balloons in a breeze. Notice how even a sensation can spark a narrative. And see if you can soften your grip on those narratives as they arise.

If you've experienced trauma or physical pain, focusing on bodily sensation might be too intense in the moment. That's OK. You can always shift your awareness to a nurturing memory, or ground yourself in the contact points between your body and a surface—the way your feet press into the ground, the way your back rests against the chair.

Once the scan is complete, take a moment to reflect. Was there a time when you became completely entangled in a thought about a sensation? How long did it last? What state of mind did it generate—anticipation, fear, judgment, curiosity? What did it feel like to try letting go of that appraisal? Perhaps, even briefly, you noticed a tiny shift—a space opening between *you* and the sensation. Between *you* and the thought. That's the doorway to transformation.

Tessa, a young designer in her first big job, described this shift in the waiting room of her dentist's office. "I had gone in for a routine cleaning, nothing major. But my legs were shaking and my mouth was dry. At first I didn't understand why. But then I realized I'd been stuck in a loop the whole drive over: *What if they find something? What if it costs hundreds of dollars? What if I can't take the time off for a filling?* My body was in full fight-or-flight, even though nothing had happened yet. I was suffering because I was living in a future that hadn't even arrived."

She paused and took a breath. "When I saw the worry for what it was—a story—I actually laughed. My muscles loosened. I stopped gripping the magazine in my lap like a life preserver. I was able to just . . . sit. Just be."

Open awareness means we don't try to escape life's difficulties but meet them from spaciousness and discernment. When we learn to recognize the body's cues, the mind's stories, and the appraisals that color our every encounter, we begin to understand how much of our suffering is optional. Not imaginary—optional. Our thoughts and judgments may feel true, but that doesn't mean they *are* true. We don't have to believe everything we think.

By placing our attention on the open field of sensation, thought, emotion, and appraisal, we begin to see the unconscious loops that keep us stuck. We begin to question them. We begin to shift. Not into a fantasy version of the self who never gets angry or anxious but toward the real, present, human self-learning to respond differently.

Try this now: As you settle from reading, take just one minute to close your eyes and breathe. Bring to mind a recent situation where you felt stressed or overwhelmed. Without diving into the story, can you recall how it felt in your body? Where did you feel it? Was there tension, heat, tightness? Can you notice any judgments or appraisals that arose in that moment—what you believed about yourself or others? Take one more breath and relate to those thoughts like clouds drifting across a vast sky. Your abiding awareness is not the cloud but the sky. Spacious. Present. Aware.

WHAT'S IN THE GAP?

> Though the ability to navigate the inner sea of our minds is our birthright, it does not come automatically, any more than being born with muscles makes us athletes. The reality is that we need certain experiences to develop this essential human capacity.[3]

This quote, from psychiatrist and author Daniel Siegel, gets right to the heart of this chapter. Just because we're born with minds doesn't mean we automatically know how to work with them. Developing this capacity to stay with our internal experience without drowning in it takes practice, patience, and a healthy dose of self-compassion.

One of the most common questions I hear in compassion training workshops is, "What if my thoughts won't stop?" To which I say—congratulations! Noticing that your mind is full of thoughts is the first step. It means you're already starting to build the skill of observing the mind instead of getting pulled along by it. Thoughts don't stop. They flicker in and out—thirty, maybe forty in a single minute. But the goal of this practice isn't to turn your mind into a blank slate. That's like asking the weather to always be seventy-two and sunny. The goal is to relate to the ever-changing mental weather with more skill, curiosity, and ease.

Settling into open awareness is like trying to fly a kite with barely a breeze—or trying to steer a sailboat directly into the wind. It takes subtlety. Instead of anchoring your attention to a single point (like the breath), open awareness invites you to release that anchor and observe the full horizon of your experience. And to prepare for that, we begin by grounding ourselves through the five senses.

You can try this with a simple practice known as 5-4-3-2-1. Wherever you are, pause and notice five colors you see. Then four sounds you hear. Three sensations in your body. Two smells. One taste. If any step isn't possible in the moment, feel free to skip or adapt it. Linger with each sense. No rush. And then—if you're ready—add a final step: Notice the thoughts arising in your mind. Are they images? Phrases? Half sentences? Can you simply observe them without clinging or pushing away?

Another practice, adapted from Daniel Siegel's SIFT method, helps bridge the gap between attention and open awareness.[4] Begin with sensation (S): Notice the weight of your body in the chair, the feeling of your shirt against your skin, the breeze through a window. Then shift to image (I): What mental pictures arise? A memory? A face? A flash of light or color? Then move into feeling (F): What emotions are present? Sadness? Boredom? Joy? Tension? And finally, thought (T): What is your mind saying? What assumptions, predictions, or judgments are floating by?

You don't need to fix or change anything. Just name what you notice. This is thinking. This is feeling. This is a sensation. This is simply what's here.

It's easy to assume that once we start meditating, we should stop feeling things—or that difficult emotions are signs of failure. That was the case with John. When he first came to our workshops, he had already done some mindfulness practice but believed that if he felt any strong emotion, he was doing something wrong. But the point of open awareness isn't to get rid of emotion—it's to relate to it differently. With interest. With kindness. With clarity.

I remember when I first read Antonio Damasio's *Descartes' Error* as a graduate student at Emory. It felt like I had found a neuroscientific mirror of the Buddhist view of the mind. Damasio tells the story of Phineas Gage, a railroad foreman who survived a horrific accident in which a metal rod pierced through his skull and frontal lobe. Miraculously, Gage lived. He could walk, talk, even return to work. But his personality had changed dramatically. He became reckless, angry, socially inappropriate. Damasio argued that while Gage's logic centers were intact, the parts of his brain responsible for processing emotion were damaged. He could think—but not feel appropriately—and this impaired his ability to reason, to choose wisely, and to engage meaningfully with others.

Damasio's research demonstrated what Buddhist contemplatives have known for centuries: that emotion isn't the enemy of reason—it's essential to it. Feelings, especially when held with awareness, allow us to discern what matters, relate with empathy, and make wise decisions. When we ignore emotion—or judge ourselves for having it—we cut off our access to the very parts of ourselves that help us live ethically and compassionately.

That's why I admire people like His Holiness and Archbishop Desmond Tutu. These are individuals who are deeply emotionally alive. They cry. They laugh. They feel grief and sadness and joy. But they don't get swept away by it. Their practice of open awareness lets them hold their feelings gently, without being hijacked. And in doing so, they remain connected—to themselves, to others, and to the larger arc of justice and love.

Back to John. He had started to apply the practice of open awareness more regularly. His first challenge? Simply noticing when frustration or sadness showed up—and resisting the urge to label those emotions "bad." It took time. But eventually, in the middle of a sit, he heard himself think, "Oh, I feel sad. I shouldn't feel this way if I'm a good meditator." That was the moment of clarity. He caught the judgment. He released it. And then, he let the sadness just be there. Not trying to change it. Not pushing it away.

Later, he told the group: "I felt some relief as the thoughts drifted away. But then I caught another thought—'Oh, that feels good! I want more of that! This is what I *should* feel if I'm doing it right.' And I had to let go of that, too."

He chuckled and shook his head. "It's like my mind is always writing reviews of how well I'm doing. But when I stop listening to the reviews, I actually start to relax. Things start to settle. It's like . . . the mind knows how to let go, if I let it."

Every time we practice this, we're stitching together those shoes for the heart. At first, we have to remember to put them on in moments we know might trigger us. But over time, they're just there. Worn in. Reliable. Capable of carrying us through every kind of weather.

THE PRACTICE OF CULTIVATING OPEN AWARENESS

This practice is an invitation into a longer, more spacious form of meditation—one that allows you to explore a quality of awareness that is less focused and more open, inclusive, and allowing. Rather than anchoring your attention on a single object, as we've done in earlier exercises, here you'll be gently cultivating open awareness: a broad, panoramic field of presence in which all experience is allowed to arise and pass without interference. Open awareness is precisely this: not guarding as defense but guarding as *tending*. Attuning to what enters through the senses and exits through thought—not to control but to *witness*. To remember that awareness itself is vast enough to include pleasure, discomfort, confusion, and clarity without needing to fix any of it.

Nothing is excluded. And nothing is clung to. You can just rest in the knowing of all that moves through this moment.

Before you begin, take a few moments to settle. Choose a posture that feels both relaxed and alert, upright but not rigid. You might let your eyes close or keep them softly open. Stretch if it feels good. Breathe deeply if it helps you land. Let your body know it can rest.

Atisha, an eleventh-century Buddhist teacher, once wrote:

> With mindfulness, monitoring awareness, and heedfulness,
> Fully guard the gateways of your senses.
> Again and again, throughout day and night,
> Examining the flow of your mind.[5]

You may find your awareness narrowing or collapsing around particular experiences. That's OK. It's natural. When you notice this, gently invite your awareness to widen again—like loosening a grip you hadn't noticed you were holding. Let yourself rest, not in any single sensation but in the open, ever-present field in which all sensations come and go.

Whether practiced with guidance or in stillness, let this be your invitation to dwell inside the natural spaciousness of your being, not as a task or performance—but as a remembering. A quiet returning to the awareness that has always been here, watching, welcoming, wise.

Open Awareness Meditation (5–7 minutes)

Once you've taken time to settle, open your attention to the unfolding inner world of thoughts, memories, and emotions, without holding on to or pushing them away, simply witnessing as they come and go.

While observing your present-moment experiences, you may let the field of your mind be like a vast sea with stillness deep down, relating to the unfolding mental activities as if they are ripples or waves of your own mind. Waves unfold on the surface of the sea when conditions are there and subside into calmness when conditions subside. Or, if you prefer, experience the mind as the clear sky through which clouds may pass.

As you observe wavelike or cloudlike inner experiences without identifying with them or judging them as good or bad, notice how they change. They may gradually subside into stillness. If this happens, you may simply rest your awareness in the unfolding calmness of the mind. If they do not subside, continue to observe without clinging to or pushing away the mental experiences as they arise and pass.

While observing the flow of your inner world, if you notice that you're caught up in an emotion or string of thoughts or stories, see if you can release that entanglement and return to being a neutral observer of your inner world. Little by little, as the gap between one thought and another expands, you can rest your awareness in that expanding space of the mind.

Finally, reflect on how helpful it can be to have more space between our impulses and our response to them. As a spark will not grow into a forest fire unless it's fanned by the wind, your impulses will not grow into emotional forest fires if you don't fan them with excessive judgments and projections.

Consider: How important is this open awareness for our own well-being? How important is it to our relationships with others? To meaningful connection?

Take a moment to dedicate your practice today to all who are suffering and longing for relief, comfort, and renewed well-being. Perhaps consider how wonderful it would be if others could experience this open, present-moment awareness and, as you are able, expand this dedication to include a widening circle of beings on this planet. Conclude by setting an intention to extend the skills and insights from this practice into everyday life in order to open the doors to meaningful connection and belonging for yourself and for others.

BRINGING THE SKILLS TO LIFE: PRACTICE BETWEEN SESSIONS

Consider establishing a few simple rituals—small, sacred pauses—to check in with your present-moment experience. Set a gentle reminder on your phone to go off three to six times a day. When it does, pause. Just for a minute. Ask yourself, *What's happening in my mind right now?* Is there a storyline running in the background? A flicker of feeling in your chest?

A memory, a worry, a to-do list, a lingering emotion? Take a breath and notice it. Not to fix or fight it—but just to see it clearly.

This act alone—of naming what is here without jumping to control it—is a quiet revolution. It shifts us out of autopilot and into presence. It loosens the knot of entanglement. And with each check-in, you might begin to notice something subtle but profound: You are not your thoughts. You are not your feelings. They simply arise and dissolve in the space of your mind.

Try catching yourself in the act of being swept away. Maybe it's an argument you keep replaying, a worst-case scenario you've mentally rehearsed ten times, or a tiny mistake that's ballooned into a spiral of shame. See if you can remember, in those moments, that these thoughts aren't solid. They're not permanent. They're not *you*. They are mental weather—passing through.

And if you find yourself in the middle of a storm—tight chest, looped thoughts, stress rising like floodwater—don't panic. Just see if you can step back. Let it all be here for a moment without jumping into the river of reaction. If it feels like too much, you're not doing anything wrong. Sometimes we need to move our bodies, call a friend, or take a break before coming back to practice. That's not failure. That's wise care.

What we're cultivating here is a new kind of connection to ourselves. One that isn't about pushing through or pretending to be unfazed but about gently choosing how we relate to our inner world. The more we practice, the more we begin to create space—between stimulus and response, between sensation and story, between emotion and entanglement. And in that space, calm begins to bloom. We find we're no longer captive to every wave that rolls through. Sometimes we can just watch them rise . . . and let them pass.

This isn't about being perfectly composed all the time. That's not realistic—and it's not the point. What *is* possible, though, is that with this new awareness, we begin to notice something else, too: the voice of self-blame. It sneaks in when life gets hard, whispering things like: *This shouldn't be happening. I shouldn't be like this. I must be the only one who struggles this much.*

That voice is not a truthful one. And in the next chapter, we'll look at how to challenge such untruths—not just with logic but with self-compassion. We'll begin to build the kind of belonging that includes even the parts of ourselves we've tried to hide. Because compassion—real, sustaining compassion that we direct toward our own tender vulnerability—starts in our ability to keep returning, again and again, to that quiet center that knows: *This, too, is part of the path.*

CHAPTER SIX

MAKING SPACE FOR SELF-COMPASSION

No one ought to feel annoyed with themselves. It just adds to the frustration. I mean, we are human beings, fallible human beings.

—Archbishop Desmond Tutu[1]

Gaining freedom from unhelpful emotional patterns and habitual reactions, we can come into a kinder relationship with both our strengths and vulnerabilities. This is one of the huge gifts of open awareness, because it creates a sense of space that helps us make different decisions and meet the ten thousand joys and ten thousand sorrows (often referred to by Buddhist teachers to reflect the duality of human experience) of the world with care and connection.

Compassion is not a merely altruistic effort. In fact, many of the Buddha's teachings carry the message that we, just as much as anyone else in the universe, are deserving of our own love and compassion. In the grip of our unchecked thoughts, it's hard to remember that every single one of us wants to feel like we're doing OK. That we're not failing. That we're good enough. And yet, it's astonishing how quickly the mind can turn against us. One misstep, one tough day, one disappointing outcome—and suddenly that quiet voice inside sharpens. "What's wrong with you?" it whispers, or maybe even screams. "You always screw things up." "Why can't you just get it together?" This is shame. This is perfectionism. This is the mind, caught in a loop of self-blame, convinced that struggle is failure and failure is personal.

Shame tells us we're unworthy of love or belonging because of something we've done or failed to do. Perfectionism convinces us that only flawlessness is acceptable—and that any mistake disqualifies us from grace. And blame—especially self-blame—is what we reach for when we're desperate to feel in control of something painful. But beneath it all is a deeper longing: to feel safe, to be accepted, to know we're not alone.

That's why this next step—self-compassion—follows so naturally from the previous one. After we've learned to focus on our sources of nurturance (those memories, people, places, and situations that help us to locate our inner refuge and motivation for doing this work to begin with), after we stabilize attention, after we've begun to widen our awareness to the full unfolding of thought, emotion, sensation—this is where we begin to change our relationship to our own pain.

Self-compassion is the quality that allows us to develop the strength to stay present with what hurts and respond with kindness rather than judgment toward ourselves. We begin to see that flaws are not failures. They are part of being human.

The Buddha, after his enlightenment, didn't shy away from the suffering of others. But he also didn't want to be worshipped as a god. He shared what he discovered, not to dazzle but to teach. When a grieving young mother named Kisa Gotami came to him carrying the body of her dead infant, begging for a miracle, he didn't tell her to toughen up or move on. He asked her to bring him a handful of mustard seeds from a home untouched by loss.

She searched high and low, knocking on door after door. But everywhere she went, she heard stories of grief. Death had visited every household. She returned to the Buddha not with the seeds but with the understanding that her loss wasn't her fault—and it wasn't hers alone. She was human. And heartbreak was an integral part of the human condition.

We often forget this. When we're struggling, it feels like we're the only ones. That everyone else has it together and we're the outlier—the one who just can't get it right. But emotional pain, disappointment, and failure are part of our shared human experience. No one is exempt. What causes suffering to intensify is the belief that we're alone in it, or worse, that our suffering is proof of our unworthiness.

This chapter is about breaking that spell.

In the face of hardship, we often think the problem is the only thing happening. And that the problem is us. But when we berate ourselves—when we spiral into "I'm a failure," "I always mess up," "I'll never get it right"—we don't get better. We get smaller. More ashamed. Less able to see clearly. Shame often begins in early experiences of disconnection—moments when we were met with punishment instead of patience, judgment instead of understanding, or silence when we needed reassurance. Over time, we internalize those reactions as evidence that there's something wrong with us. We come to believe that our flaws, our mistakes, or even our emotions make us unworthy of love or belonging. But shame isn't proof of our unworthiness—it's a signal that we've been hurt in places where we needed care. And that's exactly where compassion is most needed.

As one CBCT participant, Marianne, put it: "The patience aspects of self-compassion mitigate thoughts of harshness toward oneself and perfectionistic expectations that can fuel frustration and discouragement. Tolerance and patience help us get back up when we stumble—and maybe even laugh at ourselves when we make funny errors."

Marianne came to compassion training during what she called "the unraveling." On the surface, she was managing: leading a team at a nonprofit that was constantly lurching from one crisis to the next; shuttling her kids between school, appointments, and their father's new apartment; keeping the fridge stocked, the bills paid, the calendar in order. But underneath, she felt like a failure. Her marriage of fifteen years had ended—not with a dramatic betrayal but with the slow erosion of connection, the kind of emotional distance that accumulates when two people stop seeing each other clearly.

"I kept thinking, *I should have tried harder. I should have been able to fix it. Maybe if I'd been more accommodating, or less emotional, or more available . . .*" she recalled. "There's this unspoken narrative that women are the glue. That if a family breaks, it means we didn't hold it tight enough."

It wasn't just the end of the marriage that pained her—it was the story she told herself about what it meant. That she'd failed her children. That she wasn't resilient enough. That her exhaustion was weakness. She found herself awake at 3:00 a.m., rehashing every argument and every missed opportunity for repair. "You should have known better," her mind would hiss. "Why can't you ever get it right?"

But through the practices of open awareness and self-compassion, Marianne began to witness the machinery of her own inner torment. For the first time, she could see that her suffering wasn't just from the divorce but also from the relentless self-judgment that accompanied it. Instead of trying to silence the critical voice, she learned to listen to it with curiosity. To ask: *Whose voice is this? Where did I learn that my worth depended on holding everything together?*

It didn't happen overnight, but slowly she stopped treating her pain as proof of her inadequacy. She began greeting her grief like an old friend. She could sit with her mistakes—real and imagined—without collapsing into them. "Now when I mess up," she said, "I don't spiral. I take a breath. I remind myself that being human means getting things wrong sometimes. That doesn't make me unworthy. It makes me real."

As she grew more tender with herself, something shifted outwardly as well. She noticed the quiet despair in her colleague's rigid tone during meetings, the way her best friend masked anxiety with perfectionism. The more she saw how self-criticism showed up in others—in all its disguised forms—the more compassion she could extend. The stress didn't disappear, and the pain of the divorce still flared up at odd moments, but her relationship to it changed. She became less performative and more present. Less like someone holding up a facade, and more like someone rooted in truth. Even when the winds of chaos blew hard, Marianne had become the calm center. Not because she'd figured everything out but because she'd stopped pretending she had to.

When we stop confusing struggle with failure, we can clearly see that all of us want to feel love, safety, connection. And all of us fall short sometimes. Even His Holiness has spoken openly about feeling frustration or grief. Desmond Tutu, too, named his emotions often. Their compassion wasn't in spite of emotion—but through it. And that's what we are learning here.

We are building the emotional shoes that let us walk through life's terrain with grace. We are remembering that emotion is not a problem to be solved but a signal to be understood. And that by staying present with our imperfections—without judgment—we open the door to the ability to see ourselves clearly, kindly, and with the spaciousness to grow.

In this chapter, we'll learn how to recognize the habits of mind that keep us in cycles of shame and perfectionism. We'll uncover the unhelpful scripts—like "I should have done better" or "I'm not enough"—that keep us locked in fear. And we'll practice loosening their grip, one moment at a time.

You do not need to be perfect to be worthy of compassion. You are already worthy. And from that ground, everything can grow.

THE FEAR OF KINDNESS TO OURSELVES

Here, I want to be very clear that self-compassion follows from open awareness—it isn't a form of deluding ourselves into believing we're "perfect." Self-compassion doesn't mean we stop trying. It doesn't mean we let ourselves off the hook. It means we stop making pain harder than it already is by layering it with judgment, comparison, and shame.

In one workshop, the minute we mentioned self-compassion, a participant named Andres shot back, "Self-compassion is an oxymoron. It doesn't exist!" The room got quiet. It was a reaction that may have sounded harsh, but it was deeply human—and painfully familiar. Many of us carry a secret fear of self-compassion. We associate it with weakness, indulgence, or even laziness. "I just feel like if I let up on myself for a minute," Andres continued, "I'll get lazy and stop trying to achieve my goals.

I'm afraid I'll let myself off the hook for everything. I'm afraid of the kind of person I'll become if I'm nice to myself."

This fear is more common than we think. In many cultures, there's an ingrained belief that if we're hard on ourselves, we'll improve. That grit comes from self-criticism. That we have to earn our worthiness through relentless effort. But Kristin Neff, a leading researcher in the field of self-compassion and associate professor of educational psychology at the University of Texas at Austin, has shown through extensive research that the opposite is true. In a joint paper co-authored with psychiatrist Rick Warren and neuroscientist Elke Smeets, Neff found that self-criticism doesn't just make us feel worse—it's deeply linked with depression, anxiety, and phobias. The more critical we are of ourselves, the harder it is to recover from emotional suffering.[2] Self-blame and harsh inner dialogue are major predictors of relapse in those recovering from depression.

Being hard on ourselves makes it harder to function. The more shame we carry, the more our attention narrows, the more our nervous system becomes dysregulated, and the less able we are to solve the problems in front of us.

Take Joan, for example. One morning, she made a typo in an important company-wide email. It was a small mistake—but her reaction was anything but. She spiraled quickly: *I'm bad at everything*, she thought. Her nervous system went into overdrive. Distracted and overwhelmed by self-blame, she made more mistakes, misread people in conversation, and missed key details in her work. The shame made her feel like she couldn't breathe. At lunchtime, she slipped outside to call a friend. "I'm a failure," she sobbed. Her friend reminded her of all the things she'd done well—but Joan couldn't hear it. Not yet.

Then she returned to her desk and opened an email from a colleague: "I made a similar mistake when I first started. It happens to everyone. Don't worry—this will blow over." That message shifted her entire perspective. Suddenly, she wasn't alone. And just like that, the weight of her shame began to lift.

Shame thrives in isolation. It tells us: "I'm the only one who's this messed up. I'm the only one who keeps making mistakes." But that's not true. In fact, discovering that we are not alone—that mistakes are part of being human—can bring enormous relief. And that's one of the first steps toward true resilience.

The fear of self-compassion often stems from misunderstanding. Self-compassion isn't self-pity. It isn't weakness. It isn't self-indulgence or complacency. In fact, it's one of the most powerful tools for growth and accountability we have.[3]

In a study led by Juliana Breines and Serena Chen at the University of California, Berkeley, participants were asked to recall a recent experience that left them feeling guilty—cheating on an exam, lying to a partner, or hurting someone they cared about.[4] Participants were then assigned one of three writing exercises. One group was guided to write to themselves from the perspective of a compassionate friend. Another wrote about their positive qualities. The third wrote about a hobby they enjoyed.

The results were telling: Those in the self-compassion group were more likely to apologize and more committed to not repeating the behavior than those in the other groups. Self-compassion didn't make them avoid accountability—it made them more accountable.

Self-compassion helps us face our shortcomings without being consumed by them. It motivates us not through fear or shame but through the desire to be well.

Andres, like many others, worried that self-compassion would make him soft. But over time, through the practices of open awareness and reflection, he began to notice the toll his inner critic was taking. His sleep was disrupted; his relationships were strained. His motivation was shaky and fueled by fear. But when he practiced simply being kind to himself—just for a few moments—he felt a subtle shift. "I started to realize," he shared later, "that the voice telling me to never stop pushing wasn't actually helping me do better. It was making me feel worse."

Here, I'd like to address another common misunderstanding about self-compassion, which is often conflated with self-esteem. However, self-esteem often relies on comparison—we feel worthy when we're doing well, when we feel superior, or when others admire us. But self-compassion doesn't require us to be better than anyone else. It's not about ranking or validation. It's about recognizing that suffering is part of the human experience, and choosing to meet it with care.

Practicing self-compassion is a radical act of reclaiming our humanity. When we make a mistake, we can say: "I really messed up when I got so mad at her, but I was stressed—and I guess all people overreact sometimes." That's not weakness. That's strength. Compare that to: "I can't believe I said that. I'm such a horrible, mean person."

Which mindset feels safer to live inside? Which one will allow us to grow?

When we see ourselves clearly—without the distorting lens of shame—we reconnect with the part of ourselves that wants to try again, that wants to be better not because we're broken but because we care.

Some of the researched benefits of self-compassion include:[5]

- Greater resilience
- Less anxiety and depression
- Reduced rumination
- Less suppression of difficult emotions
- Greater ability to cope with early childhood trauma and chronic physical pain
- Greater happiness, optimism, curiosity, creativity, enthusiasm, inspiration, and excitement
- Positive associations with emotional intelligence, wisdom, life satisfaction, and feelings of social connectedness
- Promotion of personal improvement

Think about a time when you were hard on yourself—maybe after a breakup, a work mistake, a conflict at home. Then remember a moment when you realized you weren't the only one. A song lyric. A friend's honesty. A stranger's story. That spark of recognition: You belong to the human family.

That recognition can change everything:

Mistake + self-blame = stuck. Mistake + self-compassion = change.

Let these equations guide you. Let them walk you back toward the Zone of Well-Being—the place of resilience, clarity, and connection that lives inside you, waiting to be remembered.

HOW DO WE REALLY TREAT OURSELVES?

In order to shift our tendency to spiral into shame, blame, or self-doubt, we have to start with how we *see*. Not just what's happening—but what meaning we assign to it. Our minds are meaning-making machines, and many of our emotional reactions are shaped by patterns of thinking we've practiced for years—maybe even decades. That self-critical voice? It's not inevitable. It's a habit. And habits can be changed.

In the Buddhist tradition, this kind of change starts with perspective. When we're able to see our experiences more clearly—without the fog of old stories, harsh judgment, or perfectionistic ideals—we're less likely to overreact and more likely to respond in ways that are helpful, kind, and true. This is the beginning of freedom—not from difficulty but from the added suffering we layer on top.

Mateo, a project lead at a tech start-up, had one of those days that makes you want to hide under the covers. He was new to the role, eager to prove himself, and on his first major assignment he misunderstood a key directive. As a result, his team launched a version of a product that wasn't fully ready. It wasn't a disaster, but it was sloppy—and very public. His manager was curt. His team had to clean things up. And Mateo's stomach was in knots for days.

That night, after lying awake replaying every misstep, Mateo did a simple exercise from his compassion training group. He wrote two letters—one written to himself as if from a friend, and one from himself.

Letter to himself as a friend:

> *Hey man,*
>
> *I just want to say—don't be too hard on yourself. You're in a new role, you've been juggling a million things, and one honest mistake doesn't erase all the good work you've already done. Seriously. Everyone messes something up at some point. The important thing is how you respond—and I know you'll handle it with integrity. You've got this. If you want to vent or walk it off, I'm here. Don't go through it alone.*
>
> *—M*

Letter from himself:

> *Wow. You really blew it. How could you mess up something so obvious? Your team probably thinks you're incompetent. Your manager definitely does. If you can't even get this right, how are you supposed to lead anything? You always do this—you overpromise, underdeliver, and then spiral. You're embarrassing.*

Reading the two side by side, Mateo was stunned. "If I saw someone else write that second letter," he said, "I'd be horrified. But when it's to myself, it feels . . . normal?"

For many of us, being supportive and kind to *others* comes naturally. But when it comes to ourselves, especially in moments of failure or shame, we reach for the whip, not the hand.

Try the same exercise. Write a short note to a friend who's made a mistake and is feeling awful about it. Encourage them. Let them know they're not alone. Then, write a note to yourself about a time *you* messed up. Don't overthink it—just notice the tone. The language. The compassion (or lack of it).

This is a window into how you relate to yourself. And if the two letters feel worlds apart, you're not alone. Most people discover just how hard they are on themselves when they see it laid out in words. So, the real question becomes: Has being hard on yourself ever really helped? How accurate a perspective does it embody in the first place?

A BUDDHIST THEORY OF CHANGE

A lot of people come to compassion training not because they think they're doing everything right—but because they quietly fear that they're doing something wrong. Not dramatically wrong, maybe, but wrong in all the small ways that add up. They snap at their kids when they're stressed, they ignore a colleague's pain, they pretend not to notice a friend's silence. These are often caring, thoughtful people with high standards and big hearts—but their inner experience doesn't match that image. Instead, they feel like they're failing. They feel like they're falling short of their values, again and again.

That mismatch—between who we want to be and how we actually show up—can create a powerful undercurrent of self-criticism. There's a Buddhist theory of change that invites us to understand how that mismatch happens—not by blaming ourselves but by seeing clearly how our emotional and cognitive systems work. Before we proceed, in case you're unfamiliar with the term, a *theory of change* is a clear, purposeful explanation of how and why a desired change is expected to happen. At its core, it's a road map. It helps us understand the steps, conditions, and shifts required to move from where we are to where we want to be—whether that's within a social system, an organization, or our own inner life.

In the context of contemplative practice and emotional transformation, a theory of change maps out how emotional suffering arises and how we can gradually transform it. It's not wishful thinking or just hoping to "feel better." It's a structured, tested framework that guides us in:

Gaining an accurate perspective by recognizing harmful emotional habits, like self-criticism or reactivity.

Gaining insight into how those patterns arise—not just from external events but from our internal perceptions, beliefs, and mental conditioning.

Developing new perspectives, rooted in compassion, interconnectedness, and clarity.

Strengthening those new perspectives through repeated practice, so they become more than ideas—they become embodied ways of being.

When we begin to see how automatic and conditioned our reactions often are, we can start to soften the shame and blame, and build new responses that are both more compassionate and more aligned with our values.

Let's start with the first step in this theory: gaining an accurate perspective. Specifically, we're trying to get clearer about what's actually happening in our minds and bodies when we feel triggered, overwhelmed, or reactive. What causes the emotions that—when excessive—can become destructive? His Holiness has said that what we need is "a map of our emotions to develop a calm mind." His longtime collaborator, renowned emotion scientist Dr. Paul Ekman, took up that challenge.

Together, Ekman and His Holiness created the Atlas of Emotions—an interactive model that illustrates the stages of emotional life.[6] This project grew out of the Mind and Life Dialogues, a series of conversations between scientists and contemplatives that began in 1987. As a scientist, Ekman admits he was initially skeptical: "What is there to be learned from a religious person about the mind and emotions?" But His Holiness surprised him. He wasn't interested in abstract theory; he wanted practical tools that could help reduce suffering in real life. The result was the Atlas, which lays out ten different stages:

Precondition: The physiological or emotional context you bring into a situation (e.g., being tired, hungry, stressed).
Event: Something that happens internally or externally.
Trigger: The interpretation of the event through your past emotional scripts.
Perception Database: Your internal bank of memories and associations that shape how you interpret events.

Physical Changes: Bodily responses like a clenched jaw, elevated heart rate, or tension in your chest.
State: The experience of the emotion, including its physical and psychological dimensions.
Psychological Changes: The stories, thoughts, or mental habits that emerge from the emotional state.
Action: The behavior that follows, whether external (yelling) or internal (shutting down).
Post-Condition: The immediate aftermath of your response.
Selective Filter Period: How your current emotional state colors what you perceive next.

Let's make this real. Imagine Anika, a project manager at a fast-paced tech company. She's barely slept because her toddler was sick all night (**precondition**). That morning, she arrives at work and finds that a junior colleague forgot to update a key slide in their big client presentation (**event**). Instantly, her brain matches this slip to an emotional "script" from past experiences where she's had to pick up the slack (**trigger**). Her mind consults its **perception database**—a running log of frustrations—and concludes: *She doesn't take this seriously. I can't rely on her.*

Almost immediately, Anika feels her jaw tighten and her chest constrict (**physical changes**). Emotion floods in—anger, resentment (**state**). She starts to catastrophize (**psychological changes**): *Why am I always the one cleaning up everyone's mess?* She snaps at her colleague in front of others (**action**), and as the meeting ends, she's left feeling guilty and disconnected (**post-condition**). For the rest of the day, her brain enters a **selective filter period**—meaning she mostly notices things that confirm her belief that no one respects her time, while ignoring cues of support or understanding.

This is how quickly emotion can take over—not because Anika is a bad person but because her mind followed a well-rehearsed pattern. The Atlas of Emotions helps us map that internal terrain. The Buddhist tradition helps us train our awareness to navigate it. For Anika, just learning to name the stages could be a revelation. With growing awareness, she could start to see this sequence unfold in real time—not to shame herself but to interrupt the automaticity. She could learn to recognize the preconditions, spot the triggers before they escalate, and pause long enough to question the story her mind is rushing to tell. Over time, this kind of mapping can lead to a profound shift: from blame to understanding, from shame to self-compassion, from reaction to choice.

Take a moment to reflect: When was the last time you felt flooded—overwhelmed by emotion in a way that didn't feel like you? Can you break that moment down using the Atlas of Emotions sequence? What precondition were you carrying in? What memory or old story might have been activated by the event? Can you trace how your body responded before your mind had a chance to intervene?

Understanding this sequence gives us room to step in. To notice what's happening in real time. To change course. That brings us to the science of reappraisal. Psychologists Kevin Ochsner and James Gross have shown that we can shift our emotional experience—not by suppressing emotion but by consciously reframing the meaning we assign to a situation. This is what is known as *cognitive reappraisal.*[7] Remember John from chapter five? Put yourself in his shoes for a moment. If someone bumps into you and you believe it was intentional, you might react with hostility. If you later learn they're blind, your emotional response shifts dramatically. The event didn't change. Your interpretation did.

Reappraisal isn't about putting a shiny gloss on hard realities. It's about seeing more of the picture. It's the difference between thinking *I failed again—I'll never get this right* and *I didn't handle that how I wanted to, but I can learn from it.* The data is compelling: Reappraisal reduces emotional distress, builds resilience, and even has lasting effects on how likely you are to be triggered again in similar situations.

The Atlas of Emotions and the idea of cognitive reappraisal both echo what the Buddhist tradition has long taught: Emotions arise quickly, but we can train ourselves to see them more clearly, to understand their origins, and to choose our responses more wisely. We can become more aware of how our minds work—and through that awareness, more free and compassionate toward ourselves.

Change takes repetition. It takes intention. But the more we familiarize ourselves with this sequence—the more we pause, notice, and reflect—the more we build new habits of mind. Gradually, those healthier responses become more automatic. They're not always perfect, but they're grounded in a deeper understanding of ourselves and others.

If you're feeling skeptical, that's OK. This isn't about pretending life is easy or emotions are simple. It's about becoming more honest with ourselves—less reactive, more responsive. And it starts by being willing to ask questions: *What really triggered me in that moment? What was I carrying in? What script was I reenacting?*

We'll discuss cognitive reappraisal a bit later in this chapter, as it's where the work of self-compassion truly begins.

MAKING STRENGTHS VISIBLE

In *The Art of Forgiveness, Lovingkindness, and Peace*, meditation teacher Jack Kornfield recounts a powerful ritual from the Babemba tribe in Africa. When someone acts irresponsibly or unjustly, they aren't punished or shunned. Instead, they are placed in the center of the village, and every man, woman, and child gathers around. One by one, each person recalls something good the accused has done—their acts of kindness, their strengths, their better moments. The ritual can last for days. And at the end, the circle breaks into celebration, welcoming the person back into the community.[8]

The Babemba ritual doesn't erase the wrongdoing. It surrounds it with context, with love, with memory. It interrupts the human tendency to reduce people to their worst moments. And it offers something we often withhold from ourselves: belonging, even after failure.

Most of us weren't raised in villages like that. When we mess up, we don't get circled with stories of our goodness. We get quiet. We spiral. We replay our mistakes and forget everything else. We exile ourselves from our own compassion.

Psychologist Dr. Ryan Niemiec created an exercise to help us practice another way.[9] It's deceptively simple, and it works:

> Think of a time—recent or distant—when you were at your best. It might have been at work, with a friend, in a crisis, or just in an everyday moment.
> Describe what happened in detail. What did you do? How did you feel? What were the outcomes?
> Now read through your story and identify what strengths you were using. Was it perseverance? Humor? Fairness? Kindness? Creativity?

Just noticing your strengths can change your state of mind. Research shows that interventions focused on character strengths reduce depression, anxiety, and physical symptoms—and increase happiness, curiosity, resilience, and emotional intelligence.[10]

Now, pause. What does it feel like to recognize your strengths? Do you allow yourself to feel proud—or does your inner critic try to rush in with a dismissive comment?

This shift—toward naming and acknowledging our strengths—is an example of cognitive reappraisal. It's a way of reclaiming space from the negativity bias that often dominates our attention. We're not pretending everything is fine. We're balancing the picture. And this is critical when it comes to developing self-compassion. Because when we make mistakes, or feel flooded by shame, our vision narrows. We see only the bad. But when we learn to recognize the whole of ourselves—including the strength it takes to care, the courage it takes to try—we start to shift the internal story.

This is where self-compassion research, especially from Kristin Neff, becomes vital. In one study, Neff and her colleagues worked with veterans returning from Iraq and Afghanistan. Nearly half showed symptoms of PTSD. Those with higher self-compassion scores—measured by statements like "I'm tolerant of my own flaws and inadequacies"—had significantly lower levels of distress.

Self-compassion attenuates people's reactions to negative events in ways that are distinct from and, in some cases, more beneficial than self-esteem, the researchers found. Why? Because self-compassion doesn't rely on perfection. It allows for imperfection, for failure, for grief. It reduces rumination. It breaks the loop of inner hostility.

As Neff's research shows, self-compassionate people are also more likely to take responsibility for their actions—not less. They're more likely to apologize, make amends, and change course. When we respond to our suffering with curiosity instead of condemnation, tenderness instead of blame, we don't become lazy or self-indulgent. We become free to learn. Free to repair. Free to return, again and again, to what matters most.

So, take a moment. Name something you've done well recently, even if it was small. Breathe into that. Let it land. And let it remind you that you are more than your worst moment. You belong in the circle, too.

THE FIRST AND SECOND ARROWS

I've spent decades studying both Buddhist philosophy and modern science, and the more I learn, the more I see how deeply our suffering stems not only from what happens to us—but from what happens next, inside us. From how we react. That's why the Buddhist theory of change begins not with trying to control the external world (which we often cannot) but with seeking a more accurate view of our own minds and the world around us. This shift in perspective is the foundation of self-compassion.

One of the most well-known Buddhist teachings on this is the story of the two arrows. A teacher asks her student, "If someone is struck by an arrow, is it painful?"

"Yes," the student replies. "Very painful."

"And if they are struck by a second arrow, in the same place—would that be even more painful?"

"Of course," the student says. "That would be unbearable."

The teacher nods. "The first arrow is the difficulty we didn't choose. The second arrow is the suffering we create by how we respond."

The first arrow might be a breakup, a rejection, a medical diagnosis, or just a moment of disappointment or embarrassment. These are the unavoidable pains of life. But the second arrow is where our power lies. The second arrow is when we tell ourselves, "I'm not lovable," or "I never do anything right," or "This always happens to me." It's the spiral of rumination, blame, shame, or self-punishment that follows. That's the pain we add on top of pain.

I've met many people who hold themselves to standards no one else could meet. Not because they're arrogant but because they care so deeply—about being good, being kind, doing things right. When they fall short of their own ideals, even in small ways, they blame themselves relentlessly. They think: *I should be able to handle this. What's wrong with me?* That reaction can become automatic. And when it does, it feels like there's no space at all between the first and second arrows. But there can be. We can create that space with great intention.

Paul Ekman describes how emotion creates what he calls a *refractory period.*[11] It's a temporary state in which we can't see clearly. When we're angry, we can't access what we know about kindness. When we're ashamed, we can't remember our worth. When we're afraid, we interpret everything as a threat. And if we're not aware of this, we act from it—we shoot the second arrow.

Shortening the refractory period is one of the central goals of compassion training. When we learn to pause, to recognize the emotion without acting on it immediately, we begin to see what's really going on. We begin to remember that we're not our worst moments.

His Holiness once talked about being surprised the first time he learned that many people in the West experience something called "self-hatred." It isn't a concept that people grow up with in Tibetan culture. His Holiness understood doubt, confusion, and shame—but hatred toward oneself? That was new to him. But as he listened more closely, he came to understand what it meant: a deep and painful identification with one's flaws, mistakes, or shortcomings. A belief that failure is not something we experience but something we are.

This is where self-compassion becomes essential. We learn to treat ourselves with the same clarity and tenderness we would offer someone we love. We also recognize that our suffering is real, but it is not *all* of who we are.

When I teach this to students, I often share a story. A woman I'll call Nadia had just returned from a family gathering where she'd lost her temper and shouted at her sister. It wasn't the first time. Afterward, she felt terrible. "I don't even know why I reacted that way," she said. "I just snapped. And then I hated myself for it."

As we talked, I asked her to walk me through the situation using a tool from Ekman's Atlas of Emotions. We identified her preconditions: She was tired from travel, anxious about seeing family, and already irritated before the argument even began. The event? Her sister made a dismissive comment about something important to her. The perception? That she was being disrespected—again. Physical changes: heart racing, face flushed. The emotional state: anger, mixed with hurt. The action: shouting. The post-condition: shame and regret. As she mapped it out, she saw the full arc, and for the first time, she said, "Maybe I'm not just a 'bad person.' Maybe I was just . . . overwhelmed."

That realization was the beginning of a new pattern—not because she denied responsibility but because she saw the whole picture. She began to ask, "What contributed to that moment?" rather than only, "What's wrong with me?" This is what the Buddhist tradition calls *renunciation*—not in the sense of rejecting life but of letting go of the patterns that perpetuate our suffering. It's the determination to be free, and it starts with understanding what's actually causing us pain—not just the event but our reaction to it.

Self-compassion allows us to interrupt that reaction, notice when we've picked up the second arrow, and set it down.

You might try this yourself. Think of a time when things didn't go the way you hoped. A plan fell apart. A conversation turned tense. You made a mistake that still stings. What was the first arrow in that situation? What was beyond your control? Then ask: What was the second arrow? What did you tell yourself? How did you treat yourself afterward? And can you now see that your reaction, while understandable, may not have been helpful?

When we see clearly what's within our control and what isn't, we reclaim energy we've been using to beat ourselves up—and we redirect it toward wiser action. We shift from hopelessness to agency, shame to clarity, self-blame to self-compassion.

THE POWER AND PURPOSE OF ANALYTICAL MEDITATION

Most of us carry quiet burdens we rarely name out loud: the voice that says we're not doing enough, the disappointment when life doesn't unfold the way we'd hoped, the guilt that creeps in even when we've done our best. Like we've already explored, these feelings come from a mismatch between the ideals we hold and the messy reality of being human. We want to be generous, wise, patient, perfect partners or parents or professionals. And when we're not, we quietly condemn ourselves.

But just as Kisa Gotami, the grieving mother in the Buddhist parable, came to see that her loss was not unique—and in doing so, began to heal—we, too, can ease our suffering by realizing we're not alone. We're not flawed for feeling pain. We're not broken because we stumble. We are shaped by genetics, culture, upbringing, circumstance—so many forces beyond our control. And yet we still expect ourselves to be superhuman.

Compassion shows us that perfection isn't possible, and it never was. This was beautifully illustrated in a public dialogue between His Holiness and Dr. Aaron Beck, the founder of Cognitive Behavioral Therapy (CBT). Dr. Beck told the story of a brilliant physicist who came to him, deeply depressed. The man had made a great discovery for which he was expecting to win the Nobel Prize, but he didn't even receive a nomination. For him, that loss wasn't just a disappointment. It felt like proof that his life had no value. Winning the Nobel Prize "was one hundred percent important," he admitted.

When Dr. Beck asked about how the man would describe the importance of his wife and children's roles in his life by percentage, the man gave them low percentages—none more than 40 percent. He had hardly seen them, he said. He had been so focused on his work. When Dr. Beck gently asked how that made him feel, the man broke down in tears. "That was how my own father was to me," he said. "Now I see what he missed . . . and what I've missed. And what my children are missing, too."

By the end of their session, the physicist's view of himself had changed. His values shifted. His sense of self-worth was no longer tied to a prize. He could see his relationships, his love for his children, as a meaningful part of who he was. His depression began to lift. His Holiness, listening to this story, nodded and smiled. "Very wise," he said. "That method is exactly what we call analytical meditation."

Analytical meditation—the process of arriving at an insight from various angles, deepening it, and then sitting with the conviction to keep deepening it—is a primary tool for our cultivation of self-compassion. In the case of the physicist, this process shifted his view on the events of his life away from a narrow perspective on what "went wrong" and toward the neglected parts of his life where he had meaningful opportunities for personal connection, growth, and joy. To practice analytical meditation, we engage in cognitive reappraisal.

We do this by bringing to mind three perspectives evident from the above story: assessing what factors were in our control; appreciating that even if we could control more, a changed outcome was not guaranteed; and understanding that there are many causes and conditions that lead to any outcome. Taken together, these perspectives soften harsh emotional responses to external events and keep us from getting stuck focusing only on one aspect of our life, such as our mistakes or setbacks, so we can shift and sustain focus on the bigger picture.

We combine our insights with stabilizing meditation—sitting with that awareness over time, which the first three steps helped us to do—to ensure those ideas become part of our consciousness. Using the tools of stabilizing and analytical meditation, we can change our perspective. This transforms how we act and feel, bringing about a more compassionate view toward ourselves and ultimately toward others, as well. It's a deeply compassionate practice. And it's one I've leaned on myself during some of the most painful moments in my life.

In 2002, I was visiting England, traveling with other Drepung Loseling monks to give public talks, when I learned that my father had suffered a stroke. He still lived in our remote Himalayan village of Kinnaur, where hospitals were far away and care was hard to access. I couldn't just jump on a plane—I had to apply for a visa, wait, and hope it came in time. Even once it arrived, I had to get him from Kinnaur to Delhi. We moved as quickly as we could. My dear friend Geshe Thupten Dorjee met us in Delhi, helped arrange medical care. But that night, in the hospital, my father passed away.

Driving his body home the next day, I felt crushed. I had done everything I could, but it didn't feel like enough. If only I had gotten there sooner. If only I had acted faster. My chest ached with regret.

But then, I remembered the teachings. I turned to the words of Shantideva and others who reminded me to look clearly, to ask: What was within my control? What wasn't? Could I have changed the outcome? Maybe yes, maybe no. What I knew for certain was this: I did my best. There were countless forces at play—visa delays, distance, medical infrastructure—and I did everything in my power. No one factor determined the outcome. Just like a farmer can till the soil, plant the seeds, water the crops—but cannot control the sun or the wind or the weather—I had to accept that I could not control everything.

This is one of the most important insights in cultivating self-compassion: recognizing that many causes and conditions shape every outcome. This recognition doesn't erase our grief—but it does help us avoid unnecessary suffering—the second arrow. It helps us soften the harsh blame we place on ourselves when life doesn't go the way we hoped.

In analytical meditation, we compassionately shift out of self-blame and perfectionism by exploring the causes and conditions—both seen and unseen—that played a role in our experience. When we explore sincerely, and let the answers settle in the heart (not just the head), we begin to see ourselves differently. This is what allows self-compassion to take root—not as a vague idea but as a lived truth. Over time, this becomes a stabilizing force. When we combine insight with steady awareness—when we don't just think differently but feel and return to that new understanding again and again—we change.

THE PRACTICE OF MAKING SPACE FOR SELF-COMPASSION

In CBCT, we strengthen our capacity for self-compassion through powerful emotion regulation strategies that science backs and ancient traditions anticipated. A 2020 Stanford study identified three key strategies that help us work with emotion: attention deployment (shifting our focus away from what causes distress), self-distancing (stepping back from overwhelming thoughts and feelings), and cognitive reappraisal (which, as you already know, is assessing our situation from a broader, more realistic perspective).[12] CBCT draws on all three, not just in theory but in lived practice—so that over time, compassion becomes a natural response, not just a good idea.

In the first three steps, we already explored stabilizing meditation, which strengthens our ability to calm the mind and gain distance from our reactive loops. When the murky waters of thoughts and emotions settle, we start to see the deeper patterns that shape how we think, feel, and respond. From there, analytical meditation lets us engage those patterns directly—asking fresh questions, shifting perspectives, and challenging harmful habits of thought.

Here, we'll start applying these insights to how we relate to ourselves, especially in moments of failure, pain, or regret. This new mental habit is rooted in the recognition that setbacks are part of the human condition, not personal flaws. The more we connect with our own longing to be well and free from suffering, the more we soften our judgment and begin to treat ourselves with the same kindness we'd offer a struggling friend. Just like putting on our own oxygen mask first, self-compassion becomes the starting point for deeper, more sustainable compassion.

A Guided Reflection on Self-Compassion (5–7 minutes)

Once you've settled, take a moment to find a comfortable posture—seated or lying down, supported in a way that feels steady and at ease. Gently bring awareness to your body. Notice where tension lives. If you feel tightness in your jaw or shoulders, you might stretch or adjust. Let yourself arrive here with care.

If it feels natural, take a few deep breaths. Inhale slowly and imagine you're breathing in nourishment—air that fills you, steadying and calming. As you exhale, soften your muscles and let go of what you don't need in this moment: stress, self-judgment, tension.

Allow your breath to find its own rhythm, and rest your awareness on that quiet cadence. If you're having trouble settling today, consider returning to an earlier practice—perhaps grounding in bodily sensation or recalling a nurturing moment—before continuing.

Now, gently reflect: When things don't go the way you hoped—when you make a mistake, experience a setback, or fall short of your expectations—how do you tend to respond to yourself?

What emotions arise? What stories show up in your mind? Maybe they sound like: "I can't believe I did that," or "I'm never going to get this right." Maybe there's a loop of harsh self-talk: "I'm a failure. I'm useless. I always screw things up."

Let's pause here and take a step back. Even if setbacks and difficult emotions are part of life, it's common to fan the flames with self-judgment. The pain of the moment becomes amplified. The inner critic grows louder. But is it true that you're the only one who feels this way? Let's consider: Is this a you problem—or a human one?

As you reflect, see if there's a shift—however subtle—from "I'm the only one" to "I'm not alone." What does that shift feel like in the body? In the breath? In the heart?

Pause again. Now, bring to mind a time when you felt overwhelmed with harsh self-blame and thought, *There is nothing good about me*. That voice can feel all-consuming. But pause and ask yourself: Is that the full truth? We may not be good at everything—nobody is—but all of us are good at something. Let's take a moment to name some of those things now.

What are your strengths? Think about your kindness, honesty, perseverance, your creativity or humor. Maybe it's the way you show up for others, your curiosity, your love of learning, your empathy.

Pause again. Notice how it feels to remember what's going well—or even just what's going a little better. Does something soften inside you? Perhaps there's a sense of warmth, of relief, or of quiet encouragement. Let that feeling grow.

If it helps, imagine this shift as a soft, soothing light at the center of your chest. With each inhale, let that light gently expand. With each exhale, allow it to nourish your whole being.

How might this ability to step back and see the full picture—your challenges and your strengths—support your overall well-being? How might it influence your relationships? Could it shift how you show up for yourself and others?

Take a moment to connect with your deeper longing for well-being. Silently repeat: "May I be free from suffering. May I be gentle with myself. May I trust in my capacity to grow."

Then, as you feel ready, extend this aspiration beyond yourself. Call to mind someone in your life who is struggling—someone you care about. Then, widen the circle to include others in your community. And beyond that, extend it to all beings: "May we all find peace. May we all feel seen, held, and whole." Your practice has value—not just for you but for the world you touch.

As you transition out of this practice, set a gentle intention. Today, when something goes wrong or doesn't unfold the way you hoped, you might take a moment to pause. Notice what the inner critic says. And then ask: "Would I speak to a friend this way? What would I say instead?"

You might find that what you'd say to a friend applies to you, too.

If in the course of your day you find yourself knocked out of your Zone of Well-Being, you can always return to earlier practices from this book. You can ground yourself in breath or sensation. Recall a moment of connection. Or step away entirely and do something kind for your body—take a walk, sip water, step outside. This is how you begin to change the script.

BRINGING THE SKILLS TO LIFE: PRACTICE BETWEEN SESSIONS

We are not perfect. We make mistakes. We drop things, burn dinner, forget birthdays, say the wrong thing, oversleep, run out of patience. We snap at the people we love. We stare in the mirror and criticize what we see. These aren't signs of personal failure. They're signs of being human.

The invitation of this chapter has been to recognize the difference between imperfection and inadequacy. To shift the way we interpret our struggles—not as evidence that something is wrong with us but as proof that we belong to a larger story of human vulnerability and growth. Everyday mistakes become opportunities to soften the voice of the inner critic; such softening opens the door to strength—not weakness.

Sometimes the most compassionate thing we can do is just laugh in a way that recognizes the absurdity of being human. You burn the toast, you forget the password you just reset, you call someone by the wrong name—again. There's real power in being able to smile at yourself, shake your head, and say, "Of course I did." Humor doesn't erase the mistake, but it releases the grip of shame. It reminds us that we're not broken—we're just wonderfully, sometimes hilariously, human.

Self-compassion isn't just about comforting ourselves when things are hard. It's also about lightening the emotional load, loosening the seriousness, and remembering that growth doesn't have to feel like a punishment. Sometimes it looks like grace. Sometimes it sounds like laughter.

Self-compassion meets us in the mess. It doesn't ask us to have it all together. It invites us to be honest about our limits, to laugh when we can, and to rest when we need to. And when we do, we stop measuring ourselves by impossible standards, and we start making room for the truth of our experience. These shifts don't always happen overnight, but they're real—and they matter.

Lena, a caregiver for both her mother and grandmother, described how depleted and ashamed she felt when she lost her temper. "I felt terribly guilty when I would become frustrated with them," she said. "The practice of self-compassion has been essential to reframe my sense of guilt, anger, self-judgment by recognizing that they were normal in the situation. Instead of condemning myself for being human, I was able to accept my shortcomings. It made me feel freer, lighter, and more capable of continuing to care for them both."

Elizabeth, a college student, shared the pressure she put on herself to excel. "I loaded up on AP classes to prove I could handle it. When it got overwhelming, I didn't want to drop anything because I thought that would mean I wasn't strong enough. But the truth was, I was burning out. I finally gave myself permission to change my schedule—and when I did, my health and my self-respect started to come back. Admitting I needed help was actually the braver thing."

And then there's Darren, a project manager who realized how often he blamed himself when things went wrong at work. "You can't control every factor no matter how hard you try—that was my aha moment. When things went wrong at work, I turned the blame on myself and looked for the holes I should have plugged, the solutions I should have found to prevent anything from going wrong. But there's so much freedom in realizing that most of the time, no matter how hard I try to control things, so much is out of my control."

These stories reflect the core insight that excessive self-criticism and narrow judgments don't make us more capable. They make us more exhausted, more discouraged, more likely to give up. When we recognize that setbacks are inevitable—and not all our fault—we begin to relate to ourselves with greater gentleness. We stop pouring salt in our own wounds. We stop shooting the second arrow.

These are skills we can practice every day. Noticing when the inner critic shows up. Interrupting the story of "I'm no good." Naming our strengths, even in the smallest situations. Letting go of perfection and returning—again and again—to the broader truth of our shared humanity. We can call this self-compassion, but it's also just honesty: a clearer view of what it means to live in a complex world, to face uncertainty, and to still want to grow.

In the next chapter, we'll continue this journey by strengthening the perspectives that help us meet our own struggles with dignity—and begin to ask who else might be worthy of our care. Because when we stop turning against ourselves, we uncover a deeper well of compassion that naturally extends beyond our intimate circles, toward a wider, more inclusive world.

CHAPTER SEVEN

EXPANDING OUR CIRCLE OF CONCERN

From the outset establish an even-minded attitude, eliminating the bias which comes from attachment to some living beings and hostility to others. Otherwise, any love or compassion you feel will be biased; you will never feel unbiased love or compassion. So, cultivate impartiality.

—Tsongkhapa[1]

We all want to feel safe, connected, and understood. And yet, our minds often divide the world into "us" and "them." Those I trust, and those I don't. People I identify with, and people I avoid or dismiss. It's an ancient evolutionary instinct—protect the tribe. But in a world defined by complexity, migration, interdependence, and rapid change, that instinct can become a source of isolation, anxiety, and subtle (sometimes overt) bias.

In North America today, this painful split plays out in ways that feel deeply familiar. You may find yourself silently bracing when a coworker brings up politics, already assuming you're on opposing sides. Maybe you scroll past your cousin's social media posts, annoyed by their values or strident tone. Maybe someone at the gym wears a hat or a pronoun badge that makes you tense up—not because you know them but because of what you think they represent. Or perhaps it's subtler: the way you assume someone's intelligence by how they speak, their kindness by how they vote, or their trustworthiness by where they're from.

The more our world is filled with categories, the smaller it becomes. Suddenly, whole communities are dismissed as "those people." Entire stories are lost. We stay in our bubbles, talk only to people who agree with us, and wonder why we feel more disconnected and anxious. The need to protect ourselves becomes a low-grade loneliness, quietly shaping our everyday experience.

Polarization seeps inward, too. We may start to judge parts of ourselves by those same tribal codes. The parts of us that feel confused, messy, ashamed, or uncertain get pushed to the margins. We exile parts of our own humanity in the same way we exile others.

When we live in a world carved into groups of those who are "worthy" and "unworthy"—of care, of attention, of forgiveness—we don't just limit our compassion. We limit our freedom. We end up carrying the emotional weight of division everywhere we go. But there is another way: We can begin to soften those internal borders, not by pretending differences don't exist but by remembering that beneath every label is a living, breathing person—just like us.

This chapter invites us to expand our circle of concern—not just in belief but in practice. We learn to identify with people beyond our default groups. That expansion doesn't dilute our connection to those closest to us—it deepens our sense of belonging everywhere. In fact, research shows that when we increase feelings of emotional closeness toward people outside our social groups, we actually feel *less* lonely and *more* resilient.[2] The more connection we experience, the more we have to give.

This begins with recognizing that every person, no matter how different their background or beliefs, shares our most basic longings: to feel seen, safe, valued, and free from suffering. As the Buddha once said to the monk Upali—who had been taught that, as someone who was part of the "untouchable" caste, his touch might contaminate others—"My blood is the same color. How can you contaminate me?"

When the high-caste Brahmins mocked the Buddha for consorting with people of lower castes, he replied: "Nature does not discriminate.

The wind blows for everyone. The water quenches every thirst. Why, then, should we?"

These words echo across centuries—and they call out especially clearly when we look at more recent history. During the height of the AIDS epidemic in the 1980s, fear took on the form of moral panic and dehumanization. People with HIV and AIDS—especially gay men, intravenous drug users, and immigrants—were treated as if they were tainted, untouchable. Patients were refused treatment. Families were shunned. Children were pulled from schools. There was a belief, sometimes spoken and often implied, that the disease was a punishment for being who they were.

And yet—what was HIV, really? A virus. Passed through blood and fluid, yes. But more than that, it became a mirror of how willing we were to turn away from each other. To make a mockery of our shared humanity. The tragedy of AIDS was not just medical—it was spiritual. It was a time when fear disguised itself as virtue, and many chose judgment over care.

It took years of advocacy, grief, and solidarity for the tide to turn. But when it did, it wasn't just science that changed minds—it was proximity. It was friendship, protest, caregiving, kinship, and love. It was hospital rooms filled with chosen family. It was people saying, again and again, "You matter. You are not untouchable. You belong."

The Buddha's words, thousands of years old, live on in these moments. And the challenge remains with us: Can we recognize each other beyond the categories we've inherited or been taught to fear? Can we meet one another's pain without recoiling, without retreating into bias or blame?

Expanding our circle of concern is a powerful refusal to shrink from our shared humanity—even when the world tells us to draw lines and build walls. This kind of wisdom cuts through the heart of tribalism. Whether in ancient India or today's divided world, it asks us to see more clearly: not just the ways we are different but the ways we are the same.

That shared humanity becomes especially visible during moments of collective crisis. In the face of loss, injustice, or fear, we often feel our concern expand. We see someone struggling and our instinct is to help.

But we don't have to wait for crisis to practice this. Through deliberate reflection, we can train ourselves to connect with others—even those we find difficult—not because they've earned it but because we see ourselves in them.

Without a sense of kinship—without deliberately seeking common ground or nurturing the ability to recognize others as part of our shared tribe—our daily lives can become a breeding ground for sadness and conflict. We shrink into echo chambers. We protect our own and dismiss the rest. And in the process, we forget that our well-being is bound up with each other's. When we ignore a colleague's burnout because "it's not our problem," the workplace becomes heavier for everyone. When we vote only for policies that benefit our immediate circle, we contribute—often unintentionally—to the suffering of others and the breakdown of trust in our communities. When we write off entire groups as lazy, ignorant, or dangerous, we shut the door on the possibility of learning, collaboration, and peace.

Consider the ripple effects of withholding care: a neighbor going hungry while we waste food, an overwhelmed parent losing support because we assume they should be able to cope, a teen bullied online while bystanders scroll past silently. These aren't abstract issues—they shape the texture of our daily lives, our neighborhoods, our collective future.

By remembering that we're in this together, we create the conditions for our own deeper safety, connection, and joy. When we expand our circle, even just a little, we don't lose ourselves—we find more of ourselves. We loosen the tightness of fear and make room for curiosity, complexity, and care.

THE POWER OF IN-GROUP BIAS

At Christmas in 1914, just five months into the brutal trench warfare of World War I, something extraordinary happened. More than one hundred thousand soldiers—on both sides of the front—disobeyed direct orders and climbed out of their trenches into no-man's-land. They played soccer. They shared chocolate and cigarettes. They helped each other bury the dead.

These were men trained to see each other as enemies, yet for one night, they remembered that they were also sons, brothers, and human beings. They recognized something deeper than the war: their shared humanity.[3]

Moments like these are rare, but they reveal a truth we often forget. The lines we draw between "us" and "them" are real, but they are also learned. And they can be unlearned.

A few years ago, a team of psychologists including Dr. Mark Levine studied this instinct by observing fans of Manchester United.[4] After priming the participants to think about how much they loved their team, researchers staged an emergency. On the way to another part of the study, participants passed a stranger who appeared to have twisted an ankle. When that stranger wore a Liverpool jersey—or no jersey at all—only about a third of fans stopped to help. But if he wore a Manchester United jersey, almost everyone did.

The difference? Not empathy. Not morality. Just a shift in perception of who belonged.

This is how easily tribalism works. It's not always dramatic. It shows up in quiet decisions: who we greet with warmth and who we ignore, who we advocate for and who we quietly write off. If someone close to us struggles, we listen, we care, we act. But when someone outside our in-group suffers, we may not even register it—or worse, we may feel smug satisfaction.

That's the power of in-group bias. It's reinforced by brain chemistry—hormones like oxytocin actually deepen our empathy for those we identify with, while simultaneously reinforcing our suspicion of those we don't. Evolution taught us to protect our tribe. But in the modern world, this instinct often backfires.

Consider, again, the early years of the AIDS epidemic in the 1980s. In North America, fear ran rampant—not just of the disease but of the people who had it. Misinformation, homophobia, and stigma led many to believe they could be "contaminated" by sharing a cup, a handshake, even the same air. And so, people who were already suffering were met with silence, judgment, abandonment. The fear didn't protect us. What it did was override connection, which happens when we forget that *their* well-being is bound up with *ours*.

If we're chronically stressed, overworked, or afraid, our nervous systems go into threat mode. We default to habits of separation: "This person helps me, that one threatens me, that other one doesn't matter." But when we live like this—rigid, reactive, afraid—we suffer. We miss out on the beauty, insight, and strength that come from real connection. We walk past people who could have become friends. When we exaggerate the boundaries between us and others, we feed jealousy, resentment, bias, and loneliness. We become more possessive with those we love, more defensive in conflict, more judgmental in moments of difference. We lose the capacity to see nuance or imagine ourselves in another's shoes. It becomes harder to forgive. Harder to stay open. Harder to breathe.

But we are not doomed to this pattern. History reminds us that the walls can fall. So do moments of real empathy, like when a stranger holds the door open or a friend forgives us more quickly than we think we deserve. These are not grand gestures—they are small acts of reclaiming our shared belonging. Because without that, all our technological progress, our medical breakthroughs, our scientific wonders—none of it will save us from ourselves.

But expansion takes intention. It doesn't happen automatically. In a world that pulls us to judge, to categorize, to dismiss, it is a courageous act to pause and ask:

- Who do I naturally feel compassion toward? Who do I struggle to include?
- When someone in my in-group suffers, how do I respond? And how does that response shift when the person is not "one of mine"?
- Can I recall a time I judged someone quickly—and then learned something that changed how I saw them?
- What assumptions do I carry—about race, class, gender, religion,

nationality, political identity—that might be limiting the size of my circle?

- How has fear, even subtle fear, narrowed my ability to connect?
- Who are the people I walk past in my day-to-day life without really seeing?

These questions aren't meant to shame you. They're meant to wake you up—to your humanity, and to everyone else's. When we loosen the walls between "us" and "them," we come home to a world where belonging isn't earned. It's recognized. It's shared. And you don't have to start with everyone. You just have to *start*.

WHAT IS BIAS?

We're wired to connect. That's not poetry—it's evolutionary fact. Human beings are social creatures, and from the beginning, our survival has depended on being part of a group. In the wild, going it alone wasn't brave—it was dangerous. Being cast out from your tribe often meant death. So it makes sense that we developed a deep biological need for belonging. And that need still lives in us today.

You can feel it every day—in the impulse to text a friend when something funny happens, or in the relief of a warm smile from a stranger when you're having a rough day. It shows up when you scroll through social media, looking for signs that your people are doing OK. It's what draws you to join a book club, watch the same show your coworkers love just to be able to talk about it, or volunteer for a cause that gives you a sense of shared purpose.

This pull toward connection is also why rejection hurts so deeply, and why loneliness feels not just sad but painful. We don't just *want* to belong—we *need* to. And our bodies register disconnection as a threat. Studies show that social exclusion activates the same regions in the brain as physical pain. That's how seriously we're wired for relationship.[5]

While our capacity for empathy and connection is innate, it's also selective. We're naturally drawn to those who feel like "us"—people who look like us, talk like us, like the same music, eat the same food, live in the same neighborhood, vote the same way. Everyone else? They register, often unconsciously, as "other." This is what psychologists call *bias*.

At its root, bias is a tendency to favor one thing over another—often without even realizing it. It's our brain's shortcut system, helping us quickly assess who's "safe," who's "trustworthy," who's "in our group." That shortcut was helpful when saber-toothed tigers were lurking around, but in today's interconnected world, it can lead us astray.

Take empathy. As primatologist Frans de Waal points out, "In both animals and humans empathy is biased. It is always stronger for the in-group than the out-group, stronger for one's own family than for non-relatives."[6] We care more, feel more, and show up more for people we identify with—and we may not even notice how much we tune out when someone different struggles.

This starts early. Developmental psychologists at the Yale Infant Cognition Center have discovered that innate bias is an instinct we can see from infancy. For instance, babies showed a bias toward those who shared their preference for their favorite cereal.[7] Additionally, despite showing a bias or preference in general for strangers who were helpful to others, babies also demonstrated a preference for strangers who chastised those with whom they had superficial differences, even if it was as simple as not liking the same snack food. Even though babies showed an overall tendency to prefer kindness, when they found out that someone did not like the same snack as them, their responses shifted. This suggests that they preferred seeing harm come to those whom they perceived as different from them.[8] That's a little scary. But it's also eye-opening. It suggests that bias isn't something only "bad people" have. It's something all of us are susceptible to, by virtue of being human.

But the cost of dividing the world into "us" and "them" makes all of us suffer. Social neuroscientists John and Stephanie Cacioppo have shown that even the *perception* of social isolation can weaken our immune system, stress our heart, and increase our risk of death from all causes.[9] And in 2015, researchers demonstrated that social isolation is as harmful to our health as smoking fifteen cigarettes a day, and can increase our chances of dying from any cause.[10]

Our lives are no longer lived in small, homogenous tribes. We work together, live together, struggle together. If we let our unconscious biases run the show, we're clinging to an outdated script that no longer fits the reality of our lives. The invitation of CBCT isn't to feel shame for having bias but to see it clearly and choose something wiser that's deeply aligned with both our values and our future.

THE DARWINIAN DISTORTION

For generations, many Western thinkers have passed down a core belief about human nature: When crisis strikes, we revert to selfishness. The message runs deep—especially in school, where countless students are handed copies of *Lord of the Flies* and taught to see it as an accurate portrayal of human behavior. But it's worth asking: Whose perspective are we absorbing, and what shaped it?

William Golding wrote *Lord of the Flies* in the shadow of World War II, during a time when the sheer scale of violence and genocide left many searching for answers.[11] One explanation—perhaps the only one that felt possible in the aftermath—was that people are fundamentally broken. Golding himself came from a home shaped by trauma; he was raised by an abusive, alcoholic father, and later perpetuated abuse in his own life. The worldview in *Lord of the Flies* wasn't just literary—it was personal. In his story, remove the constraints of shame and social norms, and boys descend into savagery. In other words: Once the rules are gone, so is human decency.

But what if Golding got it wrong?

In his 2020 book *Humankind: A Hopeful History*, Dutch historian Rutger Bregman digs into a real-life version of *Lord of the Flies*—one most people have never heard of.[12] In 1965, six boys from Tonga were shipwrecked on a remote island for over a year. There were no adults. No rules. And yet, when they were rescued, the scene was nothing like Golding's nightmare. The boys had survived—and even thrived—by caring for one another. They found food, built shelter, tended wounds, and rotated chores. When someone got hurt, the others picked up his tasks. Decades later, they still considered each other family. The real story wasn't about descent into brutality. It was about compassion, resilience, and deep connection.

And it's that version of human nature—one rooted in cooperation, not cruelty—that Charles Darwin actually believed in.

Contrary to popular belief, Darwin never coined the phrase *survival of the fittest.* That was Herbert Spencer, a social theorist who distorted Darwin's theory of natural selection to support cutthroat capitalism and justify social inequality. Spencer's version painted the world as a battlefield where only the ruthless survive. But Darwin's writings tell a different story. He saw sympathy—not selfishness—as humanity's greatest strength. In *The Descent of Man*, he marveled at how readily humans, and even animals, put themselves at risk to help others. "This virtue," he wrote, "one of the noblest with which man is endowed . . . arises incidentally from our sympathies becoming more tender and more widely diffused, until they are extended to all sentient beings."[13]

That view is echoed in the Himalayan Buddhist culture I was raised in, where the core belief is this: Our positive qualities are stronger than our negative ones. It's easy to assume the worst about people, especially when we're overwhelmed or hurting. But if we pause, breathe, and look closely, we see a different reality unfolding in nearly every moment.

A young woman hoists a visitor's suitcase up a flight of stairs in her apartment building, saying, "I hope someone helps me when I'm older." A man in a wheelchair tips over, and before he can ask for help, five people rush in. A driver waves you into their lane. A stranger holds the elevator. A neighbor brings soup. A firefighter runs into a burning building. An acquaintance donates blood. A farmer grows food that someone across the country will eat tonight. Most of us are here because someone—often someone we didn't know—built, grew, delivered, fixed, carried, held.

And yet, it's so easy to miss all of this. The news, our own fears, and a hardwired negativity bias tell us that cruelty is everywhere. That we are alone, under threat, and better off closing our hearts. But that's not the full story. It's not even most of it.

HOW COGNITION CAN SHIFT EMOTION

Compassion is part of our biology. But cognition is what expands its reach. Let me explain.

You're handed a close-up photo of a woman's face, tears streaming down her cheeks. Instinctively, you feel sad—your empathy is triggered. You assume she's in pain. Then you're given a second image: the same woman, now seen as part of a crowd watching her child graduate from college—the first in the family to do so. Her tears, it turns out, are of pride and joy. And your emotion shifts too. You now feel uplifted.

This is the power of *cognitive appraisal*—the way our thoughts and interpretations shape what we feel (remember that cognitive reappraisal, in contrast, is our capacity to question those thoughts and interpretations, and to come up with new frameworks and beliefs).[14] Our understanding of a situation changes our emotional response to it. And often, we make these interpretations unconsciously.

Take a familiar moment: You're rushing through a crowded grocery store, your mind on dinner and a dozen other things, when someone suddenly cuts in front of you with their cart, blocking your path. You feel your frustration spike. "Seriously?" you mutter under your breath, assuming they're being rude or entitled. But then the person turns and says, "Oh, I'm so sorry—I'm actually just trying to keep up with my elderly mother behind me. She gets anxious when she can't see me." And just like that, your understanding changes. The story you told yourself shifts, and so does your emotion. Frustration gives way to empathy. Maybe even a willingness to help.

In that instant, your interpretation shifts. No one meant harm. Now you feel a pang of guilt, even tenderness. You see their vulnerability. And your emotion follows.

Cognition gets a bad rap but it's not the enemy of emotion—it's its greatest ally. The meanings we assign to situations shape how we feel and how we act. And meaning isn't fixed. It's often automatic, but it *can* be made conscious. This is what CBCT is about: deliberately shaping the meaning we give to our experiences to create healthier, more compassionate emotional responses.

But it doesn't work if it stays abstract. We have to *believe* the new meaning. And belief takes time, practice, reflection, and relevance. To truly feel that even someone we find difficult is "just like us"—vulnerable, trying to be safe, longing to be happy—requires effort. It's not a surface-level idea. It has to become a visceral, embodied truth.

This is why "cognitive" is central in CBCT—not in the cold, rationalist sense but because cognition allows us to extend compassion beyond our biological defaults. Reason and emotion aren't opposites. They inform and strengthen each other. My experience as a lifelong meditator has made this clear: Thinking deepens feeling, and feeling gives thinking its urgency.

So when people ask, "Why call it *Cognitively* Based Compassion Training?"—this is the answer. Because meaning shapes emotion. And with conscious practice, we can shift our emotional lives in a way that opens us to connection, care, and action.

THE ROLE OF LOVE IN EMBRACING THE HUMAN CONDITION

My wife and I love watching *Shark Tank*. There's something incredible about seeing everyday people come up with solutions to ease suffering—often for someone they love—and put everything on the line to bring that idea into the world. You see the vulnerability on their faces when they share what inspired them. You see their heartbreak when they walk away without a deal. You also see their joy, their tears, their awe when someone says yes. Even through a screen, we feel that surge of empathy—because we've all known what it is to hope, and to try, and to want our efforts to matter.

That same spark of identification extends far beyond the show. When I watch the Discovery Channel, I find myself rooting for a deer being chased by a tiger. I cheer when a bird learns to fly. I rejoice when someone on *Intervention* takes their first steps toward healing. Why? Because compassion and love are not abstract ideals. They're visceral responses to the suffering or success of another. When we care about someone, their happiness matters. Their pain matters.

Love, in this context, means a sincere wish for another to thrive—and compassion is what happens when that wish meets suffering. In Indo-Tibetan Buddhist philosophy, they're seen as two sides of the same coin. And you don't need a monastery to understand that; it's something we've all felt. Despite the dominant cultural messages that humans are selfish by nature, that everyone is out for themselves, these moments hint at an older truth that predates fear-based conditioning.

And yet, we also tend to categorize. Most of us divide the people around us—consciously or unconsciously—into three groups: those we're close to, those we're indifferent toward, and those we find difficult. It can feel like those categories are fixed, but they're not. A stranger can become a close friend. A friend can become estranged. Someone who once felt like a threat can become a collaborator, even a source of healing.

This awareness—that our categories are not permanent—is essential if we want to grow beyond tribalism. Often, the thing that separates "us" from "them" is simply that we haven't taken the time to notice what we share. The more visible our commonality becomes, the more instinctive it feels to include others in our circle of care. And perhaps the deepest commonality is this: Every living being wants to feel safe. Every living being wants to flourish.

When we identify with someone on the level of values—what they care about, what they long for—it creates the conditions for connection. One of those values is common humanity: the recognition that even when our views or personalities differ, we share the same fundamental drive to be free from suffering and to find meaning in our lives. It's a bridge that doesn't erase difference but allows us to see beyond it.

Since the 1930s, researchers have explored how proximity to difference can change hearts and minds. A landmark 2016 meta-analysis of more than five hundred studies showed that when people from different groups spend time together, prejudice tends to decrease. It's known as intergroup contact theory.[15] And it works because real connection dissolves imagined separation. We stop seeing people as categories and start seeing them as people—flawed, luminous, complex, just like us.

Rutger Bregman tells a powerful story about this in *Humankind.* It takes place in South Africa during the fragile, dangerous transition out of apartheid.[16] Civil war seemed likely. On one side of this powder keg was Constand Viljoen, a powerful general and the head of the Afrikaner Volksfront, an army devoted to preserving white minority rule. On the other side was his own twin brother, Abraham Viljoen, who had left their white nationalist roots behind and was fighting for multiracial democracy. Both were white Afrikaners, descendants of Dutch, German, or Huguenot settlers who fought for freedom against the British rule of South Africa in the Boer Wars, which took place a hundred years earlier. When Constand and Abraham's father was a child, he was held in a British concentration camp, where he lost his siblings. The wars ended in a brutal defeat and humiliation of the Afrikaners.

Although the brothers had grown apart over the years, during the postapartheid struggles, Abraham asked his brother to meet Nelson Mandela. Constand agreed. When the men sat down, Mandela made tea and spoke not as a politician but as a human being who understood history. He acknowledged the suffering of Afrikaners under British rule—drawing a line between their struggle and the anti-apartheid movement. He offered respect, not spite. Constand expected an enemy. What he found was kinship. And four months of secret talks that ended with the disarmament of the Volksfront. Civil war was averted.

That story doesn't end with everyone agreeing, nor does it demand that we see our oppressors as heroes or pretend that history didn't happen. What it shows is the quiet, revolutionary power of finding shared ground—even when the divide seems absolute. Mandela didn't erase difference. He made space for it, then reached through it.

Likewise, if we want to repair the frayed fabric of our world, we have to expand our circle of concern. Not by pretending we're all the same—but by grounding our connection in something deeper than sameness. In the truth that every person you encounter wants to be safe, to be loved, to be free from suffering. That includes your family. It includes people you've never met. It includes people you disagree with.

This takes critical thinking, emotional courage, and a willingness to move past our comfort zones. But as Shantideva taught, our shared longing to be free from suffering is the very reason we ought to care for one another.

We often think that expanding our circle of concern has to be some grand, ideological leap—but it happens in small, everyday ways. I see it every semester in the classes I teach. When students are invited to reflect on what brought them to the room—what shaped them, what they've been through—they're often startled by how much they share. As stories unfold, a class of strangers becomes a community. Trust deepens. There's a felt sense of psychological safety that emerges not from sameness but from a shared willingness to be seen.

We all have unique identities, cultures, and perspectives. That difference is real, and worth celebrating. But when we slow down and look deeper, we see that our preferences, our beliefs, even our personalities are shaped by particular contexts, needs, and histories. The same is true for everyone else; when we see this, it's possible to approach others with more curiosity and less judgment. Maybe we won't always agree. But we'll be more willing to listen. And more likely to find common ground.

Our neighborhoods, our companies, even our families include people with vastly different backgrounds, experiences, and worldviews. To thrive today, we need to update the instinct—to remember that our true survival depends on how well we can recognize the humanity in others, even when their lives look very different from our own.

Every person you pass on the street, argue with online, or see on the news is trying—just like you—to make sense of life and move toward something better. Some of us may have lost the thread, or gotten confused about what happiness really looks like. But the aspiration remains. It lives inside all of us. It's a thread of connection that runs underneath everything else. The more we remind ourselves of it, the more it moves from the level of thought to the level of experience. It may begin with a single moment of recognition, but when practiced, it becomes a new habit of perception. This is the heart of compassion training.

Of course, some people will still frustrate us. There are real harms in the world, and compassion doesn't mean tolerating injustice or excusing abuse. But even in difficult situations, healing won't come from doubling down on division. It will come from remembering what we share—not what sets us apart.

That brings us back to *Shark Tank*. Why do we root for the inventors, even if we have nothing in common with them? Why do we feel joy when their ideas get funded, and heartbreak when they walk away with nothing? It's because, deep down, we recognize ourselves in them. Their dream may look different from ours, but the feeling is the same. That human ache to be seen, supported, and believed in? We know it. And when we see it in someone else, our instinct isn't to turn away—it's to lean in.

THE HARMONY OF INCLUSIVE BELONGING

Think back to a time when you worked well with others—maybe during a stressful project or while showing up for someone in need. You probably felt a sense of connection, a quiet understanding that you were in it together. You may have stepped in without thinking twice, easily offering help, trusting others would do the same for you. In those moments, self-concern loosened its grip, and something more expansive emerged: the relief of shared purpose. The ease of knowing you're not alone.

For me, it's in those times that I feel most at peace—when I can set aside the running list of my own worries and allow a deeper sense of connection to take root. When I stop bracing and start trusting that we're all navigating the same fundamental truth: We all want to be happy, and we don't want to suffer. There's a harmony that arises when this understanding becomes a lived emotional truth.

Disharmony, on the other hand, begins the moment we retreat into the belief that our pain matters more than someone else's. That our needs, our views, our place in the world should take precedence. That's when the cracks start to show—when we feel justified in ignoring or dismissing others, and we forget how deeply interconnected we really are.

The more we fixate on ourselves, the more we suffer. Rumination and isolation shrink our view. But concern for others—genuine care—widens our lens and invites us out of our narrow mental loops. Even a subtle shift from "me" to "we" can open the door to greater mental well-being and emotional balance.

Of course, love is at the heart of this shift. Not love as sentimentality or attachment but the sincere wish for others to thrive. And in order to endure, love needs the grounding of equanimity. Neutrality here doesn't mean indifference—it means clarity. A steady, balanced concern that doesn't play favorites. Without it, even love can turn into blind loyalty or biased judgment.

Excessive liking, just like excessive disliking, distorts our view. When we idealize someone, we set ourselves up for disappointment. When we justify the actions of those we're close to, we lose the ability to see clearly or act fairly. A mother who cannot acknowledge her child's wrongdoing because of loyalty does more harm than good—not only to others but to the child, as well.

That's why true harmony requires more than affection—it calls for perspective. A commitment to noticing our shared reality, even with people we don't understand or agree with. The more we practice seeing this shared humanity, the more we soften the edges of bias and create room for connection.

Legal reforms and social change are vital, but they're not enough on their own. We also need a shift in mindset—a change of heart. One that allows us to extend belonging where we once saw only difference. That shift might begin in small, everyday ways: choosing to stay curious rather than judgmental when a coworker voices a political view you disagree with; pausing before making assumptions about the teenager with tattoos and a hoodie at the gas station; or resisting the urge to dehumanize the person on the other side of a heated issue online. It might mean greeting the new neighbor who speaks a different language, or sitting with the discomfort of a friend's choices without turning away. These are the moments where we practice expanding our in-group—by anchoring our relationships in the truth of what we all share: the longing to feel safe, valued, like we belong. When we pause and remember this—not just with our minds but with our hearts—we create the conditions for compassion to take root.

It reminds me of a story shared by one of our CBCT participants, Aisha, a social worker at a busy urban clinic. Her caseload was heavy—housing instability, domestic violence, substance use—and the emotional toll often followed her home. One client in particular had become difficult to face: a woman in her late fifties who showed up regularly in a storm of frustration. She refused to fill out forms, lashed out at staff, and dismissed every suggestion with suspicion.

One rainy Thursday, after a long morning of crisis management and an hour's sleep the night before, Aisha saw the woman's name on her schedule and felt her stomach drop. But as she stood to greet her, a phrase from her CBCT training surfaced quietly: *Just like me, she wants to avoid suffering and be happy.*

As the woman sat down—eyes darting, arms crossed—Aisha softened. She noticed the way the woman's hands trembled slightly when she spoke, how her anger felt more like fear with no safe place to land. Rather than jumping into logistics, Aisha paused and said gently, "Let's take this one step at a time. I'm here with you."

Something shifted. The woman's voice lowered. She listened. Together, they sorted through the paperwork and mapped out a next step. By the end of the session, the woman looked up and said, more softly than Aisha had ever heard, "Thank you . . . for helping me. Really."

Aisha walked back to her desk and sat down, stunned by how unguarded she felt. The meeting had gone better, yes—but more than that, it had felt different. There was a mutuality in it. A sense that something had opened. Not just in the client. But in her.

STEP IN, STEP OUT

One of the most powerful ways to shift our perception of others is surprisingly simple: make our similarities visible. Too often, we focus on what separates us—our preferences, politics, identities, and opinions—and overlook the deeper truths we share. But when we pause and reflect on those shared experiences, even with people we might normally ignore or avoid, something in us begins to soften. That's what this next practice is about.

In one CBCT class on expanding the circle of concern, the instructor guided participants through a physical and visual exercise that turned abstract insight into something visceral and real. It was called "Step In, Step Out."

The instructor drew a large circle on the floor and invited the group to stand around its edge. "Step into the circle," they said, "if you have a sister."

Nina, a participant in the class, stepped in. She glanced around and saw others join her. They weren't people she'd normally feel close to—but in that moment, they shared something simple and meaningful. A flicker of warmth passed through the space.

Then came another prompt: "Step in if you love coffee."

Nina stayed back—she prefers tea. She was surprised to feel a slight pang of being left out, even though it was all in good fun. Still, it revealed something: Even small preferences can create feelings of connection—or separation.

The instructor continued:

- Step in if you speak more than one language.
- Step in if you play a musical instrument.
- Step in if you belong to a religious or spiritual community.

Each prompt reshuffled the group. New bonds formed. Others dissolved. The room grew more reflective, more open.

Then the instructor said: "Step in if you've ever felt angry." A pause. Then someone moved. Then a few more. Eventually, *everyone* stepped in.

What followed were a series of prompts that everyone responded to:

- Step in if you've ever felt misunderstood.
- Step in if you've made a mistake and regretted it.
- Step in if you want to be happy and avoid suffering.
- Step in if you've longed to feel safe, seen, and loved.

Suddenly, the circle was full. No one was left standing at the edge. And that, in itself, was the point.

This exercise isn't meant to flatten difference or suggest we're all the same. Rather, it invites us to notice how even amid real differences, we are bound by our shared humanity. When we make these shared experiences visible—grief, longing, anger, hope—we begin to shift how we see one another. We remember that behind every face is a story not unlike our own. This is the beginning of connection, belonging, and compassion that extends beyond our comfort zone.

In our daily lives, we can practice this perspective shift in subtle ways:

- When a colleague frustrates us, we might recall: *They've been misunderstood, too.*
- When we pass someone we don't relate to, we might wonder: *What are they struggling with today?*

- And when we feel isolated or disconnected, we can remember: *We're not the only ones who long to belong.*

STAYING MINDFUL OF IMPORTANT DIFFERENCES

We are all vulnerable to life's challenges. But those challenges are not evenly distributed. They come with differing intensity and frequency depending on where we are born, how we are perceived, and the systems we live within. Some of us face obstacles not only because of chance or circumstance but because of deeply entrenched structures of inequality. These injustices are not erased when we reflect on our common humanity—in fact, the more we recognize what we all share, the more we may feel called to confront what makes life so much harder for some.

When we remember that each person longs to be safe, to protect their children, to live with dignity—we become more curious about what stands in the way of those rights being realized. We ask different questions. We listen more closely. We are more willing to act in solidarity, not out of pity but out of recognition.

This dual awareness—of sameness and difference—is essential. It allows us to build alliances that aren't blind to power but rooted in empathy. It helps us imagine solutions that seek justice, not just comfort. It asks us to stretch the boundaries of who we consider "one of us," and in doing so, to stretch our capacity to repair what's been broken.

That capacity was at the heart of an extraordinary friendship that emerged in the wake of unthinkable tragedy.

Bassam Aramin lived in a Palestinian village in East Jerusalem with his wife and children. One afternoon, his ten-year-old daughter, Abir, went to the corner store with friends. Nearby, an Israeli soldier responded to a disturbance. A rubber bullet was fired. It struck Abir in the head. She died two days later.

Rami Elhanan, a former Israeli soldier, lived just across the city. His daughter, Smadar, was fourteen when she was killed in a suicide bombing on Ben Yehuda Street, one of Jerusalem's busiest pedestrian zones. Rami and his wife searched for her in hospitals, only to find her in a morgue.

Both men were broken by loss. And both were raised in worlds that taught them to fear and blame the other. Rage came easily. But over time, grief gave way to something else. They met through a bereavement group for Israeli and Palestinian families who had lost children to the conflict. In that space, stripped of rhetoric and politics, they recognized something startling in one another: the same pain, the same love, the same shattered heart.

Rami recalled, "I was forty-seven. It was the first time in my life I saw Palestinians as human beings."

Bassam, too, spoke of how unexpected it was to feel friendship—true friendship—with someone he had been taught to consider an enemy.

Their bond did not erase the conflict. It didn't minimize the vast asymmetries of power or the brutal cost of occupation and war. What it did was make those realities personal. It gave them a shared purpose: to stop the cycle of hatred that had already taken too much.

"I can't forget what happened," Rami once said, "but I can choose what to do with the pain."

The story of Bassam and Rami is not a feel-good ending. It's a courageous beginning. A model for what becomes possible when we see even our adversaries not as abstractions but as parents, as mourners, as people whose blood is the same color as our own.

Compassion, in this context, is not about forgiveness without accountability. It is about building the kind of human connection that can sustain our commitment to justice, even in the most fractured places. This is what it means to expand the circle of concern: to allow ourselves to be moved not only by those we understand but also by those we don't yet know how to love.

DISTINGUISHING ACT FROM ACTOR

Bringing someone into our circle of concern is easy when they share our values or treat us kindly. But what about people we find difficult? Or those whose ideologies, actions, or beliefs seem harmful—even threatening—to us or to others?

Nearly two thousand years ago, the Indian Buddhist philosopher Aryadeva—one of the earliest commentators on compassion and a disciple of Nagarjuna—offered a powerful analogy. He wrote:

> Just as a doctor is not agitated
> With an enraged patient under the spell of disturbing emotions,
> An enlightened being sees the disturbing emotions as the enemy,
> Not the people who are under their spell.[17]

In other words, just as a physician doesn't blame a patient for symptoms caused by illness, we can learn to view others' harmful actions as the result of confusion, conditioning, or deep pain—not as reflections of their intrinsic worth.

This doesn't mean excusing harm or avoiding accountability. It means understanding that human beings are shaped by countless causes and conditions. Like us, others are vulnerable to stress, fear, bias, trauma. Like us, they've made mistakes. And like us, they are more than any single choice or belief. When we begin to reflect on our own imperfections with compassion, we can see others through a more generous lens. We can hold people accountable while also acknowledging their humanity.

This distinction—between the act and the actor—is essential. It allows us to protect ourselves from harm without being consumed by hatred. Think of it like fire: We don't hate it, but we don't put our hand in it either. We take distance when we need to, but we don't need to dehumanize the source of our pain to stay safe.

Many of our most admired leaders practiced this. Mahatma Gandhi opposed British rule with all his strength, but never stopped believing in the humanity of the British people. Martin Luther King Jr. struggled with the idea of "turning the other cheek"—especially in the face of violent racism. But after learning about Gandhi's philosophy of nonviolence, he came to believe that love and compassion were not signs of weakness. They were tools for real, lasting change.

None of this is easy. Anger can feel righteous—and sometimes, it *is* justified. But if we let it define us, it can also keep us stuck in the very cycles we long to break. Studies in neuroscience and psychology echo what many spiritual traditions have long taught: The more we fixate on resentment and judgment, the more it constricts our ability to think clearly, to heal, and to connect. It harms us as much as anyone else.

This doesn't mean we should pretend everyone belongs in our inner circle. Boundaries are vital. But there is a difference between protecting ourselves and writing others off entirely. There is a difference between holding someone accountable and reducing them to a single act.

Sheriff Sue Rahr, who led the Washington State Criminal Justice Training Commission, understood this. She designed police training that emphasized emotional intelligence and bias awareness. Recruits were taught to recognize that people often act out because they're in crisis, not because they're inherently dangerous. "You're seeing them," she said, "on the worst day of their life." Officers were trained to respond not with judgment but with steadiness, discernment, and care. In the same way, we can choose to respond to difficulty not with reactivity but with clarity and courage, which builds the conditions for trust, healing, and change.

Recall a time when you acted in a way that didn't reflect your best self. What was going on in your life at the time? How would it feel if someone judged you entirely based on that action, without knowing the context or the rest of who you are? Now think of a time when you judged someone else's actions harshly—only to learn later that there was more to the story. How did that new understanding shift your view? What might it mean for your own peace of mind to be able to distinguish harmful actions from the deeper humanity of the person who committed them? How could this approach serve your relationships, your community, or even your broader sense of justice?

THE PRACTICE OF EXPANDING OUR CIRCLE OF CONCERN

The reflections we've explored so far ask us to stretch in ways that aren't always easy: to question the edges of our empathy, to consider the possibility of connection where we once saw only distance. This next step gives us a chance to sit with those questions—not to force answers but to gently deepen our relationship to them.

The practice ahead invites us to reflect on different kinds of people in our lives: those we love, those we feel indifferent toward, and those we find challenging. But let's be clear—this is not an exercise in spiritual heroics. It's not about forcing compassion where there is still raw pain or trying to rush the healing of wounds that need time. In fact, one of the most compassionate things we can do is be honest about what feels like too much, and choose to begin somewhere softer.

If meditating on a difficult person feels overwhelming, you don't need to go there—not today, and maybe not for a long time. Start with someone you love. If you're feeling steady, you might bring to mind a stranger or someone you barely know. And if you do choose to include a more challenging person, start small: a driver who cut you off, a messy roommate, a relative whose comments irritate you—not someone who's caused deep harm. This practice is meant to be gentle, not retraumatizing. If strong emotions arise, you can always pause, return to a feeling of safety, or go back to earlier practices. The point is not to push but to build trust with yourself—so that over time, you might choose to wade a little deeper, with more confidence and care.

Widening the Circle Practice (6–8 minutes)

Take time to settle and let your body arrive. Feel the support beneath you. If there's tension anywhere, give yourself permission to move or stretch, and let your breath begin to slow and deepen. As you inhale, imagine nourishing air filling your body. As you exhale, release any lingering tightness or worry, allowing your whole being to soften. There is nothing to force here. If it's a difficult day, know that even the intention to practice is enough.

When you feel ready, bring to mind three people—one by one—from the following categories: someone you love, someone who feels neutral to you (perhaps a stranger or someone you barely know), and someone who has recently annoyed or challenged you. If it's a particularly tender day, you can stay with just one—someone who brings ease and affection. If you're feeling more steady, include all three.

As each person arises in your awareness, take a moment to notice how you feel when you imagine them experiencing joy. Do you wish them well when good things happen? Are you moved by their struggles? Do you find yourself feeling naturally warm or pulled back and distant?

It's entirely human to feel differently toward those we love, those we don't know, and those who challenge us. But when that difference becomes rigid or unconscious, it can exaggerate the distance between us and others. That's how bias grows—quietly, often without us noticing—creating disconnection where there could be care.

So now, gently reflect on what you share with each of these people. All of them want to feel safe. All of them long for meaning and belonging. Just like you, they want to avoid pain. Just like you, they have both strengths and vulnerabilities, hopes and fears. All three are human, shaped by forces we can't fully see—just as you are.

Notice what shifts when you remember this. Do they feel even slightly more familiar? More human? More connected to you—not because you agree with them or like them but because you recognize something essential and shared?

Allow your circle of concern to widen from here. Gently, sincerely, expand it to include more and more people: neighbors, colleagues, strangers, even those you've never met. Not everyone needs to feel close. But can they begin to feel *included*? Can they be part of the great web of beings who, like you, are trying to flourish in a complicated world?

And as you do this, let your heart hold the paradox: We are different, and we are the same. Our perspectives, resources, and experiences are not equal—and yet our longing to live, to be seen, to be safe is universal.

Let this understanding nourish a kind of compassion that is both fierce and wide. One that honors difference but does not let it sever connection.

To close, dedicate this practice to someone who is suffering—someone in your life or someone in the world. And if you feel able, extend that dedication outward, toward a widening circle of beings, human and more-than-human, known and unknown.

Let your final intention be this: that the clarity, tenderness, and wisdom you touched today may walk with you into your ordinary hours. May it help you meet others not just as strangers or adversaries but as fellow travelers—flawed, radiant, vulnerable, just like you.

BRINGING THE SKILLS TO LIFE: PRACTICE BETWEEN SESSIONS

Beneath our many differences, we all share a longing to be well, to be safe, to find meaning and belonging. This isn't about ignoring injustice or erasing individuality—it's about making visible what is already there: our shared humanity.

When we consciously relate to others through this lens, something shifts. Our judgments soften. Our hearts open. We begin to relate differently—to strangers, to those we find difficult, even to the people we love most. This doesn't happen all at once, and it doesn't have to be grand. But with practice, small shifts accumulate. What once felt rigid begins to soften. Our inner circle expands.

The reflections and practices below are offered as invitations—not as tasks to perform perfectly but as ways to keep returning to this perspective in your everyday life. They're small, doable, and often surprisingly powerful.

When you feel irritated by someone whose views clash with your own—or indifferent toward someone you don't know—pause. See if you can recall that they, too, are just trying to make it through their day. They, too, want to feel safe, to avoid harm, to create a meaningful life. Noticing this shared vulnerability doesn't excuse harmful behavior or erase difference, but it can soften the way you hold them. Notice how this shift in perception may change the way you relate to them—and what it stirs in you. You might even find yourself returning to your Zone of Well-Being more easily, with greater clarity and steadiness.

Look for small openings in daily life to practice seeing others through the lens of common humanity. In the grocery store, as you stand in line, pause and really see the people around you—not as extras in your day but as full human beings with invisible joys and struggles. In traffic, instead of sinking into frustration, take a moment to imagine the drivers beside you also want to get home, also carry worries, also wish for ease. Each of these moments is an opportunity to remember: "Just like me."

Pay attention to the people you idealize—those you hold close or expect too much from. Sometimes we set impossible standards for the people we love, only to feel betrayed when they inevitably fall short. When that happens, remind yourself: No one is perfect. Everyone is learning. Just like you, they are a work in progress.

Ena shared how this shift has changed the way she walks through the world: "I used to be uncomfortable around strangers. But now, when my mind wants to judge or pull away, I pause. I remind myself: Just like me, they want to be happy. Just like me, they're trying. It's helped me feel more connected—to people I once avoided—and made compassion feel more natural."

Yolanda, a seasoned attorney, reflected: "I had strong negative feelings toward members of a political party I deeply disagreed with. But CBCT helped me see that their views were shaped by their conditions, just as mine were. That allowed me to see them as human—not evil. And it helped me soften not just toward my legal adversaries but even toward my mother. Seeing how her past shaped her made space for real empathy—and it changed our relationship."

Throughout this chapter, we've focused on making visible our common humanity—a simple truth that too often goes unseen. We've seen how identifying with others at a fundamental level allows us to widen our circle of concern, loosen harsh judgments, and release unrealistic expectations. And we've explored how connecting through shared vulnerability can actually help us honor our differences more fully, without letting them divide us.

Connection isn't a luxury—it's a basic need. It's how we survive, how we grow, how we remember who we are. In the next chapter, we'll build on this foundation by reflecting on our interdependence. Together, we'll explore how recognizing the web of support around us can deepen our gratitude, our tenderness, and our capacity to love.

CHAPTER EIGHT

NOURISHING THE HEART WITH GRATITUDE AND TENDERNESS

We are caught in an inescapable network of mutuality, tied in a single garment of destiny. Whatever affects one directly, affects all indirectly.... This is the interrelated structure of reality.

—Martin Luther King Jr.

In the last chapter, we reflected on how embracing our common humanity can help us expand our circle of concern. We saw how seeing others not as "them," but as fellow humans with shared dreams, fears, and needs, allows us to soften judgment and widen the field of compassion.

Now we deepen that connection—by tuning into something even more immediate, more visceral: the web of interdependence that sustains us, and the feelings that naturally arise when we see this clearly. Namely, gratitude and tenderness.

Gratitude is the recognition that we benefit from the actions, presence, and sacrifices of others—sometimes seen, often unseen. It's a quiet acknowledgment that our lives are not ours alone. That we are not self-made. That even the simplest meal, the roads we drive on, the words we speak, the language we think in—all were given to us by others.

Tenderness is what blooms when gratitude deepens. It's a soft, warm, almost vulnerable feeling that arises when we see someone clearly in their care, their effort, their impact. Tenderness isn't pity or sentimentality—it's the openhearted response to the recognition that another being has helped us, and that help matters.

But what if you don't feel particularly grateful? What if your life feels more marked by disappointment than by abundance? What if the world around you feels distant or harsh? That's OK. This chapter isn't about forcing gratitude—it's about opening a little more space for what's already true: None of us lives in isolation. Even on hard days, someone grew the food you ate. Someone coded the software you're using now. Someone gave you a tool, a word, a lesson that helped shape who you are.

We may not always feel grateful—but the conditions for gratitude are always present.

Through both reflection and practice, we'll begin to make visible the countless ways we are supported, held, and shaped by others. We'll look not just at the obvious helpers in our lives—family, friends, mentors—but at the strangers, the unseen laborers, even the people who've challenged or hurt us. Because sometimes, what opens the heart isn't just kindness. It's difficulty that made us stronger, wiser, or more compassionate.

There's an old story in the Buddhist tradition that brings this home. When the Buddha returned to his ancestral home as an awakened teacher, he was invited to dinner with his extended family—including Amita, his aunt, who had spent much of her life undermining him. She and her son Devadatta had hoped to secure the throne for themselves and had once been consumed with bitterness.

At the end of the meal, the Buddha surprised everyone by naming the three women he was most grateful to in his life. His stepmother, who raised him with love after his own mother's death. His wife, Yasodhara, who had supported his path even at great personal cost. And—shockingly—his aunt Amita.

Perhaps he was grateful to her because her cruelty had first shown him the reality of suffering. It was her mistreatment that helped ignite his search for a path to freedom from suffering. In naming her—not to shame her but to honor how even difficulty had shaped his path—something softened. Amita's resentment began to dissolve. She saw herself anew, and she saw him anew. Respect bloomed in place of rivalry. And Devadatta, still clinging to resentment, suddenly looked very small.

This story reminds us that gratitude isn't just about praising those who've been kind to us. It's about seeing—clearly and without sentiment—how others have shaped us, challenged us, and contributed to who we've become. It might include the friend who listened without trying to fix us, the mentor who pushed us past our comfort zone, or even the colleague whose criticism forced us to grow. Sometimes, it's the stranger who held the elevator or the barista who remembered our name on a hard day. It might even be the person who disappointed us but, in doing so, clarified what we truly value. Gratitude, in this sense, is about reclaiming the full complexity of interdependence and letting that recognition open the door to connection.

In today's world, where we are often encouraged to see ourselves as self-made or separate, that kind of clarity is more important than ever. Because interdependence isn't always obvious. It's easy to forget that we are sustained by a vast, living web of people, systems, and ecologies—most of which we never see.

We may feel as though we move through life alone, responsible for everything, burdened by our own needs and unaware of how profoundly we are held by others. But interdependence is the quiet truth beneath it all, and the many examples of how it flourishes in our world could fill entire books. The phone in your pocket was built by hundreds of hands you'll never meet. The food you eat was grown, harvested, packaged, and delivered by a vast network of labor and logistics. Your ability to read these words comes from teachers, caregivers, strangers, and ancestors. Even the breath you take is made possible by trees and oceans. We don't always pause to see this—we're often rushing, distracted, overwhelmed. But when we do, our perspective shifts. Gratitude rises. Tenderness returns. And we begin to remember that we are participants in a shared and ongoing miracle.

Now, let's turn toward that remembrance with a brief reflection. Take a moment to think about a skill or quality you have that matters to you—something you're proud of or that has shaped your life. Maybe it's your ability to teach, to repair, to listen, to cook, to speak a second language, to navigate hardship. Who helped you gain this ability? Who taught you, encouraged you, challenged you, showed up for you? Hold that person—or those people—in your heart as we enter this chapter. Let the feeling of their impact guide you as we begin.

TRANSMUTING ANNOYANCE

Gratitude and tenderness are among the most transformative emotional states we can cultivate—and some of the most elusive. Study after study has shown that regular practices of gratitude can reduce stress, improve sleep, enhance relationships, and even increase life satisfaction. Gratitude doesn't just feel good—it changes us. When we express appreciation, we don't just brighten someone else's day; we actually begin to change the chemistry of our own bodies. Gratitude boosts our sense of connection and belonging, which in turn improves our mood, our health, and even how we relate to the world. In his book *Thanks! How the New Science of Gratitude Can Make You Happier*, psychologist Dr. Robert Emmons highlights a wide range of benefits linked to regular gratitude practice: better sleep, lower blood pressure, a stronger immune system, more energy, more generosity, and greater joy.[1] Gratitude, it turns out, is a powerful medicine—and one of the most accessible tools we have. And tenderness, that soft ache of recognition and care for another's vulnerability, has the power to bond us instantly to another human being. But if these are so good for us, why do they feel so hard to access, especially in everyday life?

Often, it's not the big betrayals or catastrophic events that block us from feeling grateful. It's the small, mundane irritations we let calcify in our nervous systems. It's how we greet the day after a restless night—waking up resentful of the sunlight or muttering curses when we stub a toe. It's the way we pepper our language with casual complaints: The barista was too slow, the elevator too crowded, the email tone too abrupt.

These micro-annoyances become our lens, subtly warping the way we view the world and the people around us. We may not even realize how often we reject a moment of connection simply by bracing against the world.

Annoyance often stems from a narrowed view of self—our preferences, our comfort, our schedules. When things or people disrupt our sense of control, we react with irritation rather than curiosity or compassion. And yet, in almost every situation, there is a larger context, a deeper truth we're missing.

Take Tanya and Jeff, who worked together at a law firm. They just rubbed each other the wrong way. Every meeting felt like a power struggle. Jeff felt like Tanya constantly questioned his ideas, and Tanya felt like Jeff routinely talked over her. Their tension simmered silently between them—side glances in the hallway, missed greetings, indifference coated in professionalism.

One winter evening, Jeff was driving home, tired and frazzled, when a loud noise jolted him. A flat tire. Worse, his phone had slipped between the seat and the center console—out of reach, useless. He was stuck on a dark, unfamiliar road with no one around.

Then Tanya's car appeared behind him. She had taken the same shortcut. She pulled over, rolled down her window, and said, "Everything OK?" Jeff, flustered, explained the situation. She nodded and said, "Hop in. Use my phone. I'll stay until help gets here."

There was no grand apology or dramatic reconciliation. Just a quiet act of kindness.

Thanks to her actions, Jeff was soon on his way home. And the next morning, when he saw Tanya at work, instead of the usual tightness in his chest, he felt warmth. He smiled. Not because everything had changed overnight but because he had glimpsed her differently—as someone willing to help, as someone who stayed in a moment that could have otherwise been lonely and upsetting. That moment of appreciation cracked open the possibility for tenderness.

This capacity to feel and express appreciation is not reserved for saints or sentimental people. In fact, it's so wired into us that even non-human animals show it. Alligators have been known to return, years later, to visit the humans who saved them as hatchlings.

And yet, how often do we let opportunities for appreciation pass us by? What if Jeff had turned Tanya away out of pride, or suspicion? What if he'd clung to his narrative of who she was instead of allowing the moment to soften him? Gratitude requires a measure of vulnerability. To accept help is to acknowledge need. To feel appreciation is to admit that someone else made a difference.

We often reserve gratitude for grand gestures or perfect people. But what do we have to lose by extending it further? Even if someone is rude or abrasive—what might shift if we paused and looked again? Is it possible they, too, are trying to get home? That they, too, have known fear, loss, or exhaustion?

Every being is part of the web that holds us up, whether we notice it or not. And when we do notice—when we let appreciation nourish our hearts, even for a moment—it turns strangers into neighbors. Sometimes even adversaries into friends.

THE WEB OF INTERDEPENDENCE

The ability to feel and express gratitude is something we all carry inside us, even if the pressures of daily life cause us to lose touch with it. In fact, it may be one of the most ancient emotional capacities we share, not only with other humans but even with our evolutionary relatives.

Primatologist Frans de Waal has observed that bonobos—our gentle, matriarchal cousins—show signs of gratitude through acts of grooming and sharing. A bonobo who's been groomed is far more likely to share food with their groomer. The behavior is so consistent across primate species that de Waal calls gratitude "evolution's solution to keep favors flowing."[2] Neuroscience suggests that, far from being about strict scorekeeping or transactional balancing, reciprocity is driven by connection—by a feeling of warmth and bonding that motivates us to give back.[3]

In today's world, this ancient wiring remains intact, but we often forget to access it. Our lives are busy, fragmented, and overwhelmingly digital. We're rarely encouraged to pause and consider just how much we rely on other people and on the natural world. And yet, every moment of our lives is made possible by a vast web of support that we usually don't see. We live in homes we didn't build, drink water that has been filtered and piped by invisible systems, eat food grown by farmers we'll never meet, and walk on sidewalks poured and leveled by someone else's labor. If we take a moment to trace even a simple experience—a warm slice of toast in the morning, a message sent through the internet, a safe walk to the bus stop—we'll find hundreds, maybe thousands, of people who made it possible. The teachers who gave us the literacy to read this sentence. The engineers who keep our power running. The neighbors who watered our plants while we were away.

And it's not just human labor we depend on. Without bees and bats and other pollinators, our entire food system would collapse. Yet we rarely think about these beings unless they're framed as threats or nuisances. Bats, for instance, were vilified during the COVID-19 pandemic—cast as symbols of contagion. But these same creatures are essential to our survival. They eat insects that would otherwise decimate our crops. They reduce the spread of disease-carrying mosquitoes. They fertilize forests and pollinate plants. And they do all of this quietly, without our awareness, recognition, or thanks. When we pause to reflect on the role they play, we see that gratitude isn't just about who or what we like. It's about honoring the vast, interwoven systems of care that sustain us.

This shift in perception can happen anywhere, even in the most mundane moments. I once came home to find that our toilet had overflowed into the basement. It was a mess—rank, urgent, overwhelming. My wife called a plumber, who fixed the immediate issue. But a few days later, I was driving through a nearby neighborhood and saw a sanitation crew working on a massive pipe underground. They wore the same uniforms and carried the same tools. Suddenly, I felt a swell of gratitude. These were not the same people who had come to my house, but they were part of the same system that helped my family regain comfort and safety. That gratitude stayed with me. Even now, when I pass a city worker, a delivery driver, or a repair technician, I feel tenderness toward the people whose quiet work holds my life together.

Shantideva once wrote that when we begin to see others as part of the same whole—as limbs of the same body—their needs become our concern. If your left hand is hurt, your right hand moves instinctively to help. Not out of obligation but because it belongs to you. When we practice recognizing our interdependence, our sense of "mine" begins to shift. That stranger fixing the sidewalk? That woman growing rice in another hemisphere? That overlooked pollinator keeping your garden alive? They are part of you. You are part of them.

MEETING LIFE WITH AN OPEN HEART

After all we've explored about the quiet labor of others and the unseen systems that support our lives, it's worth turning to a living, breathing example—someone who has come to know these truths not just intellectually but viscerally.

Marty, a government worker from the Northeast, lost his leg in a traffic accident in 2020. Everything changed in an instant. The physical pain was intense, but the psychological pain—the grief, the anger, the mental loop of *Why me?* and *It wasn't supposed to be this way*—was even harder to live with. For a while, he admits, he was stuck in that space: ruminating, spiraling, trying to wrestle reality into something it no longer was.

But slowly, through a mix of breathing practices, reflection, and a surprising new mantra—"I have no left foot. This pain isn't real."—Marty learned to live with the phantom pain. Even more remarkably, he learned to work with his thoughts. "Most of the problems I was obsessing over hadn't even happened," he said. "And the real ones—I just had to meet them, one at a time." These days, he focuses on accomplishing just one thing each day. And if he does that—if he makes his bed, takes a walk, finishes a task—he considers it a good day. "There's no 'supposed to be' anymore," he says. "There's just what is. And sometimes, what is . . . is OK."

But it's the practice of gratitude and tenderness that Marty credits with helping him feel joy again. Every morning, he thinks about the people who have helped him get to this point: the EMTs who got to the crash site, the surgeons who saved his life, the nurses who changed his dressings, the rehabilitation team who taught him how to move again. The engineers who designed his prosthetic. The scientists who tested the materials. The factory workers who assembled it. "I wouldn't know them if they walked past me on the street," he says. "But they changed my life. Every one of them." And once Marty began to trace those lines outward—from the team who helped him walk again to the thousands of others who grow his food, deliver his medicine, keep his lights on—his world cracked open in a new way. "I started realizing," he said, "I'm not alone. I never have been."

When he shared this reflection in a group session, another participant, moved to tears, whispered, "All of humanity is a single soul." She was quoting the Qur'an.

When we begin to see life through this lens—not of rugged individualism but of mutual belonging—we soften. A smile comes more easily. Annoyance takes a backseat to wonder. Gratitude floods in, and with it, the kind of tenderness that doesn't require sentimentality—just presence, and recognition.

Marty's story isn't a fairy tale of resilience. It's a hard-won recalibration. He's not manufacturing gratitude—he's locating it, deliberately, in the wreckage of what was lost. And in doing so, he's reentering a relationship with the world around him.

And yet for many of us, even when things are stable on the outside, something can still feel off. There's a specific kind of dissonance that comes from being surrounded by people—at work, at a party, online—and feeling invisible. Research has a name for this: *perceived social isolation.*[4] It's the experience of being psychologically alone, regardless of proximity. And it cuts deep. We can be married and feel it. We can sit with old friends and feel it. It's not about who's in the room—it's about whether we feel like we're part of the world we're moving through.

Gratitude and tenderness, in this context, are intentional tools for reconnecting to the fabric we've been frayed from.

But they are not a call to romanticize anything. They train us to see the real context we live in—a context in which we are constantly being affected by others, whether we notice or not. It's easier to feel grateful for your closest people. But the point of this practice is to challenge what we define as "ours." It's to notice how many people, most of them strangers, are part of the machinery that lets your day run at all.

We're not just talking about material needs here. Our social, emotional, and even psychological survival is embedded in systems of mutual reliance. Think about who taught you what you know. Who stocked the library? Who wired your building for electricity? Who cleaned the ICU floor when your family member was sick? None of it happens in a vacuum.

However, the intention to hold large-scale awareness of people and interlocking systems is complicated by something known as *compassion fade*, which occurs when compassion drops as the number of people we perceive to be suffering goes up. We become overwhelmed and detached when suffering feels too vast.

Research from the University of British Columbia shows that, while our brains are wired to respond to individual suffering, we often shut down when faced with large-scale pain—five hundred people, five thousand, a hundred thousand.[5] Evolutionarily, it made sense to prioritize the immediate needs of our small group. But with practice and intention, we can work around that wiring. Just as breaking a long phone number into chunks helps us remember it, mentally grouping people into meaningful roles—like the crews who maintain sewer systems or the farmers who grow our food—helps us feel warmth and concern for those we don't know personally. When we recognize how much we benefit from the people in these categories, their struggles start to matter more to us. Building these cognitive bridges toward connection helps us buffer against compassion fade. Because when one part of the system falters, the whole web trembles. If these people stopped showing up, our lives would unravel fast. This training invites us to start seeing those links—clearly, consciously—and to let that recognition move us.

Staying aware of all this—especially when we're stressed, annoyed, or depleted—requires effort. So, start simple. Choose one item you rely on every day. A phone, a pen, a pair of shoes. Set a timer and write down everyone you can imagine who played a role in getting that thing into your hands. The longer your list gets, the more the isolation starts to wear thin.

You can still dislike your job, still be furious at the political system, still feel grief about what's broken. But gratitude adds dimensionality. It reminds us there are others, everywhere, holding up parts of the world we don't see. And when we make that visible—when we practice tuning into the invisible labor and lives around us—we don't become more virtuous. We just become a little less alone.

SELF-ABSORPTION: THE BANE OF GRATITUDE

Recognizing our interdependence can awaken a natural sense of gratitude, tenderness, and care for others. But one of the greatest barriers to sustaining that awareness—indeed, one of the most entrenched habits of our time—is self-absorption. The more we center our lives around our own preferences, perceptions, and projections, the more difficult it becomes to remain attuned to the ways we're held, impacted, and supported by the world around us. In this way, self-absorption becomes the enemy of connection.[6]

Instead of building lives anchored in community, reciprocity, and shared commitment—the things we most deeply yearn for—we've learned to equate freedom with self-maximization, to prize autonomy over interdependence. The result is not liberation but fragmentation. The only way out is to rebuild a culture that steers people back toward relationality and responsibility, a culture in which our personal fulfillment is tied not to our personal brand but to our capacity for care.

Reflecting on interdependence naturally softens a narrow self-focus. The more we see how much others contribute to our lives, the more our attention shifts away from the ego's demands and toward a sense of relational value. In *The Great Treatise on the Stages of the Path to Enlightenment*, the fourteenth-century Tibetan scholar Tsongkhapa writes that one of the central obstacles to cherishing others is the assumption that they are unrelated to us—that their joys and struggles bear no weight in our own lives.[7] When we see others as irrelevant, we disconnect from them. And when we disconnect, tenderness dissolves.

Tsongkhapa identifies two particular obstacles to cultivating genuine care. The first is our habit of categorically distinguishing between ourselves and others—treating our suffering as urgent and theirs as optional. But this mindset is misguided. He explains that self and other are mutually dependent: "When you are aware of self, you are aware of others; and when you are aware of others, you are aware of self." The second obstacle is the belief that we have no reason to alleviate others' suffering because it doesn't directly affect us. This, he says, is like refusing to save money in your youth because you can't yet feel the hardship of old age. Or like ignoring pain in your foot because your hand isn't hurting. To act as though the well-being of others is unrelated to our own is to misunderstand the very nature of interconnection.

This misunderstanding has profound consequences. Without a widespread sense of mutual concern, even material progress cannot save us. We risk becoming more emotionally estranged, mentally unwell, and culturally unstable. Mental health challenges—many of which are rooted in chronic disconnection—may be just the beginning of what a society without gratitude and tenderness looks like. If we cannot shift this paradigm, we will pay the price in isolation, mistrust, and the slow erosion of the social fabric we all depend on.

And yet, gratitude and other-oriented concern can seem so obvious in theory that we're left wondering why they don't arise more naturally in our lives. Why, in moments of stress, do we so easily revert to self-protective thoughts? Why do we lose sight of the innumerable ways we've been helped and held?

Part of the reason lies in habit. Excessive self-focus is not just a personality quirk—it's a trained reflex. And it's a risky one. Studies have shown that heightened self-referential thinking is associated with lower psychological well-being and greater risk for depression. While attending to our own needs is necessary, when that concern becomes excessive—when every encounter is filtered through the lens of "How does this affect me?"—we become more anxious, less generous, and less able to experience the healing force of connection.[8]

Consider two very different case studies—each illustrating the long-term effects of orientation, one toward the self, and one toward others.

Kenneth Lay, the former CEO of Enron, managed his employees through a regime of fear and humiliation. At weekly meetings, he singled out those who didn't meet performance targets and publicly shamed them. His fixation on winning—on maintaining power and appearances—eventually fostered unethical behavior that led to the company's collapse. Lay was once seen as a philanthropic businessman, but behind the scenes, his relentless self-interest and refusal to consider broader impacts destroyed thousands of jobs and livelihoods. He died before sentencing, having been convicted of ten counts of securities fraud.

Even someone intelligent, hardworking, and outwardly generous can lose their moral bearings when absorbed in the pursuit of personal gain. Self-absorption doesn't always look cruel, though—it can wear the mask of ambition. But when left unchecked, it hollows out relationships and robs our lives of meaning.

Now consider Bob Chapman, CEO of Barry-Wehmiller. When his company was struggling financially, he didn't double down on pressure or performance metrics. Instead, he reimagined leadership as a form of caregiving. He trained his managers to see their employees not as tools of productivity but as someone's precious child. He encouraged reflection on the human dignity of each team member and invited genuine connection—sharing stories, listening deeply, creating space for vulnerability. This shift transformed the company culture. People began to thrive. The business rebounded. A company on the brink of bankruptcy became a model of well-being and resilience—not because it prioritized profit but because it prioritized people.

One man collapsed a system through self-focus. Another rebuilt one through relational care. Their stories show us what's at stake—and what's possible.

So, what does this mean for us?

It means we can look closely at our own patterns. When have we seen someone fall into the trap of self-absorption? What did that do to their relationships, their effectiveness, their health? And when have we seen someone truly care for others—not at their own expense but from a place of grounded generosity? How did their life shift? How did those around them flourish? And most importantly: What are we cultivating?

Our goal here is not to negate the self but to decenter it—just enough to remember the web we belong to. In a culture that conditions us to think always of the self first, this is radical work. But it is also essential. As Daniel Goleman writes in *Social Intelligence*, "Self-absorption in all its forms kills empathy, let alone compassion. When we focus on ourselves, our world contracts. . . . But when we focus on others, our world expands."[9]

The shift from self to other is not a sacrifice. It is a widening. A return. A deepening of what it means to be fully human.

ALTRUISM, RECIPROCITY, AND INTERDEPENDENCE

Building on the previous chapter's invitation to widen our circle of concern, we now explore how cultivating gratitude and tenderness can help us do that. When we begin to notice how much of our daily well-being depends on the efforts, presence, and care of others—many of whom we will never meet—we create the conditions for warmhearted connection to arise. These emotions aren't just pleasant by-products of a good mood; they are powerful openings. They expand our capacity to care, helping us include more people—beyond our immediate circle—in our field of empathy and concern. Gratitude and tenderness become tools for softening our habitual self-focus and forging deeper, more inclusive bonds.

This is where altruism, a selfless concern for the well-being of others, comes in. In recent decades, scientists have been studying the conditions under which altruism arises.[10] Evolutionary biologists have identified two natural roots of altruistic concern.[11] The first is kinship-based altruism: We instinctively tend to care for those we perceive as our own. A lioness feeds her cub before herself; a parent stays up all night with a feverish child. Yet kinship is not always determined by blood. There are documented cases of animals caring for the offspring of others—like birds raising chicks that aren't theirs. Even in human hospitals, children switched at birth are raised with the same care and love, because the bond is real even if biology is mistaken. The sense of kinship depends on perception, not fact. And that perception can be expanded.

The second root is reciprocity. Even when relationships aren't familial, animals often help those who have helped them in the past—or whom they anticipate may help in the future. Lions share the spoils of a hunt even with those who didn't contribute that day, because cooperation matters. In human life, these dynamics play out constantly. We appreciate our coworkers when they help with a project. We feel warmth toward neighbors who pick up our packages, friends who check in on us when we're sick. These acts of reciprocity create trust and deepen our sense of connection.

But what makes us uniquely human is that we can use our insight and intelligence to stretch these instincts even further. We can reflect on our shared humanity and recognize kinship not just with our families or closest friends or even the people we'll never meet but whom we can appreciate from a distance but with the people we live and work beside every day—especially those we might otherwise overlook. A neighbor who doesn't return your waves but always puts your trash bins back upright after a storm. A coworker whose personality grates on you but who stays late to make sure the team meets a deadline. A teenager on the subway who offers their seat to someone older. These moments, if we're paying attention, reveal how much we actually do for each other—how much effort and care flows between us, even if it often goes unnoticed or unspoken.

In many theistic religions, the idea that we are all created in the image of God becomes a moral mandate to treat one another with respect and care. Tenderness is not reserved only for those we like but extended to all of God's creation. In Tibetan Buddhism, the belief in infinite lifetimes gives rise to radical empathy: Every person has at some point been our parent and cared for us. Meditation practices invite us to reflect on this and expand our feelings of gratitude and warmth to all beings.

Even outside religion, we find similar insights. Albert Einstein once wrote in a letter to a grieving friend:

> *A human being is a part of the whole, called by us "Universe," a part limited in time and space. He experiences himself, his thoughts and feelings as something separated from the rest—a kind of optical delusion of his consciousness. . . . Not to nourish the delusion but to try to overcome it is the way to reach the attainable measure of peace of mind.*[12]

As you deepen your awareness of interdependence—through observation, reflection, or practice—you may notice a glimmer of tenderness even for those you once found distant or difficult. Perhaps you will get a few glimpses of people, even strangers on the streets, "walking around shining like the sun," as did the Trappist monk Thomas Merton.[13]

These moments aren't sappy and sentimental—they are revolutionary. When we allow ourselves to feel tender toward others, even briefly, we are stepping out of the shell of isolation that our culture so often reinforces. We're awakening to a deeper current of connection—and to the possibility that compassion can occur, moment by moment, in the lives we already live.

THE PRACTICE OF NOURISHING THE HEART WITH GRATITUDE AND TENDERNESS

As we deepen our exploration of gratitude and tenderness in the following pages, it's natural for certain questions and hesitations to arise. These emotions, after all, can feel vulnerable or even inappropriate in a world that's often indifferent, unjust, or hurried. You may wonder: *Do I have to feel grateful for things I didn't ask for? Should I really extend tenderness toward people who have hurt me—or people who don't seem to care? What if gratitude feels forced, or inaccessible?*

It's easy to feel grateful when someone goes out of their way to help—when a friend brings soup while we're sick, or a stranger helps pick up something we dropped. But sometimes we believe that gratitude should only be reserved for intentional acts of kindness. Take, for example, a delivery driver dropping off a package of life-saving medicine. It might be tempting to think, *They're just doing their job. They don't deserve my gratitude.* But that logic quickly falls apart. We wouldn't think twice about feeling grateful for the medicine itself, even though it has no intention at all. The act of helping us, whether performed by a person or an inanimate object, can still evoke appreciation—because it's the *benefit*, not the intent, that often triggers the feeling.

Gratitude is a warm, expansive response that arises when we focus on what's helpful, meaningful, or life-sustaining. And it changes *us*—not necessarily the person we're grateful for. As we grow in awareness of how many people contribute to our lives without ever meeting us, we start to soften our sense of separateness. Gratitude starts to bind us to others, even in moments where the connection is invisible or impersonal. And that bond, even if it lives only in our own hearts, helps buffer the loneliness and disconnection that modern life often breeds. In fact, cultivating this kind of sustained appreciation lays the groundwork for compassion—especially for people outside our inner circle.

Still, there's a natural tension here. Is it realistic to feel gratitude or tenderness for everyone—including people who've harmed or hurt us? CBCT never asks us to force this. There is no moral pressure to include anyone in our reflections before we're ready. If there's a person who brings up nothing but pain or resistance, it's perfectly valid to leave them out of our practice. These categories—close ones, strangers, difficult people—can shift over time, but there's no need to push that change.

That said, if there's a part of us that wants to soften toward someone challenging, CBCT offers a path. We begin by reflecting on their basic humanity: They want to be safe, just like we do. They've likely been shaped by circumstances they didn't choose. They have losses, regrets, fears—just like us. From there, we can explore whether anything in our lives has shifted or improved *because* of their presence. Maybe they taught us a hard lesson. Maybe we gained resilience, new relationships, or just a sharper sense of our own boundaries. These are not excuses for harmful behavior—they're simply ways of honoring the complexity of what we've lived through. Even our hardest experiences can offer meaning and growth. And sometimes, that meaning becomes a gateway to unexpected tenderness.

Shantideva, the eighth-century Indian philosopher, wrote extensively on patience. He posed a powerful idea: If we truly value patience, then shouldn't we value the people who give us opportunities to practice it? If everyone were kind and easy, how would we ever develop the strength to stay steady in the face of difficulty? In his eyes, our greatest teachers are often those who challenge us most—not because they are right or good but because they help us grow.

And when it comes to meditating on the web of interconnectedness that can bring up feelings of gratitude and tenderness, another aspect arises: Not all interdependence feels good. Reflecting on the systems that support our daily lives often brings us face-to-face with painful truths. Take your smartphone. Behind this device are hundreds—maybe thousands—of people. Engineers, designers, shipping workers, retail clerks. But also underpaid laborers working in dangerous mines. Children who are part of a global chain of exploitation. In the face of that reality, gratitude can feel inappropriate or even naïve.

But the point of reflecting on interdependence is not to glorify the system. It's to make it visible. Sometimes, seeing the suffering woven into our lives stirs the very ground of compassion. We may start to feel a responsibility to act, to care more deeply, or to seek change.

For now, what matters is the clarity that arises when we begin to pay attention. Gratitude and tenderness are not about ignoring harm or pretending everything is OK. They are about noticing what's true. They are about recognizing that we are beneficiaries of vast, complex networks of care and labor, and that even in the messiest of human relationships, there are often moments—however small—worth appreciating.

Deepening Gratitude and Tenderness Practice (6–8 minutes)

Let your body be at ease, your spine upright but not stiff. With each inhale, invite spaciousness. With each exhale, release what's no longer needed. Allow your mind and body to settle into this moment.

When you feel ready, call to mind a person who, despite their own vulnerabilities and limitations, has cared for you in some way. This might be someone who has attended to your physical or emotional needs—a friend, a parent or guardian, a teacher, a caregiver, or perhaps someone whose act of kindness seemed small at the time but stayed with you. Let this person come to mind gently, without force.

As you hold their image or presence in your awareness, reflect on the ways in which their support has been meaningful to you. What have they offered you—time, wisdom, presence, protection, encouragement, nourishment? How has this shaped you? How has it contributed to your own strength, your sense of safety, your growth?

As you rest with this memory, see if you notice any warm feeling beginning to arise. Perhaps a quiet sense of tenderness, appreciation, or affection. If any of these feelings surface—even in the faintest flicker—let yourself linger with them. Sit with them. Breathe into them. Allow them to soak into your heart and your body, moment by moment.

Now gently expand your awareness beyond this person. Reflect on how interconnected your life is with the lives of others. Every resource, comfort, or skill you enjoy has come into being through the efforts of many people. Consider, for a moment, something simple—like your breakfast this morning. Who helped grow or transport that food? Who stocked the shelves, prepared the ingredients, or made the utensils and appliances you used? Allow yourself to glimpse the vast web of people who made that moment possible.

Take a few moments now to call to mind a skill or ability you cherish—something that has shaped your identity or well-being. It might be your ability to read or write, to cook, to solve problems, to listen, to nurture, to build, to lead. Who helped you gain this skill? Who supported your learning? Who made the learning environment possible? Who encouraged you when it felt hard?

Begin with those closest to the development of that skill, and gradually widen your focus. Include mentors, teachers, peers, and eventually even those you'll never meet—those who designed the books or tools you used, who paved the roads that got you there, who funded the institutions or cared for you so that you could focus.

As this web of support comes into view, notice what arises in your body and mind. Do you feel a shift? A deeper sense of appreciation? A warm glow in your chest? Perhaps a sense of humility or belonging? Let yourself rest with these feelings—let them settle in your heart.

Now, begin to sense how this awareness of interdependence may nourish your feelings of connection to others. Can you feel how many people are part of your story? Can you sense how even strangers—people you may never meet—have touched your life in meaningful ways?

Allow your heart to open, as much as feels safe and possible, to include them in your circle of gratitude. Imagine this warmth spreading outward, not only toward those you know and love but also toward those you've never met, and even those you may find difficult. You're not being asked to force affection—but simply to acknowledge that they, too, are part of this shared world.

Finally, bring to mind someone you know—or a group of people—who is in need of healing, care, or support. Silently dedicate this practice to them. Then gently widen that dedication to include others beyond your immediate circle. To the overlooked, the overwhelmed, the helpers, the harmed, and to all beings whose lives touch and are touched by others. May they be well. May they be safe. May they be free from suffering. May they know tenderness.

Take a deep breath in . . . and slowly exhale. As you prepare to close this practice, set an intention. It might be quiet or small: to notice moments of gratitude throughout the day. To extend warmth when it feels possible. To stay aware of the many hands that hold you, even when you feel alone. To let tenderness guide your attention.

When you're ready, gently return your awareness to your body . . . to the room . . . to this moment. You may wish to stretch, to place a hand over your heart, or to simply sit for a few more breaths.

Carry the insights and feelings of this reflection with you—into the day, into the world, into your next conversation.

May this practice serve you. May it serve others through you.

BRINGING THE SKILLS TO LIFE: PRACTICE BETWEEN SESSIONS

As we come to the close of this section, the practice becomes even more essential. If we want to deepen our capacity for gratitude and tenderness—not just as fleeting emotions but as inner resources—we must bring awareness into our daily lives.

Start by attuning to your interdependence. Catch yourself when you feel isolated or disconnected from others. In those moments, try shifting your awareness to the simple truth that your life depends on the kind efforts of many. Let that awareness work on you. Let it soften the edges. Let any feelings of warmth or appreciation deepen and grow.

Another practice is to keep a positive events log. To offset the brain's natural negativity bias, keep a log of all the good things that happened each day for one week. Each night, before bed, list at least five things that went well, no matter how small. Maybe the barista smiled at you. Maybe a stranger held the door. Maybe you laughed at something ridiculous. If your mind starts focusing on what went wrong, gently bring it back to what went right. You can also ask yourself: What caused this good thing to happen? Often, you'll discover other people at the root—revealing, once again, the invisible web of support that surrounds us.

You might also consider a gratitude visit. Write a letter to someone who positively influenced your life but whom you never really thanked. Be specific. Tell them what they did and how it mattered. If you can, deliver the letter in person and read it to them. It's a powerful way to make your appreciation real—and it's often just as transformative for you as it is for them.

There are those who've lived this practice, not in abstract terms but in moments of deep personal difficulty. Take Marcus, for example, who lost both of his parents in a short span of time. Things at home were hard. The weight of grief and responsibility bore down on him. The one place he found solace was canoeing—the simple rhythm of paddling down the river behind his house. But one morning, after a storm, he discovered his canoe had come loose and smashed on the rocks.

He said: "At that moment, I called to mind my lifelong best friend, someone with whom I could always find comfort and happiness, a refuge in the otherwise unrelenting storm. I was grateful for that friend's constant presence in my life. From there, I continued to think of my gratitude for others: my sister, brother, cousins with whom I am close, coworkers, and even strangers. It felt so much better to be filled with love and warmth and gratitude rather than anger and depression. And now I realize I have a tool to rely on when things get tough. Doing this meditation really helps. Even though the worst had happened—the loss of family, and the loss of my source of joy—it wasn't the end of everything. It was just another obstacle that I could handle with the help of my support system. Being conscious of gratitude and love, even in the worst times, can make life seem far more manageable."

And there was Lila, a journalist, who shared something quieter but just as powerful. She'd spent years harboring resentment toward her mother—a slow, steady bitterness that colored their every interaction. But one day, during a CBCT practice, a new light dawned.

She shared, "Shifting from resentment to gratitude, I was able to soften toward my mother. Rather than keep the running list of what I hadn't received, I focused on what I did receive. I realized that it was my mother who taught me to read. As a journalist, remembering that, and focusing on how my mother had given me the gift that would determine my career, helped me drop the last of my resentment. Gratitude provided a spark of warmth and affection that infused the relationship with kindness and patience."

These stories remind us that even in the midst of difficulty, gratitude and tenderness are possible. Love can coexist with pain. And in remembering what we've received, we may find our way back to connection.

In the next chapter, we'll explore how this warmhearted connection naturally unfolds into a compassion that is both realistic and responsive, rooted in clear seeing rather than sentimentality. For now, remember you have nothing to lose by letting gratitude and tenderness touch your life. In fact, you may discover they were quietly sustaining you all along.

CHAPTER NINE

EASING THE SUFFERING OF THE WORLD

No kind action ever stops with itself. One kind action leads to another. Good example is followed. A single act of kindness throws out roots in all directions, and the roots spring up and make new trees. The greatest work that kindness does to others is that it makes them kind themselves.

—Amelia Earhart

By now, you've learned to return to a sense of inner balance. You've widened your circle of concern. You've cultivated tenderness, gratitude, and a growing awareness of just how deeply your life is intertwined with the lives of others. This final chapter asks something bold of you—not to retreat from the world's suffering but to turn toward it with clarity, strength, and openhearted resolve.

For many of us, this idea raises questions before it offers answers. You may already be carrying a lot—trying to pay rent while the cost of living soars, navigating mental or physical health challenges, trying to make sense of a job that exhausts you or a world that seems to careen from crisis to crisis. How do we show up for the world when we feel like we're barely holding it together ourselves?

It's exactly because life is hard that compassion matters. Compassion is not a soft-spoken virtue reserved for saints and saviors. It is the courage to stay present, the creativity to solve real problems, and the deep human strength to care. Compassion, in its truest form, is not just about soothing pain; it's about transforming it.

I recall meeting a CBCT participant: A father, having just learned that his newborn son would grow up blind, felt a surge of tenderness so powerful it moved him to act—not only to comfort his child but also to prepare him for a world that might not always be kind. That is compassion.

It can feel more natural to act compassionately toward those closest to us. But when we recognize how others share our hopes, our vulnerabilities, and our need for dignity, we begin to understand that compassion doesn't have to stop at the edge of our family or community. Our tenderness can stretch outward, encompassing those we've never met, as well as those we find difficult to understand or relate to as fellow journeyers on the path.

And compassion doesn't always look the way we expect. It's not just a hand on the shoulder or a quiet nod. Compassion is active, strong, solution-oriented. It begins in the heart, but it doesn't end there. Real compassion holds suffering, yes—but it also mobilizes to address its roots.

Consider Adeeb Barqawi, who left a PhD program at Johns Hopkins to become a teacher through Teach for America. Assigned to one of Houston's lowest-performing schools, he expected hardship—but he wasn't prepared for what he heard one day when he found a normally attentive student falling asleep in class.

"My mother was murdered last night," she told him.

"Why did you come to school, then?" he asked.

"I had nowhere else to go," she replied.

Soon, Adeeb heard more. "We don't have any food." "My dad's in jail." "I haven't eaten in days." "I'm taking care of my siblings alone." He was overwhelmed. Panicked. *What do I do? What do I do? What do I do?*

That response wasn't compassion. That was *empathic distress*—a state of overwhelm that paralyzes rather than empowers.

But Adeeb found a way through. Drawing on his background in data systems, he and a team created a platform that allowed schools to track student needs and connect them with vetted agencies that could provide food, housing, and support. He didn't fix everything. But he made it possible for others to help. He transformed pain into action. That's compassion.

Compassion is aware. It listens deeply. It observes what hurts. It may arrive as a gentle hand or as a protective roar. It may look like tending to a sick loved one—or organizing for housing justice. It may be as simple as holding space for a friend's grief, or as complex as reimagining an entire system. But always, as I shared toward the beginning of this book, compassion contains three elements:

- A warmhearted sense of connection
- An awareness of what others are up against
- A desire to help ease that suffering

Compassion asks us to see more clearly what others are facing: children without food or shelter; neighbors crushed by medical debt; strangers tormented by racism, addiction, or loneliness; entire communities strained by systems that harm rather than help.

And then it asks: *How can I be part of the healing?*

Yes, it can feel like too much. You're just one person. But what if you stopped asking what you can't do—and started asking where you *can* help?

Maybe it's checking in on someone who's struggling. Maybe it's offering money or time to a cause that matters to you. Maybe it's changing your habits, or speaking up when you normally wouldn't. Maybe it's just listening more deeply.

Compassion isn't a performance. It's the quality of your presence, which is cumulative. One person alone can't solve the housing crisis or rebuild the climate—but if we all decide we're powerless, then nothing changes. If we each do something, however small, the ripple grows. Oceans, after all, are made one drop at a time.

There's an old story I like to return to, from American writer/anthropologist/naturalist Loren Eiseley's beautiful essay "The Star Thrower":

> One day, a man was walking along the beach when he noticed a boy picking up things and gently throwing them into the ocean. Approaching the boy, he asked: "Young man, what are you doing?" The boy replied, "Throwing starfish back into the ocean. The surf is up, and the tide is going out. If I don't throw them back, they'll die." The man laughed to himself and said, "Do you realize there are miles of beach and hundreds of starfish? You can't make any difference." After listening politely, the boy bent down, picked up another starfish, and threw it into the surf. Then, smiling at the man, he said, "I made a difference to that one."[1]

As the Talmud says, "Do not be daunted by the enormity of the world's grief. Do justly now. Love mercy now. Walk humbly now. You are not obligated to complete the work, but neither are you free to abandon it."

Just for a moment, find a comfortable seat and gently close your eyes, if that feels safe. Take one slow, steady breath. Now, bring to mind someone in your community who may be struggling. They don't need to be close to you—just someone whose challenges have come to your awareness. See if you can imagine what this person might be feeling. What needs are not being met? What might they be longing for? Without judgment, without trying to fix, just allow yourself to witness.

Now ask yourself: *Is there anything I can do—however small—to ease their burden, even slightly?* A gesture, a message, a shift in your own behavior?

Rest for a moment in that quiet space of care.

In the pages that follow, we'll explore how to move from empathy into wise, sustainable action. You'll learn how to guard against overwhelm, how to harness compassion's full strength, and how to contribute to a more just and loving world—one choice, one connection, one starfish at a time.

THE DIFFERENCE BETWEEN EMPATHY AND COMPASSION

Researchers generally agree there are three main types of empathy, each engaging different parts of the brain—and each carrying different possibilities and risks:[2]

Emotional Empathy (Emotion Resonance): This is the contagious kind. When you wince because someone stubbed their toe, or cry during a movie. It's automatic, visceral, ancient. Frans de Waal writes about how animals—yes, even bonobos—yawn when their peers do, or cry when one of their own is distressed. Babies do it, too. This is a foundational part of group living. But it can leave us stuck in others' pain without knowing how to help.

Cognitive Empathy (Perspective-Taking): This is what happens when you imagine what it's like to be someone else. You might think about the future of your children—or even of generations not yet born—and feel concern. It's how we relate to people we've never met, in different parts of the world. It helps us make wise choices about politics, climate, education, and health care. But on its own, it doesn't always lead to action or care. The same perspective-taking is also used by psychopaths to manipulate their victims.

Empathic Concern: This is the kind of empathy that activates compassion. It's not just about feeling someone else's suffering or understanding it—it's about caring. About wanting to reduce their pain. This kind of empathy fuels everything from volunteering at a shelter to comforting a friend to designing a better health care system. And unlike empathic distress, empathic concern doesn't burn you out—it can actually energize you and bring you a deep sense of purpose. But, divorced from discernment, such a concern can also overwhelm us at times.

So often, when we talk about being "empathetic people," we mean we feel others' pain. But without tenderness and motivation, that feeling alone can become heavy and even unhelpful.

Many of us know what it feels like to take on the emotions of someone else. A friend is grieving, and your own chest tightens. You see a child crying in the grocery store, and suddenly you feel overwhelmed, too. This is empathy—our innate ability to sense and mirror the feelings of others. But sometimes empathy alone can backfire. Instead of moving us toward care and connection, it can leave us paralyzed or drained. We shut down. We tune out. We walk away because it hurts too much to stay.

This is what researchers call *empathic distress*—what Adeeb experienced at first when he heard his students talk about their lives. Empathic distress is what happens when we feel another person's pain so intensely that it becomes our own—and we start to suffer *with* them, instead of being able to show up *for* them. It occurs when our emotional resonance with another's suffering pushes us beyond our personal Zone of Well-Being. This tipping point—where shared emotion overwhelms rather than connects—can be profoundly taxing, especially when sustained over time.

In professions like nursing, firefighting, caregiving, and teaching, this reaction isn't rare. It's chronic. When empathic distress becomes prolonged, it can lead to trauma, burnout, and emotional depletion. The more we care, the more vulnerable we may become. But ironically, the more we are consumed by distress, the less able we are to help. As Jamil Zaki writes in *The War for Kindness*, "Easily distressed people avoid others' suffering . . . refusing volunteer opportunities that will put them in emotional situations. People who tend to feel concern are willing to engage in helping."[3] In his research, people who experienced distress would help only if it was the only option—but withdrew if given an out. Those who felt empathic concern (which I'll share more about shortly), on the other hand, helped even when they didn't have to.

This doesn't mean empathy is a problem to be eliminated. Far from it. It is what alerts us to another's pain—it's the human tuning fork. But if the resonance becomes so loud it drowns out everything else, it pulls the focus inward. We become emotionally dysregulated, uncomfortable, irritable. And we lose the very thing that brought us into the connection in the first place: our ability to care clearly, compassionately, and sustainably.

THE THREE DIMENSIONS OF COMPASSION

When neuroscientist Tania Singer placed French Tibetan Buddhist monk Matthieu Ricard—often called "the happiest man in the world"—in an fMRI scanner at the Max Planck Institute, she was curious to see how his brain responded to suffering. First, Ricard was shown upsetting images and asked to focus on the pain of others. The pain circuits in his brain lit up like a flare. It was intense. But then, Ricard shifted into a mode of compassion—focusing not just on the suffering but on the desire to help. The pain subsided. The areas related to reasoning and positive mood activated. He reported joy. In fact, Singer and her colleagues concluded that compassion results in positive feelings similar to eating chocolate!

Singer expanded her research by comparing untrained individuals with those who had undergone compassion training. The untrained participants responded to distressing images with stronger activation in brain areas linked to negative affect and pain empathy. But those trained in compassion experienced a boost in positive emotions, social bonding, and neural activity associated with love and affiliation. The takeaway? While empathic resonance can lead to empathic distress, compassion offers a learnable, powerful way to sustain care without collapse.[4]

Compassion is not just empathy. It is empathy plus agency—a warm, wise engagement with suffering that doesn't get stuck in it. And when the three parts of compassion come together—affective, cognitive, and motivational—compassion becomes a powerful force. It connects you emotionally, informs you mentally, and moves you to respond skillfully and generously. That means you can shift from being overwhelmed by pain to being rooted in love. You can cry with someone, feel their heartache, and stay grounded in a warm, steady presence. You don't have to drown in an emotional flood in order to be fully human.

So, if you're someone who's ever felt too much, loved too hard, or found yourself collapsing under the weight of other people's pain, know that your sensitivity is not the problem. It is the gift. But that gift must be stewarded with care. Because when we learn to shift from empathic distress into compassion, we don't shut down—we open.

Of course, when we bear witness to another's suffering, the line between compassion and empathic distress can be perilously thin. We may arrive with the desire to help, only to find ourselves overwhelmed—emotionally hijacked by pain we cannot fix. But there is a difference between being flooded by suffering and being rooted in care.

Mara learned this difference while volunteering to support a teenage burn patient undergoing painful reconstruction. Her role required presence during wound care and debridement—procedures that left the student trembling with pain. "I was apprehensive about my ability to self-regulate," Mara recalled. "I needed to be able to assist with dressing changes and care, as well as emotional and spiritual support."

She knew that if she let herself become overwhelmed by the girl's agony, she wouldn't be able to offer anything helpful, only empathic distress. Instead, Mara turned to her CBCT practice for grounding and inspiration.

"During one particularly difficult moment," she said, "I found that the practice helped me sense into the strength and courage and resource of compassion, and the ability to stay present and grounded and provide care."

What emerged was a quiet, sturdy presence—a warm resolve that allowed her to stay. "The boundlessness and strength of compassion was very real and accessible in that difficult circumstance," she reflected, "and I recognized that it arose from the practice."

Mara didn't shut down. She didn't flee. She found that compassion, when embodied, doesn't drown us. It steadies us. "I'm still very grateful," she said. "It gave me confidence in compassion that is also a resource."

Right now, someone you know is hurting. Maybe it's someone you love deeply—or maybe it's someone you struggle to like. Maybe it's you. Pause for a moment. Who comes to mind? What would it feel like to connect with their pain without being overtaken by it? To understand it, and to want to help—not out of guilt or obligation but because your heart simply says yes? That's compassion. It doesn't mean fixing the world in a day. It just means showing up with intention, openness, and care.

WHAT'S LOVE GOT TO DO WITH IT?

We often hear that compassion and love are "two sides of the same coin." And they can be—when we're talking about a very specific kind of love: the kind that arises from deep care, rather than need. Think of this as *agape*, a Greek word that refers to altruistic love—a love rooted in the sincere, warmhearted wish for someone else to flourish. It's expansive, generous, and doesn't hinge on what we get in return.

English is a tricky language, especially when it comes to the word *love*. We use it for everything: "I love ice cream," "I love my partner," "I love sleeping in." These uses point not so much to altruism but to *attachment*—desire that centers around how something or someone makes us feel. We say we love things when they bring us pleasure, validation, comfort, or excitement. And in relationships, it's incredibly common for these two threads—altruistic love and attachment—to be intertwined. As Indo-Tibetan Buddhist psychology puts it, they are often "mixed like milk and water."

That's not necessarily a bad thing. When we love people, especially romantic partners or close friends, our love often includes both a genuine care for their well-being and a desire for how they make us feel. But becoming more aware of which one is leading—altruism or attachment—can be incredibly clarifying.

Here's one way to reflect on it: When you think about someone you love, are you primarily focused on their happiness and what would help them grow—even if it doesn't include you? Or are you mostly focused on what they bring into your life: how they make you feel, what they give you, what you fear losing?

Romantic relationships, in particular, can easily tip into attachment-heavy territory. We start to see the other person as essential to our happiness, maybe even telling ourselves that we couldn't be happy without them. It may feel like devotion, but if we look closer, it's often about meeting our own emotional needs—understandably so.

CBCT doesn't ask us to judge or reject this kind of love. These feelings are normal, and there's no need to pretend we're above them. It's natural to find joy in being cared for, to feel fulfilled by companionship, to light up when someone we love makes us feel safe or seen. But it's helpful to distinguish that kind of affection from the kind that says, "I want you to thrive, no matter what." That's altruistic love—and cultivating it can be a powerful shift in how we relate to others.

There's another layer here, too: a pattern called *pathological altruism*. It can look like altruism on the surface—lots of giving, serving, and sacrifice—but underneath, it's driven by the desire to be liked, to be needed, to be seen as "the good one," or to control the well-being of others. Sometimes we overextend ourselves in the name of helping, but we're really chasing reassurance, validation, or a sense of control. That doesn't make us bad people. These are deeply human impulses, especially for those of us who have been raised to measure our worth by how useful we are to others.

The invitation is to reflect gently, without self-blame: *What's motivating my care for this person? Is it truly about them—or is it about how I want to be seen, or what I'm afraid of losing?* The more clearly we understand ourselves, the more space we create for genuine, sustainable compassion—the kind that nourishes both giver and receiver.

A quick note for clarity: When I talk about *attachment* here, I don't mean the kind of healthy attachment that psychologists refer to between a child and their caregiver. That kind of bond is vital for a child's development and for the parent's well-being. What I'm referring to here is emotional clinging—the kind of grasping that can cloud the ability to love freely and wisely.

So, love fully. Let it be tender. Let it be joyful. And with practice, let it become increasingly spacious—less about holding on, and more about helping someone become who they're meant to be.

SEEING CLEARLY, ACTING WISELY: SYSTEMS THINKING AND DISCERNMENT IN COMPASSION

You care. You want to help. But how?

That's the question many of us ask when we see suffering all around us—on the news, in our families, in our neighborhoods, and within ourselves. Whether we're staring down injustice, burnout, climate collapse, or heartbreak, the scale of pain in the world can feel paralyzing.

Compassion is the force that moves us, but without clarity and discernment, that movement can falter. Intention alone is not enough. As His Holiness writes in *Beyond Religion: Ethics for a Whole World*,

> While sound compassionate motivation is the foundation for ethics and spirituality, a further factor is crucial if we are to achieve a balanced and genuinely universal system of ethics.... While intention is the first and most important factor in guaranteeing that our behavior is ethical, we also need discernment to ensure that the choices we make are realistic and that our good intentions do not go to waste.[5]

This is where *systems thinking* becomes indispensable. It's the practice of zooming out and mapping the many interlocking forces—individual, cultural, structural—that shape a given experience. Systems thinking invites us to see the full ecology of suffering, and from there, to determine what actions are not just well-meaning but well-placed.

You might think of a time when you tried to help someone and it didn't go the way you expected. Maybe your advice fell flat, or your efforts were misinterpreted, or you were burned out before you even made a difference. That's not uncommon. Compassion without discernment can feel like flailing in the dark. But compassion *with* discernment? That's a light strong enough to guide you toward effective, sustaining care.

This starts with cognitive empathy—our capacity to see from someone else's point of view. Without it, we'd never fully grasp what others are up against. This kind of understanding is what makes compassion actionable. But it's also double-edged. Cognitive empathy alone—without warmth or tenderness—can be weaponized. Political operatives, con artists, and manipulative marketers often use deep understanding of people's fears to exploit, not support. That's why insight must be guided by care.

We've already explored how to open our hearts through recognizing our shared humanity and interdependence. Now, we deepen that tenderness by making visible what others are facing. What's holding them back? What pain or pressure is shaping their behavior? What hidden forces—personal, social, systemic—are stacked against them?

Sometimes the struggles are clear: poverty, illness, heartbreak. But much of the time, they're not. A coworker who seems aloof may be battling anxiety. A neighbor who keeps to themselves might be grieving. A successful-looking friend may be internally unraveling. When we don't see these inner realities, we risk withholding compassion simply because the suffering isn't loud or obvious.

I often speak of three levels of suffering afflicting human society:

Obvious struggles: Physical or emotional pain that's visible and clear.

Suffering from the illusion of permanence: The pain that comes from clinging to what's always changing, like relationships, youth, or status.

Suffering from the illusion of independence: The deepest level, rooted in the mistaken belief that we exist separately from everything else. This false sense of isolation causes enormous inner pain.

When we understand these layers, our compassion deepens. We begin to see how even someone who appears "fine" may be suffering profoundly. A friend constantly chasing success may be struggling with grasping for permanence. A community member with extreme views may be acting from unseen wounds or inherited systems of thought. Instead of judging from the surface, systems thinking invites us to look beneath.

And it's not just about understanding individuals. It's about recognizing that systems—cultural norms, economic policies, historical traumas—shape people's lives in profound ways. When we begin to notice how race, class, gender identity, immigration status, or disability intersect with systems of power, we see suffering that may have once been invisible to us. And our compassion expands.

Take, for example, the young generation of activists fighting for climate justice. Many of them aren't just looking at today's problems—they're imagining the world their children and grandchildren might inherit. Their compassion extends forward in time, toward people they may never meet. That's what cognitive empathy, fueled by systems thinking, can do: It turns vague concern into bold, visionary action.

But discernment isn't just for policymakers or activists. It's for all of us. A doctor can't always prevent a patient's death, but she can sit beside them, ease their pain, or comfort a family member. A teacher can't fix a student's home life, but they can create a classroom where that student feels seen. A therapist can't repair a broken system, but he can help someone survive it.

When we look at the entire ecosystem of a problem, we often find *some* place where we can act. The key is not to solve everything. It's to stay engaged, curious, and responsive.

I once brought a group of students to Dharamsala, India, to meet with His Holiness. One student asked how millennials could possibly address a crisis as massive as climate change. His Holiness took a moment to reflect and replied that, while the problem was indeed overwhelming, the response need not be. "Look at the causes and conditions," he said. "Then focus on what you can do where you are."

THE RIPPLE EFFECTS OF COMPASSION

You don't have to be a superhero to make a difference. A nurse eases pain through care. A friend offers presence. A journalist tells a story no one else has noticed. A neighbor checks in on an elder down the hall. Each of these actions is rooted in compassion, shaped by the context, skills, and circumstances of the person giving.

Even when there's no immediate solution, our presence matters. Holding someone's hand, witnessing their struggle, offering silence without judgment—these quiet acts are part of the work. They tell others: "You are not alone."

Sometimes, we won't know what to do. But if we sustain the compassionate wish—if we stay open, alert, and attuned—opportunities arise. History offers countless examples of this kind of presence—of people who didn't set out to change the world but simply responded to what was right in front of them, with clarity, courage, and compassion. Sometimes, a quiet gesture ends up shifting the course of hundreds of lives.

During World War II, a young stockbroker named Nicholas Winton saved more than six hundred children from Nazi-occupied Czechoslovakia.[6] He quietly arranged transport, visas, and housing—and then told no one, not even his family. Decades later, his actions came to light, and he was invited to a surprise gathering in London. There, in an auditorium packed with people, he discovered that nearly every adult present was either a child he'd saved or the child of someone he had. He couldn't save everyone. But by focusing on what he *could* do, he changed hundreds of lives—and, through them, thousands more.

Compassion doesn't always come with a spotlight. It doesn't always mean sweeping solutions. But when we act from the heart—even in small, specific ways—we send out ripples that reach further than we'll ever know.

We've all heard the phrase *pay it forward*, and we've likely seen it in action. One person does something kind, and the next person feels moved to do the same. In one remarkable example, a customer at a Starbucks drive-through chose to buy coffee for the person behind them. That sparked 378 people to do the same, creating a chain that lasted eleven hours.[7]

Even small gestures—holding a door, listening well, forgiving someone, donating a few dollars—can create a wave of kindness far beyond what we see. Indigenous traditions have long understood this. In the Haudenosaunee Confederacy, the Seventh Generation Principle teaches that every decision we make should benefit people seven generations into the future. Even if we'll never meet them, we hold their well-being in mind. This is compassion with discernment. It's how kindness becomes culture.

Let's make this personal. Think of a time someone did something kind for you. Maybe it was small—an unexpected compliment, a ride when you were stranded, a teacher who noticed you were struggling. Maybe it was something bigger.

Write it down. What was the act? Who offered it?
Trace the impact. How did it affect your life? Did it change your mood, your choices, your direction? Did it inspire you to show up differently for someone else?
Go even further. Challenge yourself to imagine the full ripple effect. What long-term shifts might have been set in motion?
Reflect. What arises in your body as you sit with this memory? Warmth? Grief? Joy? Let it be.
Ask yourself: What small act might you offer next?

GOING WHERE YOU ARE NEEDED

We end with an essential paradox: The wish to help is enough. And it isn't.

It's enough to stay rooted. To remind us of our values. To keep our hearts open, even when action feels impossible. But it's also not the end of the story. Sustaining the warmhearted wish makes us ready. We're poised to act when the time comes. We don't turn away.

Martin Luther King Jr. once said, "Life's most persistent and urgent question is: 'What are you doing for others?'"[8]

Compassion changes us. It keeps us motivated even when the work is long. It prevents burnout when it centers meaning and connection. It gives strength in struggle and purpose in chaos. And most powerfully, it reminds us: We are never powerless. We may not see the end of the story. But we help shape it.

Building on the deep truth that compassion uplifts both giver and receiver, you may find yourself asking: *Now what?* You care, you feel, but the scope of suffering in the world can seem dizzying. *Where do I even begin?* The climate is collapsing, mental health crises are rampant, people are more divided than ever—and here you are, just one person with one life and limited time.

The invitation here, the one that allows you to help shape the story of our collective future, isn't to try to solve everything but to focus your care. To choose something that moves you, that stirs your compassion, and start there. You don't have to fix global warming—but maybe you can start composting in your apartment building or teaching kids in your neighborhood about pollinators. You might not cure loneliness for everyone, but perhaps you can make weekly tea dates with your elderly neighbor who lost her partner last year. You won't end the mental health epidemic, but you can volunteer an hour a week on a crisis text line, or advocate for better school resources in your district.

When we connect our warmhearted wish to *one* issue, one community, one area of impact, it becomes less abstract and more actionable. Try this:

Think of a few issues that matter to you—anything from the climate crisis to social isolation to food insecurity. Choose the one that hits closest to home or feels most urgent right now.

Ask yourself: *What's the change I want to see?* Make it simple and clear—more access to clean water, stronger community ties, safer schools.

Now, make it personal. Who do you know who would be affected by this positive change? Your cousin navigating unemployment? Your friend struggling with anxiety? Your own future child? Picture their faces. Let that picture deepen your commitment.

With that goal in mind, draw a small map: In the center, place the issue you chose. Around it, place the factors that contribute to the issue—from large systemic causes to smaller, day-to-day ones.

Look closely. Which piece of this web do you actually have the ability to influence? Do you have skills, connections, resources, or time that could shift one small link in the chain?

Write down one small action you *could* take. Could you cook an extra meal for a food-insecure family? Could you share a resource? Could you mentor someone younger than you? Picture yourself taking that step. How does it feel?

Often, we find that the paralysis of "too big" starts to loosen when we make things tangible. And no act of compassion is wasted. A warm meal, a shared ride, a handwritten note, a voter registration drive—these are drops that ripple outward in ways you may never see. The key isn't *what* the action is—it's that you choose something that matters, and offer it with care.

THE PRACTICE OF EASING THE SUFFERING OF THE WORLD

His Holiness often recites a centuries-old prayer by Shantideva. Though simple in form, its words carry the full weight of what it means to live compassionately:

> May I be a guard for those without one,
> A guide for all who journey on the road,
> May I become a boat, a raft or bridge,
> For all who wish to cross the water.
> May I be an isle for those desiring landfall,
> And a lamp for those who wish for light,
> May I be a bed for those who need to rest,
> And a servant for all who live in need.[9]

This prayer is a call to be someone who meets suffering with care, someone who brings light where there is darkness. Even when we don't know exactly how to help, even when we're not sure how to fix what's broken, the simple desire to relieve suffering and offer warmth makes a real difference. Compassion begins with that wish.

In the Buddhist tradition, the wish to see others happy is called *love*. The wish to see them free from suffering is called *compassion*. For the people closest to us, these wishes arise naturally. But through practice, we can expand them outward—to include strangers, communities, and even the Earth itself.

You don't need to force a feeling. Just cultivate the wish. Over time, that wish strengthens into something steady and radiant. You'll find yourself less overwhelmed by suffering—not because you're numb but because your desire to help has become grounded in purpose and love.

Sometimes people ask, "Why can't I just skip to the final step and not do the earlier ones?" It's a fair question. But it's a little like planting seeds in a garden without preparing the soil. Without the earlier chapters—stabilizing your attention, developing self-compassion, reflecting on our interdependence and shared humanity—you might find it hard to stay present with someone else's pain. You might shut down, pull away, or feel overwhelmed.

Returning to the foundational practices gives you strength. If you find yourself rattled by another person's suffering, you can ground yourself again. If someone difficult comes to mind and you feel resistance, you can revisit your practice of seeing common humanity—or return to the well of self-compassion. These earlier reflections become like muscles: The more you use them, the stronger they get.

Eventually, compassion stops feeling like an effort. It becomes your default setting. The earlier practices create the internal conditions where compassion doesn't have to be manufactured—it flows naturally.

Harnessing the Power of Compassion (5–7 minutes)

When you're settled in and ready, take a few grounding breaths and gently bring your attention inward. Begin to call to mind the people in your life who have supported or touched you in some way—those who've shared love, kindness, laughter, or even moments of challenge that helped you grow. Let yourself feel the tenderness that comes with remembering all that connects you.

Slowly, let your awareness expand. Include not only your loved ones but also acquaintances, strangers, and—when you're ready—even those whose actions or values you may not agree with. Try not to force anything. Just open the door a little wider.

As you hold these individuals in your awareness, ask: *What are they up against?* What fears or heartbreaks might they be carrying? What daily burdens or unseen challenges might they be navigating? How, like you, might they be vulnerable to life's many uncertainties?

Notice what arises in you as you reflect. Does concern stir? Do you feel a desire for their struggles to ease, even a little? Whatever feelings emerge—warmth, sadness, connection—just let them be. You might imagine this compassionate urge as a pearl of light glowing at the center of your chest. With every in-breath, see that light grow. With each out-breath, offer it to those you hold in your heart, radiating ease, nourishment, and well-being.

To deepen this practice, you may choose to repeat silently: *May you be free from suffering and the causes of suffering. May you have happiness and the causes of happiness.*

Pause here. Allow these wishes to move through you as heartfelt intentions. Let them soften you. Let them shift how you feel in your body and your mind.

Then, ask yourself: *How might this growing tenderness support not only my relationships but my own greater well-being? How might I carry this into the world—not just in my imagination but in action?*

You may wish to dedicate this practice to someone you know who is struggling. Then, extend that dedication outward—to all those facing similar pain. Let the ripple expand. The world is full of people—many you will never meet—who might be uplifted by even a whisper of your compassion.

To close, set a gentle intention to carry this awareness into your day. Let it shape how you speak, how you listen, how you move through the world.

Today, as you move through the ordinary rhythms of life, look for small ways to turn this wish into action. Greet someone with genuine warmth. Send a check-in text to a friend. Offer help to a neighbor or stranger. These don't need to be grand gestures. Let your kindness be humble, but real.

You might also consider someone with whom things have felt strained—a colleague, a relative, a friend. Using what you've explored through this practice, ask yourself: *What small step could I take toward reconnection?* Could it be a kind message? A moment of listening? A willingness to let go of a grudge?

Write down a few possibilities, and if it feels right, choose one and act on it today.

Every time you extend compassion—even in the smallest of ways—you reinforce a truth we often forget: that healing, change, and connection begin right where we are, with what we already have.

Let your intention be simple: to be a source of care in a world that needs it. One breath. One action. One connection at a time.

BRINGING THE SKILLS TO LIFE: PRACTICE BETWEEN SESSIONS

Compassionate action doesn't have to be grand or heroic. It often begins with something much simpler: the willingness to pause, reflect, and connect with our heart's desire to see others flourish. Here's how you can slow down, reengage with your values, and apply discernment and kindness in grounded, tangible ways.

Apply discernment. When you feel overwhelmed or indifferent in the face of others' pain, notice that impulse—and don't rush past it. Return to your breath. Settle your body and mind. Then, gently reconnect to your tenderness for that person or group, even if it's just a glimmer. Remind yourself of your wish to see them thrive. From this more centered place, ask: *What might be contributing to their suffering? What social, cultural, emotional, or structural factors might be at play?* As you reflect, see if there is anything—no matter how small—you can do. If nothing external seems possible, remember that simply sustaining a compassionate wish for them is already a meaningful act.

Perform small acts of kindness. Acts of kindness are a powerful antidote to despair—and a reminder that we always have the capacity to ease suffering in some way. This week, brainstorm three small, specific acts of kindness you could carry out. Maybe it's making a warm meal for someone who's grieving, checking in with a colleague who's been quiet lately, or offering to run an errand for a neighbor with limited mobility. Write them down. Choose one and commit to doing it. Afterward, take time to reflect: *How did it feel? What changed, if anything, in you or the other person?* Need inspiration? Visit www.kindspring.org and explore their twenty-one-day kindness challenges, designed for individuals, families, or organizations. You can even request free "smile cards" to leave behind after anonymous kind acts, inviting others to pay it forward and keep the ripple going.

Connect with your motivation. Sometimes we face more complex situations—ethical dilemmas, moments of conflict, or decisions that force us to weigh multiple values. In those moments, discernment becomes essential. His Holiness describes his process in *Beyond Religion: Ethics for a Whole World*, offering a method both simple and profound:

> In my own case, when called upon to make a difficult decision, I always start by checking my motivation. Do I truly have others' well-being at heart? Am I under the sway of disturbing emotions, such as anger, impatience, or hostility? Having determined that my motivation is sound, I then look carefully at the situation in context. What are the underlying causes and conditions that have given rise to it? What choices do I have? What are their likely outcomes? And which course of action, on balance, is most likely to yield the greatest long-

> term benefit for others? Making decisions in this way, I find, means they are not the cause of any regret later on.[10]

You can use this process too. The next time you face a tough decision—personal or professional—pause to check your motivation. What are you hoping to bring about? What emotional currents might be pulling you? From there, consider the causes and context. Weigh your options, not only for immediate outcomes but for their long-term effect on others. Let your action be guided by wisdom and care, rooted in clarity rather than reactivity. With practice, this kind of discernment becomes a way of life: not about always having the right answers but about staying grounded in your values and being willing to grow wiser through each choice.

As we come to the end of this journey, you may still wonder what it means to live with compassion—not just in grand, heroic gestures but in the soft, daily moments of being human with one another.

Jordan, a longtime practitioner of these teachings, worked at a library branch in a small city and had just entered her sixties when she began to ask a quiet but pressing question: "How can I be of service to people who are nearing the end of life?" She wasn't sure what form this calling would take—she wasn't in a position to change careers or become a hospice volunteer—but she knew she wanted to show up more courageously when her friends, neighbors, and coworkers began facing illness, aging, or loss.

"CBCT practices have been very helpful," she said. "They help me to confront and be present with suffering in a constructive way. I am reminded that there is always something I can do. Maybe not directly, but I can always be with the suffering and be with the person who suffers. I can always offer a compassionate heart."

In the past, she admitted, her instinct had been to freeze or fumble—dropping off a casserole, but then avoiding the person afterward because she didn't know what to say. She feared saying the wrong thing, or making their pain worse. But after several months of daily practice, she began sitting beside people with a steadier heart—when a friend lost her spouse, when a colleague broke down at the reference desk, when an elderly neighbor began declining. She no longer rushed to fix or cheerlead. She simply refused to turn and look away.

"I've found that, by looking at suffering directly and not turning away," she said, "I'm able to find the joy that is present in almost every situation. In this way, I find that I am more able to 'weather' the suffering that is all around me."

It's easy to underestimate how powerful it can be simply to remain—to bear witness with a steady, loving heart. But it is precisely that presence that opens the door to healing. And, as Jordan discovered, it is also what makes joy more visible, even in sorrow.

We close the seven steps of CBCT not with certainty or solutions but with this invitation: to keep your heart soft, your awareness clear, and your presence steady. In a world that so often turns away, may your compassion become a refuge—for others, and for yourself.

CONCLUSION

THE CALL FOR A COMPASSION REVOLUTION

We need a revolution of compassion based on warmheartedness that will contribute to a more compassionate world with a sense of oneness of humanity. The entire human family must unite and cooperate to protect our common home.[1]

—His Holiness the Fourteenth Dalai Lama

Lodi Gyari, the longtime special envoy to the United States for His Holiness, once told me a story that stayed with me—not because of its historical weight but because of the quiet, astonishing clarity of heart it revealed.

It was 1979. His Holiness, after twenty years in exile following China's occupation of Tibet, had finally received a visa to visit the United States during the Carter administration. This was no small opportunity. It was his first chance to bring the suffering of the Tibetan people to the attention of the world's most powerful nation. Journalists flocked to cover his visit, and his advisors, understandably, saw this as the moment to amplify Tibet's plight. But something surprising happened: Instead of focusing solely on the politics or the injustices, His Holiness began speaking more and more about something else—about how to work with suffering itself. He talked about the emotional pain people carried in their daily lives. About depression. About burnout. About the modern condition.

Lodi, who had worked tirelessly to bring Tibetan voices to the world stage, grew concerned. He gathered his courage and brought his concern directly to His Holiness. "We have this incredible opportunity," he said. "People are listening. Shouldn't we be talking more about Tibet?" His Holiness listened quietly, then responded with the compassion and clarity that would define his global role for decades to come:

"It is true that there is the opportunity for me to talk about our grievances. But these people coming to me are coming with their own struggles. I feel when people are coming with their own suffering, for me to instead of providing them some hope—some way to deal with that, to offer some help and support, or insights to help relieve that suffering—to add onto it with our own suffering doesn't feel right."

That moment, Lodi said, changed everything for him. It reframed his understanding of leadership, of advocacy, and of what it means to truly serve humanity. His Holiness was not abandoning the Tibetan cause. He was elevating it. He was placing it within a greater human cause: the urgent need for a global compassion revolution.

And what is this revolution? It is a revolution of the heart.

Despite our remarkable scientific and technological advancements, we are, as a species, still deeply unwell. His Holiness has said, again and again, that we need more than intellect. We need ethical wisdom. In a 1998 commencement address at Emory University, he described education as a tool—not inherently good or bad but shaped by the heart of the one who uses it. "If one comes with warmheartedness and a compassionate heart," he said, "then they will use it for a constructive purpose."

This moral revolution, this compassion revolution, begins inside each of us. His Holiness refers to it as "secular ethics"—human values like compassion, forgiveness, contentment, and self-discipline that don't require religious belief but are available to every human being by virtue of our shared nature.

We don't need to believe in God or Buddha to believe in goodness. We don't need to join a religion or a movement to change the world. We simply need to wake up to our shared humanity—and take responsibility for how we relate to it.

We need compassion in our schools, in our hospitals, in our governments, in our neighborhoods, and in our homes. We need it in the ways we parent, partner, and lead. We need it not just as a response to crisis but as a practice—a daily choice.

"Now is a critical time for us to make a difference, and to protect the future of humanity," His Holiness has said. "This effort involves each one of us."

It may seem like too much, but each of us has a role to play. Sometimes that role will be big and bold. Other times, it will be quiet and humble. But it matters.

The beauty of the Compassion Shift is that it doesn't require permission from those in power. It doesn't wait for institutions to change or for world leaders to issue a decree. It begins wherever you are—at the breakfast table with your child, on the sidewalk with a stranger, in a difficult conversation with a friend or coworker. It begins when you choose not to react from habit but from presence. When you listen, when you stay, when you remember that the person in front of you—no matter how "wrong" they seem—is a human being shaped by struggle and longing just like you.

And in a world that seems determined to magnify our differences, this kind of compassion becomes a radical act of belonging. It reminds us that behind every label is a person. Behind every opinion is a story. Behind every mask of indifference or hostility is a heart that has been hurt, dismissed, or unseen. Compassion doesn't erase difference, but it does reveal our shared vulnerability, our shared hopes, our shared longing to be known, accepted, and loved.

Compassion dissolves the illusion that belonging is something we earn by being the same. Instead, it shows us that belonging is something we build by holding space for difference, with dignity. It's in the soft eye contact between two people who disagree, the silent comfort of standing beside someone in grief, the willingness to keep showing up for one another even when it's hard. Compassion gives us a way home to each other. It returns us to the truth that we are not separate, and never were. It recalibrates what's possible between people.

Compassion is the source of real power—not dominance or control but the kind of power that multiplies through care. When compassion is no longer outsourced to institutions or reserved for saints but reclaimed by each of us in our daily lives, the world begins to change—not from the top down but from the inside out.

It is true that the world is heavy with suffering. We are bombarded by reminders of all that is broken. But I have also seen, again and again, that people are capable of transformation. A single shift in how we perceive or relate to ourselves and others can ripple outward in ways we can't even begin to imagine.

So, if you're reading these words—having journeyed through this book, reflected on your own life, and maybe even opened your heart in ways that feel unfamiliar—I want to thank you. And I want to tell you something important: You matter. Your efforts, no matter how small they may seem, matter.

I want to leave you with the wisdom of *Ubuntu*—a philosophy from Southern Africa that roughly translates to, "I am because we are." Ubuntu is not simply a cultural sentiment; it is a worldview, a way of being that affirms our shared humanity and insists that our individual well-being is bound up in the well-being of others. It offers a powerful compass for how we might reimagine our systems—education rooted in care and interdependence, health care that treats the whole person with dignity, art that awakens empathy and connection, environmental stewardship that honors our kinship with the Earth, governance that is relational rather than extractive, and technology that amplifies the best in us rather than exploits our vulnerabilities.

Compassion is the thread that weaves through all of these possibilities. It is not a sentimental luxury—it is infrastructure for a livable future. And we are already seeing glimmers of this world coming into being. The work of CBCT is quietly and powerfully taking root in schools, hospitals, community justice initiatives, corporations, and even government programs. It's showing us that compassion is not only teachable but scalable. That when we commit to training the heart with the same seriousness with which we train the mind, we begin to transform culture from the inside out.

Compassion is not a soft sentiment or lofty ideal. It is a steady practice, a discipline for the most courageous hearts. And each time you choose to respond with tenderness instead of aloofness, with clarity instead of indifference, with care instead of cynicism—you are helping to shape a more just, more compassionate world.

We are not helpless. We are not too late. We are here, now, standing on the edge of what's possible. And if each of us begins to live from a place of warmhearted compassion, then together, we will become the medicine this world so desperately needs.

FINAL REFLECTIONS: THE VALUES TREE

When we turn our lens inward and bring greater clarity to our inner lives, we begin to understand the values that quietly guide us. The Values Tree is a reflection tool we use in our training programs to explore the relationship between personal values and collective flourishing. By envisioning a single, core value as the "trunk" of a living tree, you can begin to trace how that value is supported, how it expresses itself, and what it ultimately yields.

You may be wondering why we're exploring the Values Tree at the end of this book. It's meant to be both a source of inspiration and a reminder: You are the tree. As you continue to cultivate compassion—for yourself and for others—and spread a deeper sense of belonging in your life and communities, this practice offers a way to root into your values and grow from them.

You can use the prompts below to articulate your vision—start with one value you hold dear, and let your answers grow from there. By imagining your value as the "trunk" of a living tree, you'll begin to trace what nourishes it, how it expresses itself in society, and what fruits it bears over time. Let your responses grow organically, grounded in the truth of what matters most to you and what you long to see flourish in our collective future.

- **Trunk:** What is one overarching value you would like to see for yourself and our society?
- **Roots:** What would we need to realize this value? What are the key contributing factors?
- **Branches:** When this value is achieved, in what forms or fields would it manifest in society and systems?
- **Fruits:** What would be the enduring outcomes that grow from the flourishing of this value?

When I share this practice at trainings, the answers vary widely and powerfully. Some people name *justice*, *truth*, or *freedom* as their trunk value. Others choose *joy*, *courage*, *wisdom*, *resilience*, or *dignity*. The beauty of the Values Tree is that each person's vision is entirely their own, yet deeply connected to the whole.

And I always end by saying this: Compassion is at the root of them all.

Compassion is what allows justice to be enacted with care, freedom to be held with responsibility, joy to be shared without guilt, and truth to be spoken without cruelty. Compassion is not a soft add-on—it is the animating force that makes all other values human. It is what keeps us from turning ideals into weapons or isolation. It grounds us in mutuality. It reminds us that we belong to one another, and that the flourishing of one is bound up with the flourishing of all.

APPENDIX

ADVICE ON DAILY PRACTICE

Developing a regular practice of CBCT (Cognitively Based Compassion Training) requires consistency, care, and self-awareness. These appendices provide guidance and insights into how to establish and deepen your meditation experience in a way that honors both your unique life circumstances and the wisdom of the CBCT framework. Whether you're new to contemplative practice or returning to deepen your understanding, the following guidance is designed to supplement your knowledge and to support your continued journey.

GETTING STARTED WITH COMPASSION PRACTICE: SIMPLE WAYS TO BEGIN

People come to CBCT with all kinds of backgrounds—some have long-standing meditation practices, while others are trying it for the first time. Wherever you are, it's OK. Over time, many people find that the tools of this training become part of their everyday life, supporting them through difficulty and helping them connect more deeply with others. The same can be true for you.

CBCT offers two kinds of practice: *formal* and *informal*. Formal practice—what we often think of as meditation—is a way to deliberately train the mind, typically done in a quiet space, whether seated, lying down, standing, or walking. Informal practice is about weaving insights into your daily life: pausing to reflect, journaling, or recalling gratitude during a conversation. Both are essential and reinforce each other.

If you're new to meditation, the idea of sitting still with your thoughts might feel daunting. Cassy, a former participant, shared how overwhelming it felt at first. "I thought it was making things worse," she said. "But really, I was finally seeing what had been there all along." She started by simply counting ten breaths. That was enough. Then she did a minute. Then two. Slowly, her inner world became less chaotic, and she felt more at ease.

To build a habit, try setting up a dedicated space; a chair, cushion, candle, or photo can help create a sense of calm and ritual. Pick a regular time, like first thing in the morning or before bed. And if it helps, anchor the practice to something you already do—like meditating after a daily walk.

Even in the best conditions, your mind might wander or get sleepy. That's natural. If you're distracted, gently refocus. If you feel dull or foggy, take a few energizing breaths or let more light in. These are skills you'll build over time.

All formal practices begin with three settling steps:

Supportive posture: Find a position that feels both relaxed and alert. Sitting is most common, but standing or lying down is fine, too. Let your spine be tall, your body soft. Eyes can be open or closed.

Grounding sensations: Feel the support of the chair or floor beneath you, the weight of your body, the touch of your clothes or hands. Let your awareness settle here.

Settling breaths: Take a few long, steady breaths. Let each inhale refresh you, and each exhale release tension. If you feel anxious or scattered later on, you can always return to these breaths or grounding sensations.

Above all, be gentle with yourself. If it ever feels too much—emotionally or physically—pause. Get some air, stretch, call a friend. There's no right pace. You're allowed to stop. You can always begin again.

THE CBCT MODEL OF CHANGE

When it comes to building the habits of heart and mind that support compassion, intention alone is not enough. We may deeply wish to respond to others with kindness, or to view our own struggles with more understanding, but in the rush and stress of daily life, we often fall back on old habits.

One of the things that helps us cultivate compassion is integrating new views into our ways of thinking. However, taking on new views—even when we want to—does not always happen easily or right away, especially when the views are different from the ones we currently hold. The CBCT Model of Change presents a process by which we can deepen perspectives to foster lasting and meaningful shifts over time. This model draws on a comprehensive approach from the *lojong* tradition called *ta-gom-cho-sum* in Tibetan, which translates to "view-familiarization-behavior."

View refers to us gaining a more accurate perspective on things, or arriving at a deeper or broader understanding of a situation, which in turn can help us have a healthier response to that situation. *Familiarization* is the process of deepening these perspectives so that they become gradually embodied. Once embodied, these views naturally lead to an enduring shift in *behavior*. Here, "behavior" includes both the emotional responses and the subsequent actions on account of these emotions. The more we embody these accurate views through deliberately engaging in the familiarization process, the more spontaneous our healthier responses become.

This approach can be powerful for changing an unwanted habitual reaction—a harmful behavior, an emotional hang-up, a prejudice, a cycle of frustration with a family member, a tendency to excessively self-criticize—and for cultivating a healthier reaction that contributes to our well-being or to the well-being of others. Such changes take time and practice. To fully take on a new or broader view, the model offers a step-by-step approach to move through three levels of understanding, as explained below:

Level 1—Content Knowledge: To reshape our views, we first need to understand them at an intellectual level. This first level of understanding comes from receiving content knowledge—hearing or reading about a new or broader view on a given topic. We gain this knowledge through activities such as reading informative books, listening to podcasts, or attending classes or talks. This level of understanding is reached when the information we receive makes logical sense to us and we are able to recall it in detail. While this is an important first step, this is insufficient to bring about changes to deeper, ingrained habits of thinking and behaving on its own.

Practical Integration: Make space in your week for conscious learning. That might mean highlighting key insights in a book, saving podcasts, or journaling about what stands out during CBCT practice. Start by asking yourself: *What view am I currently holding? How might this new information offer a healthier or more realistic alternative?* Try paraphrasing new insights into your own words—it's a great way to begin processing them.

Level 2—Personalized Insight: Personalized insight is the second level of understanding, where we resonate with the knowledge and connect it to our lived experience. This is developed through critical thinking and reflective practices, including insight activities and formal analytical meditations, along with informal practices where we bring the insights into our daily lives. These practices are designed to inspire "aha" moments, connecting the content knowledge to our lived reality, and moving our understanding from the head to the heart. At this level, we experience increased meaning, motivation, and conviction, and for this reason, personalized insight has much more impact than content knowledge alone. But even so, these insights can be fleeting and in themselves may not lead to lasting changes.

Practical Integration: Take five to ten minutes at the end of your meditation session or evening routine to reflect on a concept and connect it to your lived experience. For example, if you've learned that "all beings wish to avoid suffering," think: *When did I last ex-*

perience suffering? How did I respond? Have I seen others go through something similar? Let the idea meet your reality, and notice the “aha” moments that follow.

Level 3—Embodied Understanding: Embodied understanding is the third and final level of understanding. Here, the insights have fully soaked in and become second nature. We move toward this level by continuing the process of familiarization—examining the personalized insights from new or different angles, applying them to diverse situations, and then deliberately sustaining these insights in our awareness. This is done through formal practices that combine stabilizing and analytical meditation, along with informal practices that bring the insights into our daily lives. Embodying more realistic and helpful views leads to spontaneous, healthier emotional and behavioral responses. Through this process, desired habits become our new disposition, and we can start to leave unwanted habits behind.

Practical Integration: At this stage, your goal is not just to remember insights but to live from them—naturally and consistently. Begin by creating rituals of recall: moments in your day that prompt you to return to the insight, even for a few seconds. Post a sticky note on your mirror with a grounding phrase like “Just like me, they want to be happy,” or set a phone reminder that asks, “What’s shaping my response right now?” Identify everyday situations where the insight can be practiced—commuting, waiting in line, interacting with coworkers or loved ones. Use these moments to deliberately pause and reflect: *Can I see the shared humanity here? Can I remember what matters most?* Also, reflect at the end of each day. Ask yourself: *Where did the insight show up naturally? Where was it absent?* Don’t judge—just notice. Over time, this gentle, consistent repetition deepens your felt sense of the view until it becomes second nature—guiding your emotions, shaping your habits, and softening your reactivity. This is how insight becomes embodiment.

This model can apply to many areas of life. For example, let's imagine we want to learn how to swim. We might start off by reading instructional books to inform us on technique—how to tread water, how to kick our legs and move our arms through the water. This learning is the first level of understanding—content knowledge. While this helps us gain an understanding of how to swim, it is challenging to fully grasp the concepts until we're in the water and trying for ourselves. Moving our legs about in the shallow end of the pool, practicing the backstroke, we gain a personal and felt understanding of the content. This experience, and the associated "aha" moments, constitutes the second level of understanding—personalized insight. But even still, going in the water once or twice won't be enough to become a natural swimmer. It will take many times getting into the water and practicing the techniques for them to become second nature. This process of familiarization leads us to the final level of understanding—embodied understanding.

IF YOU'RE HAVING TROUBLE SETTLING: STAYING IN OR RETURNING TO THE ZONE OF WELL-BEING

Sometimes, no matter how well we understand the value of compassion or insight, we find ourselves too agitated, distracted, or shut down to actually practice. In these moments, we don't need more analysis—we need grounding. Before we can meditate, reflect, or tap into a deeper source than our current circumstances, we need to come back into a state of balance within ourselves.

Developed by Elaine Miller-Karas, a collaborator with the Emory Compassion Center and the creator of the Zone of Well-Being (ZOW) concept, the following trauma-informed practices can help us throughout the CBCT process. These tangible, body-based activities are powerful tools to help us access our inner resources when we feel stuck:

Grounding is a practice in which we notice how it feels to make physical contact with an object or surface. Grounding can include things we touch with our hands or feet or other parts of the body when in contact with something solid and supportive, such as your back against a chair.

Grounding can be a very helpful tool for calming the body and mind. Most of us have already unconsciously developed many grounding techniques that help us feel relaxed, secure, safe, and more comfortable. These may include things like leaning against a wall or on a table, sitting in a certain way, folding our arms in a certain way, holding objects we like, lying a certain way on a couch or in bed, and so on. However, we may not be aware of using these intentionally to calm our bodies and return to our ZOW.

Tracking refers to the practice of noticing sensations in the body. During a grounding practice—and for any of the practices of CBCT—we will be checking in from time to time to notice what sensations our body is experiencing. For example, if we are grounding ourselves by sitting in a chair with our feet flat on the floor, we would also attend to the sensations that our feet are experiencing, that our body is experiencing as our weight is supported by the chair, the feeling of our hands resting on our lap, etc. Tracking sensations can help to bring us into the present moment and can sustain us in (or help return us to) our ZOW.

Shift and Stay occurs when we track our sensations in any practice and notice that a sensation is pleasant, unpleasant, or neutral. If we find pleasant sensations, resting our attention on that part of the body can sometimes allow the feeling to deepen and the body to relax and return to the ZOW. If we find neutral sensations, focusing attention on these can also help us come back to the ZOW. However, if instead we become aware of an unpleasant sensation, we can "shift and stay"—meaning, we can scan the body to find an area that feels more comfortable (either neutral or pleasant) and then rest our attention on that new location instead. Our ability to shift and stay will become enhanced even more as we cultivate skills of attention and awareness.

Help Now! Strategies can be used to help us quickly return to our ZOW when we find ourselves in the high or low zone. They all involve engaging in a task and tracking our sensations during that experience. These strategies are designed to activate calming sensations and feelings, but every person will have their own responses to each strategy. I strongly recommend trying each of these out and discovering the ones you find the most calming and helpful for you. You can then return to those strategies whenever you're in need of additional support.

Walk: Notice the sensations of your body moving and feet touching the ground as you walk.

Listen: Name all the sounds that you can hear around you.

Look: Name five or more colors or shapes you can see.

Drink: Drink a glass of water slowly, paying close attention to the sensations you feel (in your mouth, throat, and stomach) as you drink.

Count Backward: Count backward from twenty as you walk around.

Push: Notice the sensations of your muscles pushing against a wall or a table.

Touch: Feel different textures of objects around you and attune to those sensations.

SPECIAL CONSIDERATIONS FOR MENTAL HEALTH CONDITIONS

There is one group of experiences that might result from formal practice that requires special care and caution. These are experiences that can happen when practitioners have an ongoing mental health issue. For example, people with bipolar disorder or other severe mental illness may have increased experiences of symptoms such as agitation, mania, delusions, and even hallucinations.

Another area of caution concerns symptoms of traumatic stress or post-traumatic stress disorder (PTSD) due to interpersonal violence or a catastrophic illness or loss. During meditation, it is possible to reexperience memories that lead to intense fear, flashbacks, or other difficult experiences. Several research studies have shown that CBCT can help people who have difficult issues like PTSD from combat or assault, depression, suicide attempts, and breast cancer. But just because CBCT is helpful for some does not mean it will be helpful for all.

Depending on the challenges you're facing, it can be good to acknowledge a powerful truth: Meditation is not a one-size-fits-all path. For those navigating mental health challenges, it can offer profound benefits—but it can also bring up discomfort or even retraumatization. Knowing what's right for you is part of the wisdom that CBCT encourages.

Please keep in mind that CBCT is not therapy and should not be used as a replacement for professional mental health services. If you have any concerns, it is important to discuss whether meditation is safe for you with your physician or a mental health professional before beginning a CBCT program. In addition, if enrolled in a class, you should feel free to mention these concerns to your CBCT teacher.

Be honest with yourself about your needs, and seek counsel if you have any doubt. In CBCT, we believe that a beneficial meditation program (or teacher) will not try to insist on certain progress or manipulate you into doing things that you don't want to do. In the end, the decision of what and how to practice is yours. Be careful if you ever feel that your decisions are being dictated or imposed on you by others.

THE CENTER FOR CONTEMPLATIVE SCIENCE AND COMPASSION-BASED ETHICS

At the heart of Emory University, a quiet revolution is taking place—one that blends ancient wisdom with cutting-edge science to explore one of humanity's most vital questions: How do we live with greater compassion?

The Center for Contemplative Science and Compassion-Based Ethics

(CCSCBE) was born out of the Emory-Tibet Partnership, a decades-long collaboration between Western academia and Tibetan contemplative traditions. But today, it stands on its own as a vibrant academic center committed to integrating compassion into education, health care, business, and beyond.

The work of the center isn't about promoting any one religion or ideology. Instead, it's rooted in a shared human aspiration—to live with kindness, clarity, and care for one another. Whether through classrooms or research labs, teacher trainings or global outreach, the CCSCBE seeks to support both individual flourishing and collective well-being by helping people reconnect with their deepest values.

This approach is rigorously evidence-based and wholly human-centered. The center's work is grounded in a unique blend of interdisciplinary science and contemplative practice. That means asking not only how compassion feels but also how it functions—what happens in the brain, in the body, and in society when we nurture empathy and ethical awareness.

Compassion Shift®: Advancing a Global Culture of Compassion

Responding to His Holiness the Dalai Lama's call for a compassion revolution, the CCSCBE launched the Compassion Shift—a global initiative to create a more compassionate world, one classroom, workplace, and community at a time. At its heart are three educational pillars: the Emory-Tibet Science Initiative (ETSI), SEE Learning® for children, and CBCT® for adults.

Emory-Tibet Science Initiative

Equipping Tibetan Buddhist contemplative scholars with a scientific knowledge and research methodology, this initiative seeks to advance the fundamental understanding of contemplative practices, including compassion. Now that it's been implemented in more than a dozen major Tibetan Buddhist monasteries and nunneries, monastics are already engaging in innovative studies in the field of contemplative science and are publishing their research findings.

SEE Learning®

In a world where kids are facing stress and complexity at younger and younger ages, emotional intelligence is no longer a "nice to have"—it's essential. SEE Learning (short for Social, Emotional, and Ethical Learning) equips students with the tools to navigate not just academics but life itself.

Developed at Emory University for use around the globe, SEE Learning expands on the best in social-emotional learning by integrating topics like attention training, compassion training, resilience, trauma-informed care, systems thinking, and ethical discernment. The result is a powerful, holistic program that helps students of all backgrounds thrive.

In just six years since its global launch, SEE Learning has reached more than twenty million students in more than one hundred thousand schools across seventy-eight countries. Teachers consistently report that it not only supports student growth but also transforms classroom culture—fostering compassion, curiosity, and connection.

Whether you're an educator, a parent, or simply someone who cares about the next generation, SEE Learning offers an inspiring vision for what education can be: not just a transfer of knowledge but the cultivation of wisdom and character.

CBCT®

If you've connected with the practices in this book, you've already been introduced to the heart of CBCT. This secular, research-backed training program offers a rich, structured approach to strengthening compassion from the inside out.

CBCT draws inspiration from the tradition of Indo-Tibetan Buddhism but is adapted for anyone—regardless of background or belief. It weaves together contemplative practices with insights from modern psychology, neuroscience, and evolutionary biology. And it's not just theory.

Over the past two decades, CBCT has become one of the most extensively researched compassion training programs of its kind, with robust findings that demonstrate measurable improvements:

- Reductions in stress, inflammation, depression, PTSD symptoms, and loneliness
- Increases in hope, empathy, compassion, and self-kindness
- Strengthened immune responses and emotion regulation

What sets CBCT apart is its depth. Participants explore topics like attention and emotional regulation, common humanity, interdependence, and, ultimately, engaged compassion. The practices go beyond surface-level mindfulness—they are transformative tools for reshaping how we relate to ourselves and others.

To make CBCT more accessible than ever, the program is now available through Compassion U, a dynamic digital learning platform that brings CBCT to learners around the world. Through interactive video content, guided practices, live online sessions with certified teachers, and a growing global community, Compassion U is making it easier to engage with compassion as a daily practice. For more information about these programs, visit the following websites: SEE Learning (seelearning.emory.edu); CBCT (compassionshift.emory.edu); and the Emory-Tibet Science Initiative (tibet.emory.edu).

It is my deepest hope that SEE Learning, CBCT, and the broader work of the center can help build what so many of us are longing for: a more grounded, connected, and compassionate world, not just in moments of crisis—but in everyday life, across generations and borders. These practices transcend self-care; they are about world-care. And they are here for you, whenever you are ready to begin.

ACKNOWLEDGMENTS

This book is the result of my lifelong journey of learning and reflection, shaped by two great traditions of understanding the human condition and cultivating the inner qualities essential for flourishing—the ancient wisdom of Buddhism and the insights of modern science. I am deeply grateful to the countless individuals who have worked tirelessly for millennia to advance these traditions. I stand on the shoulders of so many, and it is because of their work that I find myself at a point where I can attempt to show how these two domains of knowledge not only complement each other but also mutually reinforce our understanding of compassion and well-being.

I would like to thank my parents, who have been a consistent lived demonstration of love and compassion. Their care and example nurtured in me the very qualities this book seeks to explore and honor.

The path my life has taken would not have been possible without His Holiness the Dalai Lama. From a remote Himalayan village that did not even have a proper school, two other young boys and I were brought to a world of great possibilities through the kindness of His Holiness. Since I was fourteen years old, His Holiness has supported my academic, emotional, and spiritual growth, and throughout my life, he has guided me with boundless wisdom and compassion. In this book, however imperfectly, I try to share what His Holiness has inspired over so many years. His writings—offering a clear, systematic path to cultivating compassion and fundamental human values—inspired me to find the courage to develop a compassion program.

I also express my deep gratitude to all my teachers, from both the Tibetan tradition and the Western academic world. In particular, Gen Lobsang Gyatso, who shaped my thinking in my most formative years, and Dr. Robert Paul, my teacher and mentor in the West.

So much of what I offer in this book has been shaped and informed by those who have given their precious time to hear what I am sharing—notably my students at Emory University and the many individuals around the world who have engaged with the work of the Emory Compassion Center. Their interest, insights, and belief that these teachings could be of benefit to humanity have inspired my ongoing efforts. In particular, I want to thank my former student Molly Harrington, who in 2003 was leading a movement to destigmatize mental health problems at Emory. She recognized that the Tibetan Buddhist knowledge and contemplative practices she was learning in my class, if presented in a more secular way, could be healing for students who were struggling more than ever with anxiety, depression, and isolation. It was her deep conviction and persistent encouragement that inspired me to develop the rationale and method for a secular compassion training program that could be practiced by people of any, or no, religious faith.

I owe a debt of gratitude to my colleagues at the Emory Compassion Center who have been instrumental in supporting the development, implementation, and global dissemination of our programs. Their tireless efforts and dedication continue to make this work possible.

Particularly, I want to acknowledge the work of the CBCT® (Cognitively Based Compassion Training) and SEE Learning® (Social, Emotional, and Ethical Learning) programs, as well as the Emory-Tibet Science Initiative. I am deeply grateful to His Holiness for providing the opportunity to advance his vast vision for humanity through these programs.

I am also deeply indebted to Charles Raison, PhD, and Thaddeus Pace, PhD, who helped me design and launch the initial research studies on CBCT. I would like to thank them for the early conversations and the bold exploration of how compassion might be approached from psychological and scientific perspectives. Together, we hypothesized, conceptualized, and laid the foundation for research on CBCT, which is now one of the most widely researched compassion training programs in the world. Additionally, my thanks go to Teri Sivilli for her important contributions as the coordinator for the CBCT research in the intial years. Though too numerous to mention, I extend my gratitude to the many other scientists who have carried out CBCT research with diverse populations in the years since.

As a non-native English speaker, I have received instrumental support from a number of individuals who helped to beautifully translate my vision for this book into a compelling narrative. I am grateful to Amy Hertz for her help in structuring the book conceptually, and to Nirmala Nataraj for her extensive editorial efforts in refining the book. I would like to thank Mark McGill, Ariel Lierman, Michelle Liberman, Tsondue Samphel, and Carol Beck for their thoughtful editing, proofreading, and essential feedback along the way. I also offer my gratitude to my agent, Elizabeth Kaplan, and my publisher, Simon & Schuster—and particularly my editor, Lauren Marino.

Finally, to my beloved wife, Irene Lee, who has been my bedrock and a true pillar of support for me personally and for my work. Her strength, patience, and unwavering encouragement through years of travel and commitments have sustained me more than any words can express. I would not have been able to advance this work without her.

And to all who have contributed in seen and unseen ways, thank you. This work is yours as much as it is mine.

ENDNOTES

1. Dalai Lama and Victor Chan, *The Wisdom of Compassion: Stories of Remarkable Encounters and Timeless Insights* (Riverhead Books, 2012).

Chapter One: Compassion—The Greatest Nourishment of All

1. Dalai Lama, "Compassion and Education," talk at Kalindi College, New Delhi, India, January 28, 2015, posted May 1, 2019, by Dalai Lama Archive, YouTube, https://youtu.be/yiSlzyggCOw?si=r_DVV3fy73h8EdRT&t=1510.
2. Lynn Margulis, *Symbiotic Planet: A New Look at Evolution* (Basic Books, 1998).
3. Charles Duhigg, "What Google Learned from Its Quest to Build the Perfect Team: New Research Reveals Surprising Truths About Why Some Work Groups Thrive and Others Falter," *New York Times*, February 25, 2016, https://www.nytimes.com/2016/02/28/magazine/what-google-learned-from-its-quest-to-build-the-perfect-team.html.

Chapter Two: Ancient Source, New Science

1. Acharya Shantideva, *A Guide to the Bodhisattva's Way of Life* (Bodhicaryāvatāra), trans. Stephen Batchelor (Library of Tibetan Works & Archives, 1979).
2. Aino Saarinen et al., "Compassion Protects Against Vital Exhaustion and Negative Emotionality," *Motivation and Emotion* 45, no. 4 (2021): 506–17, https://doi.org/10.1007/s11031-021-09878-2.
3. Emma Seppala, "Compassionate Mind, Healthy Body," *Greater Good Magazine*, July 24, 2013, https://greatergood.berkeley.edu/article/item/compassionate_mind_healthy_body.
4. "Meditation Dramatically Changes Body Temperatures," *Harvard Gazette*, April 18, 2002, https://news.harvard.edu/gazette/story/2002/04/meditation-dramatically-changes-body-temperatures/.
5. Thaddeus W. W. Pace et al., "Effect of Compassion Meditation on Neuroendocrine, Innate Immune and Behavioral Responses to Psychosocial Stress," *Psychoneuroendocrinology* 34, no. 1 (2009): 87–98, https://doi.org/10.1016/j.psyneuen.2008.08.011.
6. Daniel Goleman and Richard J. Davidson, *Altered Traits: Science Reveals How Meditation Changes Your Mind, Brain, and Body* (Avery, 2017); Pace et al., "Effect of Compassion Meditation."
7. Thaddeus W. W. Pace et al., "Cognitively-Based Compassion Training Reduces Peripheral Inflammation in Adolescents in Foster Care with High Rates of Early

Life Adversity," *BMC Complementary and Alternative Medicine* 12, no. S1 (2012), https://doi.org/10.1186/1472-6882-12-S1-P175; and Boghuma K. Titanji et al., "Cognitively Based Compassion Training for HIV Immune Nonresponders—An Attention-Placebo Randomized Controlled Trial," *Journal of Acquired Immune Deficiency Syndromes* 89, no. 3 (March 1, 2022): 340–48, https://doi.org/10.1097/QAI.0000000000002874.

8. Sanna K. Tirkkonen and Ruth Rebecca Tietjen, "Loneliness and Radicalization," *Philosophy & Social Criticism* (2025), https://journals.sagepub.com/doi/10.1177/01914537251334550.
9. National Academies of Sciences, Engineering, and Medicine, "Evaluating the Evidence for the Impacts of Social Isolation, Loneliness, and Other Aspects of Social Connection on Mortality," in *Social Isolation and Loneliness in Older Adults: Opportunities for the Health Care System* (National Academies Press, 2020), https://www.ncbi.nlm.nih.gov/books/NBK557977/.
10. Pace et al., "Effect of Compassion Meditation"; Thaddeus W. W. Pace et al., "Engagement with Cognitively-Based Compassion Training Is Associated with Reduced Salivary C-Reactive Protein from Before to After Training in Foster Care Program Adolescents," *Psychoneuroendocrinology* 38, no. 2 (February 2013): 294–99, https://doi.org/10.1016/j.psyneuen.2012.05.019; Pace et al., "Cognitively-Based Compassion Training"; Thaddeus W. W. Pace et al., "Innate Immune, Neuroendocrine and Behavioral Responses to Psychosocial Stress Do Not Predict Subsequent Compassion Meditation Practice Time," *Psychoneuroendocrinology* 35, no. 2 (February 2010): 310–15, https://doi.org/10.1016/j.psyneuen.2009.06.008; Sheethal D. Reddy et al., "Cognitive-Based Compassion Training: A Promising Prevention Strategy for At-Risk Adolescents," *Journal of Child and Family Studies* 22, no. 2 (2012): 219–30, http://dx.doi.org/10.1007/s10826-012-9571-7; Titanji et al., "Cognitively Based Compassion Training for HIV Immune Nonresponders"; Jennifer S. Mascaro et al., "Meditation Buffers Medical Student Compassion from the Deleterious Effects of Depression," *Journal of Positive Psychology* 13, no. 2 (2016): 133–42, https://doi.org/10.1080/17439760.2016.1233348; and Ariel J. Lang et al., "Compassion Meditation for Veterans with Posttraumatic Stress Disorder (PTSD): A Nonrandomized Study," *Mindfulness* 11, no. 1 (2017): 63–74, https://doi.org/10.1007/s12671-017-0866-z.
11. Sally E. Dodds et al., "Feasibility of Cognitively-Based Compassion Training (CBCT) for Breast Cancer Survivors: A Randomized, Wait List Controlled Pilot Study," *Supportive Care in Cancer* 23, no. 12 (2015): 3,599–608, https://doi.org/10.1007/s00520-015-2888-1; and Jennifer S. Mascaro et al., "Compassion Meditation Enhances Empathic Accuracy and Related Neural Activity," *Social Cognitive and Affective Neuroscience* 8, no. 1 (2012): 48–55, https://doi.org/10.1093/scan/nss095.
12. Stephen Trzeciak and Anthony Mazzarelli, *Compassionomics: The Revolutionary Scientific Evidence That Caring Makes a Difference* (Fire Starter Publishing, 2019).

Chapter Three: Finding Your Sources of Nurturance

1. John Bowlby, *A Secure Base: Parent-Child Attachment and Healthy Human Development* (Basic Books, 1988).
2. Viktor Frankl, *Man's Search for Meaning: An Introduction to Logotherapy* (Washington Square Press, 1963).
3. Tannistha Sinha, "The Life and Times of LaTonya Goffney," *Defender*, January 12, 2025, https://defendernetwork.com/news/education/la-tonya-goffney-superintendent-aldine-isd/.
4. Elaine Miller-Karas, *Building Resilience to Trauma: The Trauma and Community Resiliency Models* (Routledge, 2015).
5. "Stress Effects on the Body," American Psychological Association, November 1, 2018, https://www.apa.org/topics/stress/body.
6. Kevin N. Ochsner and James J. Gross, "The Cognitive Control of Emotion," *Trends in Cognitive Sciences* 9, no. 5 (2005): 242–49, https://doi.org/10.1016/j.tics.2005.03.010.
7. Lukas Novak et al., "Neural Correlates of Compassion—An Integrative Systematic Review," *International Journal of Psychophysiology* 172 (2022): 46–59, https://doi.org/10.1016/j.ijpsycho.2021.12.004.
8. Kazuo Mori and Hideko Mori, "Another Test of the Passive Facial Feedback Hypothesis: When Your Face Smiles, You Feel Happy," *Perceptual and Motor Skills* 109, no. 1 (2009): 76–78, https://doi.org/10.2466/pms.109.1.76-78.

Chapter Four: Developing a Clear and Stable Attention

1. Gerald Zaltman, *How Customers Think: Essential Insights into the Mind of the Market* (Harvard Business School Press, 2003).
2. Paul Ekman, *Emotions Revealed: Recognizing Faces and Feelings to Improve Communication and Emotional Life*, 2nd ed. (Owl Books, 2007).
3. Vasubandhu, *Abhidharmakosha*, chap. 5, verse 34, translated by the author.
4. Matthew A. Killingsworth and Daniel T. Gilbert, "A Wandering Mind Is an Unhappy Mind," *Science* 330 (2010): 932, https://doi.org/10.1126/science.1192439.
5. Craig A. Moodie et al., "The Neural Bases of Cognitive Emotion Regulation: The Roles of Strategy and Intensity," *Cognitive, Affective & Behavioral Neuroscience* 20, no. 2 (2020): 387–407, https://doi.org/10.3758/s13415-020-00775-8.
6. Nicole D. White, "Mindfulness-Based Cognitive Therapy for Depression, Current Episodes, and Prevention of Relapse," *American Journal of Lifestyle Medicine* 9, no. 3 (2015): 227–29, https://doi.org/10.1177/1559827615569677.
7. Goleman and Davidson, *Altered Traits.*
8. Jia Wei Zhang and Serena Chen, "Self-Compassion Promotes Personal Improvement from Regret Experiences via Acceptance," *Personality and Social Psychology Bulletin* 42, no. 2 (2016): 244–58, https://doi.org/10.1177/0146167215623271.

Chapter Five: Practicing Open Awareness

1. Paul Ekman, *Emotions Revealed: Recognizing Faces and Feelings to Improve Communication and Emotional Life*, 2nd ed. (Owl Books, 2007).
2. Michael Ussher et al., "Immediate Effects of a Brief Mindfulness-Based Body Scan on Patients with Chronic Pain," *Journal of Behavioral Medicine* 37, no. 1 (2014): 127–34, https://doi.org/10.1007/s10865-012-9466-5.
3. Daniel J. Siegel, *Mindsight: The New Science of Personal Transformation* (Bantam Books, 2010).
4. Daniel J. Siegel, *Brainstorm: The Power and Purpose of the Teenage Brain* (Penguin Group, 2013).
5. Atisha, "A Bodhisattva's Garland of Gems," translated by the author.

Chapter Six: Making Space for Self-Compassion

1. Dalai Lama and Desmond Tutu, *The Book of Joy: Lasting Happiness in a Changing World* (Avery, 2016).
2. Rick Warren, Elke Smeets, and Kristin D. Neff, "Self-Criticism and Self-Compassion: Risk and Resilience: Being Compassionate to Oneself Is Associated with Emotional Resilience and Psychological Well-Being," *Current Psychiatry* 15, no. 12 (2016): 18–32, https://self-compassion.org/wp-content/uploads/2016/12/Self-Criticism.pdf.
3. Kristin D. Neff, "The Five Myths of Self-Compassion," *Greater Good Magazine*, September 30, 2015, https://greatergood.berkeley.edu/article/item/the_five_myths_of_self_compassion.
4. Juliana G. Breines and Serena Chen, "Self-Compassion Increases Self-Improvement Motivation," *Personality and Social Psychology Bulletin* 38, no. 9 (2012): 1,133–43, https://doi.org/10.1177/0146167212445599.
5. Kristin D. Neff, "Self-Compassion: Theory, Method, Research, and Intervention," *Annual Review of Psychology* 74 (2023): 193–218, https://www.annualreviews.org/content/journals/10.1146/annurev-psych-032420-031047; Adrián Pérez-Aranda et al., "Impact of Mindfulness and Self-Compassion on Anxiety and Depression: The Mediating Role of Resilience," *International Journal of Clinical and Health Psychology* 21, no. 2 (May–August 2021): 100229, https://www.sciencedirect.com/science/article/pii/S1697260021000107; Imogen C. Marsh, Stella W. Y. Chan, and Angus Macbeth, "Self-Compassion and Psychological Distress in Adolescents—A Meta-Analysis," *Mindfulness* 9 (2018): 1,011–27, https://link.springer.com/article/10.1007/s12671-017-0850-7?fromPaywallRec=false; Madeleine Ferrari et al., "Self-Compassion Interventions and Psychosocial Outcomes: A Meta-Analysis of RCTs," *Mindfulness* 10 (2019): 1,455–73, https://self-compassion.org/wp-content/uploads/2019/08/Ferrari2019.pdf; Sarah J. Egan et al., "A Review of Self-Compassion as an Active Ingredient in the Prevention and Treatment of Anxiety and Depression in Young People," *Administration and Policy in Mental Health and Mental Health Services Research* 49 (2022): 385–403, https://doi.org/10.1007/s10488-021-01170-2; Maria Hughes et al., "Self-Compassion and Anxiety and Depression in Chronic Physical Illness

Populations: A Systematic Review," *Mindfulness* 12 (2021): 1,597–610, https://link.springer.com/article/10.1007/s12671-021-01602-y; Regina Hiraoka et al., "Self-Compassion as a Prospective Predictor of PTSD Symptom Severity among Trauma-Exposed US Iraq and Afghanistan War Veterans," *Journal of Traumatic Stress* 28, no. 2 (March 2015): 127–33, https://pmc.ncbi.nlm.nih.gov/articles/PMC5032642/; Fiona Purdie and Stephen Morley, "Self-Compassion, Pain, and Breaking a Social Contract," *Pain* 156, no. 11 (November 2015): 2,354–63, https://pubmed.ncbi.nlm.nih.gov/26164588/; Derrecka M. Boykin et al., "Barriers to Self-Compassion for Female Survivors of Childhood Maltreatment: The Roles of Fear of Self-Compassion and Psychological Inflexibility," *Child Abuse & Neglect* 76 (February 2018): 216–24, https://www.sciencedirect.com/science/article/abs/pii/S0145213417304180; Karina Prentice, Clare Rees, and Amy Finlay-Jones, "Self-Compassion, Well-Being, and Distress in Adolescents and Young Adults with Chronic Medical Conditions: The Mediating Role of Emotion Regulation Difficulties," *Mindfulness (NY)* 12, no. 9 (July 2021): 2,241–52, https://pmc.ncbi.nlm.nih.gov/articles/PMC8311066/; Susanna Torbet, Michael Proeve, and Rachel M. Roberts, "Self-Compassion: A Protective Factor for Parents of Children with Autism Spectrum Disorder," *Mindfulness* 10 (2019): 2,492–506, https://self-compassion.org/wp-content/uploads/2020/08/Torbet2019.pdf; Kristin D. Neff, "Self-Compassion: An Alternative Conceptualization of a Healthy Attitude toward Oneself," *Self and Identity* 2, no. 2 (2003): 85–101, https://psycnet.apa.org/record/2003-03727-001; Laurie Hollis-Walker and Kenneth Colosimo, "Mindfulness, Self-Compassion, and Happiness in Non-Meditators: A Theoretical and Empirical Examination," *Personality and Individual Differences* 50, no. 2 (January 2011): 222–27, https://www.sciencedirect.com/science/article/abs/pii/S0191886910004769; Mary Heffernan et al., "Self-Compassion and Emotional Intelligence in Nurses," *International Journal of Nursing Practice* 16, no. 4 (August 2010): 366–73, https://pubmed.ncbi.nlm.nih.gov/20649668/; Kristin D. Neff, "The Role of Self-Compassion in Development: A Healthier Way to Relate to Oneself," *Human Development* 52, no. 4 (June 2009): 211–14, https://www.ncbi.nlm.nih.gov/pmc/articles/PMC2790748/; Kristin D. Neff, "What Is Self-Compassion?" Self-Compassion.org, https://self-compassion.org/what-is-self-compassion/; Breines and Chen, "Self-Compassion Increases Self-Improvement Motivation"; and Meredith L. Terry and Mark Leary, "Self-Compassion, Self-Regulation, and Health," *Self and Identity* 10, no. 3 (July 2011): 352–62, https://www.researchgate.net/publication/232968819_Self-compassion_self-regulation_and_health.

6. Paul Ekman and Eva Ekman, "Atlas of Emotions," AtlasofEmotions.org, https://atlasofemotions.org.
7. Kevin N. Ochsner, Jennifer A. Silvers, and Jason T. Buhle, "Functional Imaging Studies of Emotion Regulation: A Synthetic Review and Evolving Model of the Cognitive Control of Emotion," *Annals of the New York Academy of Sciences* 1251 (2012): E1–E24, https://doi:.org/10.1111/j.1749-6632.2012.06751.x.

8. "Tools and Practices: Remind People of Their Goodness," Fetzer Institute, https://fetzer.org/resources/practice-remind-people-their-goodness.
9. Jack Kornfield, *The Art of Forgiveness, Lovingkindness, and Peace* (Bantam Books, 2002), 42–43.
10. Ryan M. Niemiec, "Mental Health and Character Strengths: The Dual Role of Boosting Well-Being and Reducing Suffering," *Mental Health and Social Inclusion* 27, no. 4 (2023): 294–316, https://doi.org/10.1108/MHSI-01-2023-0012.
11. Paul Ekman, "Emotional Bias," Paul Ekman Group, November 20, 2020, https://www.paulekman.com/blog/emotional-bias/.
12. Craig A. Moodie et al., "The Neural Bases of Cognitive Emotion Regulation: The Roles of Strategy and Intensity," *Cognitive, Affective & Behavioral Neuroscience* 20, no. 2 (2020): 387–407, https://doi.org/10.3758/s13415-020-00775-8.

Chapter Seven: Expanding Our Circle of Concern

1. Tsongkhapa, *The Great Treatise on the Stages of the Path to Enlightenment*, trans. the Lamrim Chenmo Translation Committee, ed. Joshua W. C. Cutler and Guy Newland (Snow Lion Publications, 2000).
2. Ashley E. Ermer and Christine M. Proulx, "Associations Between Social Connectedness, Emotional Well-Being, and Self-Rated Health Among Older Adults: Difference by Relationship Status," *Research on Aging* 41, no. 4 (2019): 336–61, https://doi.org/10.1177/0164027518815260.
3. Editors of National Geographic, "The Christmas Truce of 1914: What Historians Say Really Happened," *History Magazine*, December 20, 2023, https://www.nationalgeographic.com/premium/article/christmas-truce-world-war-i.
4. Mark Levine et al., "Identity and Emergency Intervention: How Social Group Membership and Inclusiveness of Group Boundaries Shape Helping Behavior," *Personality and Social Psychology Bulletin* 31, no. 4 (2005): 443–53, https://doi.org/10.1177/0146167204271651.
5. Ethan Kross et al., "Social Rejection Shares Somatosensory Representations with Physical Pain," *Proceedings of the National Academy of Sciences of the United States of America* 108, no. 15 (2011): 6,270–75, https://doi.org/10.1073/pnas.1102693108.
6. Stefan Stürmer, Mark Snyder, and Allen M. Omoto, "Prosocial Emotions and Helping: The Moderating Role of Group Membership," *Journal of Personality and Social Psychology* 88, no. 3 (2005): 532–46, https://doi.org/10.1037/0022-3514.88.3.532.
7. J. Kiley Hamlin et al., "Not Like Me = Bad: Infants Prefer Those Who Harm Dissimilar Others," *Psychological Science* 24, no. 4 (2013): 589–94, https://doi.org/10.1177/0956797612457785.
8. Ibid.
9. John T. Cacioppo et al., "The Neuroendocrinology of Social Isolation," *Annual Review of Psychology* 66 (2015): 733–67, https://doi.org/10.1146/annurev-psych-010814-015240.

10. Julianne Holt-Lunstad et al., "Loneliness and Social Isolation as Risk Factors for Mortality: A Meta-Analytic Review," *Perspectives on Psychological Science* 10, no. 2 (2015): 227–37, https://doi.org/10.1177/1745691614568352.
11. Rutger Bregman, *Humankind: A Hopeful History*, trans. Elizabeth Manton and Erica Moore (Little, Brown and Company, 2020).
12. Ibid.
13. Charles Darwin, *The Descent of Man, and Selection in Relation to Sex* (John Murray, 1871).
14. Dalai Lama and Paul Ekman, *Emotional Awareness: Overcoming the Obstacles to Psychological Balance and Compassion* (Times Books/Henry Holt & Co., 2008).
15. Thomas F. Pettigrew and Linda R. Tropp, "A Meta-Analytic Test of Intergroup Contact Theory," *Journal of Personality and Social Psychology* 90, no. 5 (2006): 751–83, https://doi.org/10.1037/0022-3514.90.5.751.
16. Bregman, *Humankind.*
17. Aryadeva, *Four Hundred Verses on the Middle Way*, translated by the author.

Chapter Eight: Nourishing the Heart with Gratitude and Tenderness

1. Robert A. Emmons, *Thanks! How the New Science of Gratitude Can Make You Happier* (Houghton Mifflin Harcourt, 2007).
2. Frans de Waal, *The Age of Empathy: Nature's Lessons for a Kinder Society* (Three Rivers Press, 2009).
3. Robert A. Emmons, "The Psychology of Gratitude: An Introduction," in *The Psychology of Gratitude*, ed. Robert A. Emmons and Michael E. McCullough (Oxford University Press, 2004), 1–15.
4. Adnan Bashir Bhatti and Anwar ul Haq, "The Pathophysiology of Perceived Social Isolation: Effects on Health and Mortality," *Cureus* 9, no. 1 (2017): e994, https://doi.org/10.7759/cureus.994; Erin York Cornwell and Linda J. Waite, "Social Disconnectedness, Perceived Isolation, and Health Among Older Adults," *Journal of Health and Social Behavior* 50, no. 1 (2009): 31–48, https://doi.org/10.1177/002214650905000103; and Louis C. Hawkley and John T. Cacioppo, "Loneliness Matters: A Theoretical and Empirical Review of Consequences and Mechanisms," *Annals of Behavioral Medicine* 40, no. 2 (2010): 218–27, https://doi.org/10.1007/s12160-010-9210-8.
5. Daniel Västfjäll et al., "Compassion Fade: Affect and Charity Are Greatest for a Single Child in Need," *PLOS One* 9, no. 6 (2014): e100115, https://doi.org/10.1371/journal.pone.0100115.
6. David Brooks, *The Second Mountain: The Quest for a Moral Life* (Random House, 2020).
7. Tsongkhapa, *The Great Treatise on the Stages of the Path to Enlightenment.*
8. Robin M. Kowalski, "Complaints and Complaining: Functions, Antecedents, and Consequences," *Psychological Bulletin* 119, no. 2 (1996): 179–96, https://doi.org/10.1037/0033-2909.119.2.179.
9. Daniel Goleman, *Social Intelligence: The New Science of Human Relationships* (Bantam Books, 2006).

10. De Waal, *Age of Empathy.*
11. Frans de Waal, *Good Natured: The Origins of Right and Wrong in Humans and Other Animals* (Harvard University Press, 1996).
12. Albert Einstein, "Letter to Robert J. Marcus," in *The New Quotable Einstein*, ed. Alice Calaprice (Princeton University Press, 2005).
13. Thomas Merton, *Conjectures of a Guilty Bystander* (Doubleday, 1966).

Chapter Nine: Easing the Suffering of the World

1. Loren C. Eiseley, *The Unexpected Universe* (Harcourt Brace Jovanovich, 1985).
2. Jamil Zaki, *The War for Kindness: Building Empathy in a Fractured World* (Broadway Books, 2019).
3. Ibid.
4. Tania Singer and Matthias Bolz, eds., *Compassion: Bridging Practice and Science* (Max Planck Society, 2013), https://www.compassion-training.org.
5. Dalai Lama, *Beyond Religion: Ethics for a Whole World* (Houghton Mifflin Harcourt, 2011).
6. Stephen Bates, "Sir Nicholas Winton Obituary," *Guardian*, July 1, 2015, https://www.theguardian.com/world/2015/jul/01/sir-nicholas-winton.
7. Paulina Firozi, "378 People 'Pay It Forward' at Starbucks," 11Alive.com, August 21, 2014, https://www.11alive.com/article/life/378-people-pay-it-forward-at-starbucks/85-253208559.
8. Martin Luther King Jr., *Strength to Love* (Harper & Row, 1963).
9. Acharya Shantideva, "Bodhicary¯avat¯ara: An Introduction to the Bodhisattva's Way of Life," chap. 3, trans. Adam Pearcey, Lotsawa House, 2007, https://www.lotsawahouse.org/indian-masters/shantideva/bodhicharyavatara-3.
10. Dalai Lama, *Beyond Religion.*

Conclusion: The Call for a Compassion Revolution

1. Dalai Lama, with Franz Alt, *Our Only Home: A Climate Appeal to the World* (Bloomsbury, 2020).

INDEX

ABOUT THE AUTHOR

Lobsang Tenzin Negi, PhD, is a cofounder and the executive director of the Center for Contemplative Science and Compassion-Based Ethics at Emory University, where he also teaches in the Department of Religion. The developer of CBCT® (Cognitively Based Compassion Training), Lobsang is a contemplative practitioner and investigator whose research has focused on the relationship between emotions and well-being. A former Tibetan Buddhist monk, Lobsang has spearheaded multiple innovative programs, including the Emory-Tibet Science Initiative, CBCT®, and SEE Learning®—programs at the intersection of science and spirituality. He has received numerous awards for his pioneering work, including Emory University's Thomas Jefferson Award and an honorary Doctor of Science degree from Rutgers University.